Thanksgiving 101

Celebrate America's Favorite Holiday with
America's Thanksgiving Expert

Rick Rodgers

Broadway Books titles may be purchased for business or promotional use or for special sales. For information, please write to: Special Markets Department, Bantam Doubleday Dell Publishing Group, Inc., 1540 Broadway, New York, NY 10036.

BROADWAY BOOKS and its logo, a letter B bisected on the diagonal, are trademarks of Broadway Books, a division of Bantam Doubleday Dell Publishing Group, Inc.

Library of Congress Cataloging-in-Publication Data
Rodgers, Rick, 1953–
     Thanksgiving 101 : celebrate America's favorite holiday with America's Thanksgiving expert / Rick
  Rodgers. —1st ed.
    Includes index.
    ISBN 0-7679-0136-3
    1. Thanksgiving cookery.   I. Title.
TX739.2.T45R63   1998   98-6290
641.5′68—dc21   CIP

FIRST EDITION

Designed by Pei Loi Koay

Illustrations by Wendy Wray

02 03 04 05 06 20 19 18 17 16 15 14 13 12 11

The Genuine Spirit of Thanks

*T*hanksgiving, or as we prefer "Turkey Day", is *the* genuine American holiday.

It's about stopping to recognize and appreciate the bounty we enjoy, regardless of race or religion, hometown or job title. It's about the things we share; not the things that divide us.

Wild Turkey is the perfect spirit to honor the occasion. It's handcrafted, the old fashioned way, using ingredients from all across the land. The corn is harvested in Kentucky and Indiana, the rye in the Dakota plains, and the barley grows under Montana's spacious skies. And, of course, the sturdy oaks from the Ozark Mountains that are used to make our barrels and the cool crystal limestone waters of Kentucky can be tasted in each sip.

The recipe for a perfect Wild Turkey is probably the easiest thing you can prepare this season. It's great neat, on the rocks or with a splash of water, mixed with cola or in one of these simple drinks.

WILD TURKEY TODDY

This hot and steamy combination of Wild Turkey, orange juice, sugar, butter and cloves is a delicious treat.

2 oz. Wild Turkey
1 oz. Orange juice
1 tsp. Granulated sugar
1/4 pat of Butter
1 Clove

Place all ingredients in a mug. Fill with boiling water and stir. Float a quarter of a pat of butter on top.

RARE MANHATTAN

The Perfect Classic Cocktail

2 1/2 oz. Wild Turkey Rare Breed
3/4 oz. Sweet Vermouth
1/2 oz. Dry Vermouth

Mix well in a shaker filled with ice. Strain into chilled martini glass. Garnish with cherry or lemon twist.

In the spirit of Thanksgiving, we'd like to offer genuine thanks to you, our customers, and ask that you enjoy Wild Turkey responsibly.

Broadway Books
New York

Dedicated to Dick and Eleanor,
Steve and Cynthia, Ron, and Patrick

Contents

Turkey and Friends 29
The Main Event

Stuffings and Dressings 63
The Stuff That Dressings Are Made Of . . .

Desserts 109
How Many Ways Can You Say "Pumpkin"?

Leftovers 138
There's Got to Be a Morning After . . .

Thanksgiving Menu Planner 147

Index 157

Acknowledgments

In order to keep up with creating new recipes for my cooking classes, I have to work well ahead of my annual autumn tour. I have prepared many a Thanksgiving meal in July—often in other people's kitchens. Harriet Bell tops this list of people who have happily lent me their kitchens and tastebuds. Not only is she a cookbook author's dream editor (and the guiding hand behind this book), she's been a great friend over the years, too. And we shared the fun of deep-frying a turkey—a bonding experience if ever there was one. Steven and Cynthia Stahl and Ron Dier were always generous with their kitchens, friendships, and dishwashing talents during the many years of wonderful Thanksgivings we've shared. And, of course, my parents, Dick and Eleanor Rodgers, who produce a flawless Thanksgiving year after year, and showed me how fun and easy it can be.

Many cooking schools throughout the country allowed me to hone my Thanksgiving dinner–making skills. These people shopped, chopped, and cooked beside me and provided teams of great kitchen assistants to help us get the meal on the table, often for forty or fifty hungry students at a time. Thanks to Ruth Henderson, Sandy Daniels, and Beth Castellano at The Silo, New Milford, Connecticut; Bill Wallace at Draegers' Markets (with special thanks to the hardworking Laura Gates and our cohort, Edna Frescura), Menlo Park, California; Phyllis Vaccarelli (and Liz and JoAnn) at Let's Get Cookin', Westlake Village, California; Doralece

Lipoli Dullaghan (and Sarah and Michelle) at Sur La Table's California locations; Jeannie Rader (and Lisa Larsen, Lorene Greer, and Nancy Lorenz) at Dierberg's School of Cooking, St. Louis, Missouri; Bernard Kinsella and Heather Arvello at Kroger's Markets, Atlanta, Georgia; Sue Sell of Cook 'n' Tell, Colt's Neck, New Jersey; Arlene Ward (and Maria, Paul, and Inez) of Adventures in Cooking, Wayne, New Jersey; David Martone of Classic Recipes in Westfield, New Jersey; Sigrid Laughlin at The Complete Kitchen in Darien, Connecticut; Bev Gruber of Everyday Gourmet at Larry's Markets, Bellevue, Washington; Heidi Blenkhorn at Gelson's Markets, Calabasas, California; and the cooking school staff at King's Markets in New Jersey. And while I certainly can't list all of my students by name, there are special ones who always show up, year after year, to taste and collect the current recipes, and I am especially thankful for their loyalty and appetite. Susan Wyler, cookbook editor and friend, encouraged my affection for turkey and stuffing by providing projects on those subjects that helped establish me as the expert on Things Thanksgiving.

For researching assistance and permissions to use their companies' products and recipes, I am grateful to: Linda Compton (Ocean Spray Cranberries), Ann Marie Murray (Campbell Soup Company), Roz O'Hearn (Nestlé USA/Libby's Pumpkin), and Cynthia Giorgio (General Foods/Jell-O and Kraft Philadelphia Brand Cream Cheese). Thanks to Valerie Tully of the National Turkey Federation for the turkey industry statistics and information. For the history of American food companies and eating habits, two books proved invaluable: James Trager's *The Food Chronology* (Henry Holt, 1995) and Jean Anderson's *The American Century Cookbook* (Clarkson Potter, 1997).

In my test kitchen, nothing would ever get done if it weren't for Diane Kniss. Her helpfulness and dilligence are combined with a sense of humor that makes her the kind of coworker that makes you want to get to work so you can try to top yesterday's laughs. Thanks, as always, to my agent Susan Ginsburg, and her assistant, John Hodgman. And, my Thanksgiving dinner is always best when the party is cohosted by Patrick Fisher.

Thanks to the many people at Broadway Books who contributed their professionalism to make this book the best it could be. Copy editor Judith Sutton has helped me through the grammatical jungle on other books, and I am again beholden to her. Thanks to Roberto de Vicq de Cumptich, Pei Loi Koay, Caitlin Connelly, Skip Dye, and Harriet's assistant, Alexis Levenson. I'll save a piece of pumpkin pie for each of you.

Thanksgiving 101

Introduction

Talking Turkey

For each of the last eight years, I have prepared more than thirty Thanksgiving dinners for more than one thousand people. Turkey addict? Pumpkin pie groupie? A victim of gravy obsession syndrome? Yes, but there is a better reason. I travel all over the country teaching a cooking class called Thanksgiving 101. Now, everything I teach in my classes is in this book, with my favorite recipes, make-ahead tips, anecdotes, organization secrets, and insights into what makes this holiday so different from all others.

How did I become a Thanksgiving guru? In 1985, I started a catering company, Cuisine Americaine, and specialized in cooking regional American foods. And what is more American than Thanksgiving dinner? My customers loved my holiday spreads. In 1990, when Perdue Farms, one of the East Coast's largest poultry producers was looking for a media spokesperson to represent their turkey products, they came to me. I learned everything there is to know about turkey, spending lots of time on turkey farms and in the kitchen, and even wrote a cookbook on the subject.

Since then, I have traveled all over the country teaching Thanksgiving cooking classes and making television and radio appearances on how to have the perfect Thanksgiving meal. Everyone, from friends to television producers, calls me "Mr. Thanksgiving" or "The Turkey Meister."

One of the best things about my work as a cooking teacher is that I am in personal contact with our country's home cooks—I am not a restaurant chef who is out of touch with how people actually cook. No matter where I go, from Seattle to Miami, I ask my students about their personal Thanksgiving dishes and customs. First, *Thanksgiving 101* is a collection of these favorite recipes—even if some of them start with a can of soup or a box of Jell-O. Some of Thanksgiving's most cherished recipes are brand-name specific. I call these "Classic Recipes," and I include some background on how they rose to the top to become holiday icons.

We all know the generic recipes that form the backbone of the quintessential Thanksgiving dinner. Mashed potatoes, gravy, piecrust, and stuffing all fit into this category. With practice, these dishes become simple, but they can intimidate novices and elude practiced cooks looking for the perfect version. These recipes are labeled "101," and if they seem long, it's because I have included extra details that even old hands can learn from.

Certain Thanksgiving foods have achieved almost religious significance, and must be served at that meal on the fourth Thursday of every November. While researching recipes for my classes, I became fascinated with how these particular foods became so important. These are discussed in the sections en-

titled, "It Wouldn't Be Thanksgiving Without . . . ," where you'll find information on classics such as cranberries, pumpkin, gelatin salads, and, of course, turkey.

What I hear most from my students is that they are desperate for help in *organizing* the meal. So, in addition to a host of tips, I've provided suggested complete menus with preparation and cooking timetables.

My students also tell me that these recipes are too good to reserve for just one day of the year, and I agree. Thanksgiving isn't the only time when turkey makes an appearance—it's perfect for a Sunday supper, creating leftovers to use for other meals, and many families serve the bird with fixings for Christmas and Easter, too. You'll savor many of the other dishes year-round, too, especially the side dishes and desserts. For example, I rarely serve grilled pork chops without a cranberry chutney (I keep a stash of frozen cranberries to use when they're out of season). Because most of my Thanksgiving first-course soups and salads feature seasonal ingredients, I use them often during cool months. No matter what the season, hardly a party goes by without one of the appetizers from this book. And it certainly doesn't have to be Thanksgiving to make apple pie!

I have been gathering the recipes for this book for years, listening to thousands of American home cooks tell me about the fun (and fear) they experience while getting the big meal on the table. I promised them I would write a *practical* guide on this beloved holiday. Many of these recipes are downright simple, but that doesn't make them any less delicious. *Thanksgiving 101* is a culinary insurance policy to having the best Turkey Day ever.

Happy Thanksgiving!

Getting It Together

Everyone loves Thanksgiving. But, even experienced cooks look at making Thanksgiving dinner with a mixture of trepidation and nostalgia. After all, it has probably been 364 days since the last time they were asked to make such a huge meal. Some of those dishes are made on Thanksgiving and Thanksgiving only, so it is like starting from scratch. Someone once asked a famous Wagnerian soprano how she performed her long, grueling roles night after night. "No problem," she modestly replied. "All you need is a good pair of shoes." When people ask me how I pull off my Thanksgiving dinners, I know how that singer felt. I want to say, "All you need is a good pair of shoes . . . and a plan!"

The happiest Thanksgiving cook is the most organized. No one ever sees the pile of lists that guides me through the organization and preparation of the meal. It's not enough to just *want* to serve a delicious holiday dinner—you'd better think about how to get all of that food on the table at the same time. Plot it out on paper, and you'll be one giant step closer to serving a perfect meal. A written plan is reassuring—you can look it over as many times as you want to check and double-check, or make the changes that will inevitably occur.

Lists, Lists, and More Lists

Thanksgiving Rule Number One:

You can never have too many lists. And nothing feels better than seeing every item checked off. You will need the following lists:

• **Guest List:** Invite your guests, by mail or phone, at least three weeks ahead. As soon as possible, try to get your friends to let you know if they are bringing guests. I always plan on one last-minute phone call with someone saying, "I just found out that so-and-so at the office has nowhere to go. Can I bring them along?" Especially for large gatherings, keep track of RSVPs. When necessary, include directions to your house with the invitation.

• **Grocery Lists:** You should have at least three grocery lists and a beverage list. Spread out the shopping over a couple of weeks so you're not one more person standing in line at the supermarket with an overflowing cart. Buy as many nonperishables as possible before that Tuesday or Wednesday. That way, you'll only need a quick trip to the market pick up the fresh items. My goal every year is to be able to stand in the express lane on Thanksgiving Eve, and I have accomplished this more than once.

The first grocery list should be nonperishables that can be purchased two or three weeks ahead of the dinner. You may not know exactly how many people are coming yet, but you can get candles, coffee filters, guest towels and soap, cocktail napkins, camera film, paper towels, aluminum foil, plastic wrap, bathroom tissue, and other incidentals. Play it safe and buy staples like flour, sugar, salt, and such. Buy coffee and put it in the freezer. If you are grilling your turkey, put charcoal or propane gas on this list.

The second grocery list is for the week before the meal. By now (hopefully), your guest list is confirmed. You know what your menu is, and what groceries you'll need. Buy all the produce that will keep for a week (like onions, garlic, potatoes, yams, carrots, lemons, and limes), dairy items (cheese, eggs, and butter), canned goods, and spices. When you write down the groceries, try to organize them by category (or if you are really familiar with your market, by aisle location), so you don't have to run all over the store. If necessary, order your turkey and other meat or seafood items. Call the bakery to reserve your pies and dinner rolls (if you're not baking them yourself).

The last grocery list is for Tuesday or Wednesday's shopping, which will include only fresh turkey, cream, milk, vegetables, and fruit, and maybe a couple of extra bags of ice. If you can, purchase your produce at a greengrocer—the line will be shorter and the produce better than most supermarkets.

In states where alcohol is sold in grocery stores, your beverage list can be part of the second shopping list. Otherwise, make a separate list for the liquor store. Don't forget mixers and nonalcoholic beverages and any garnishes, like celery for the Bloody Marys.

- **Prep Lists:** There are a lot of cooking chores that can be done well ahead of time. Look at your menu for potential freezable items. I am not a big "freezer person," mainly because I don't have a large freezer, but, I do freeze a few quarts of home-made turkey stock, and maybe some piecrusts.

Be realistic about how much time it will take for you to make each dish. Only you know how fast you can chop. Also, schedule in cleaning time. It is much easier to clean as you go along than to wait until the dishes are piled so high you can't stand it anymore.

- **Utensil List:** French chefs call this a *batterie de cuisine.* It means all the pots, pans, basters, spoons, roasting racks, coffee makers, measuring cups, rolling pins, pie pans, and other things that you'll need to get the dinner on the table. Check all of the recipes and be sure that you have everything you need. If a recipe calls for a 9 x 13-inch baking dish, and yours is a different size, you can either buy the right pan or throw caution to the wind and hope that the recipe turns out all right in your pan. I vote for buying the new dish. I have made every effort to use pots and pans that can be found in the average home. Where necessary, unusual equipment is listed after the ingredients list in a recipe.

Be sure to have plenty of large self-sealing plastic bags on hand. Whenever possible, store food in the plastic bags instead of bowls. You'll save lots of refrigerator space that way.

- **Tableware List:** Check to see that you have all of the serving dishes and utensils you need. Many items may be stored away, so take them out and get them washed. To keep all of those bowls and platters straight, list what food goes in what dish. This way, in the heat of the battle, when a helper says, "What dish do the mashed potatoes go into?" you can say "The blue one!" not, "I don't remember!" If you have silver to be polished or linens to be washed and pressed, schedule those jobs well ahead of time.

If you don't have enough china and silver, try to avoid using paper plates and plastic utensils. Restaurant supply shops sell inexpensive dishes and silverware, or, borrow from friends and family. You may not have a matching set, but at least the gravy won't seep through the plates. Along the same lines, use real napkins, not paper ones—it's a festive holiday.

Everything has its place—but even more so at Thanksgiving. Draw a "map" of the table that includes the serving dishes and centerpiece to be sure everything will fit. If it doesn't, figure out where you will put the excess. If you don't have enough chairs, borrow from a friend or rent them. If you need to move any furniture to make room, take note and add it to another "To Do" list.

If you are having a buffet, think about where to put the plates and eating utensils. You may want to put them on a separate sideboard or table. If you have a large crowd, pull the table away from the wall if necessary. Make two stacks of plates, and place them on opposite sides of the table, so there can be two lines and guests can serve themselves from both sides. Put two utensils in each bowl so guests can serve themselves faster. To save space, roll the forks and knives in napkins and tie with ribbons, then stack them in a basket. Place the basket at the end of the buffet, so guests don't have to juggle the utensils while they are trying to fill their plates.

- **The Bill of Fare:** It sounds silly, but I always have the complete menu, including beverages and appetizers, taped up on the refrigerator door to double-check that everything makes it out to the table. More than once, after the meal, I have found a bowl of cranberry sauce hidden in the refrigerator (and my guests were too polite to say, "How chic! No cranberries!" to remind me).

Your Menu and You

There are many variables that make a menu the right one. Sure, personal taste comes into play, but more important are the logistics. Do you have enough refrigerator space? Do you only have one oven? How big is it? How many people can you really seat, even with the card table? Brutally assess your cooking skills. Some people are entranced by what they see on television cooking shows (or read in cookbooks), and overdo it. Instead of enjoying your guests, you see a lot of your kitchen.

Most of the recipes in this book are for eight to twelve servings. (A serving is an average-sized portion. I can't say "Serves Eight," because if your eight guests have big appetites, and take big spoonfuls, the eight servings become four.) With the exception of the desserts, all of the recipes can be multiplied or divided to fit your guest count. Desserts have to be prepared by the unit—you wouldn't bake only half a pie to get four extra servings.

If you are new to the Thanksgiving routine, concentrate on one or two dishes (like turkey and gravy) and learn to do them well. Let guests bring side dishes and desserts or pick them up at a takeout place. Next year, expand your repertoire to include cranberry sauce and pumpkin pie. Pretty soon, you'll be able to execute the entire menu.

Being a slave to fashion is bad enough, but being a slave to the traditional Thanksgiving menu is worse. You don't have to serve the exact same meal that Mom made. Design a balanced meal with different colors, textures, and flavors. If you think there are too many sweet things or starches on the menu, scratch one off and replace it with something else. In my opinion, most people just serve too much food. Thanksgiving should be about visiting with loved ones over a special meal, not about how much turkey you can eat in twenty minutes because the football game is about to come on.

And speaking of football, my heart goes out to you cooks whose meal has to vie for attention with the

Pilgrim's Progress

In the middle of all the planning and festivities, keep in mind what Thanksgiving is about. It's not about football, or pumpkin pie, or even turkey. The Pilgrims used the first Thanksgiving feast as a celebration to give thanks for the good in their lives, in spite of the fact that it had been a very difficult year. But it was no solemn occasion. One professor of American history has said that Thanksgiving "was a party, and a three-day party, at that!"

The Puritans wanted to purify the Church of England of rituals that had their roots in Catholicism. They were driven from England by James I, and fled to Holland in 1608. Twelve years later, tiring of Dutch customs and language, they made the difficult decision to emigrate to the New World, where they could practice their own customs and speak their own language. One hundred and two passengers made the sixty-six-day journey on the Mayflower, landing in Provincetown Harbor (not Plimouth Rock as is often assumed) in Cape Cod on November 21, 1620. Exactly one month later, after exploring the area, they chose Plimouth as the settling spot.

By harvest time the next year, forty-six of the original group had succumbed to scurvy or pneumonia. However, the autumn crop had been good, mainly because of the help of one Pawtuxet Indian, Squanto, who taught the settlers much about farming in their new home. Squanto, who had been a slave in Spain but had escaped to England, spoke English. He had returned to his native village only six months before the Puritans arrived.

The Puritans were familiar with harvest festivals, which were common in England. So, it was a natural turn of events for Governor William Bradford to declare a thanksgiving feast. The exact date has never been established. According to Bradford's own history, *Of Plimouth Plantation,* on September 18, he sent men to trade with the Indians. The harvest was gathered after they returned. The first written mention of the party was in a letter by another settler on December 11. But, with all of the outdoor activities described in the original sources, the event probably happened while the weather was still reasonably warm.

As for the menu, we know that Bradford sent "four men fowling" to gather wild poultry for the feast. They returned with ducks and geese and a "great store of wild Turkies." However, to the Puritans, *turkey* meant any kind of guinea fowl, which also roamed the wilds of the Atlantic coast, and we can't be sure that our familiar turkey was served. Venison was surely on the menu (the Indian chief Massasoit sent braves into the woods who "killed five Deere which they brought to our Governour"), along with lobsters, clams, sea bass, corn, boiled pumpkin, watercress, leeks, and dried fruit. Corn cakes, fried in venison fat, were served as the bread, as there was no wheat. It is assumed that cranberries, an Indian favorite, would have been included, probably cooked in maple syrup. As there were no cows, there wouldn't have been any dairy products, like butter, milk, or cheese. Contrary to popular belief, the Puritans did drink alcohol, although they did not tolerate drunkness, and quaffed a strong beverage that probably resembled brandy.

After the meal, a little exercise was in order. Of

course, football hadn't been invented yet, but the Indians and Puritan soldiers played other games. Marksmanship was exhibited with both the bow and arrow and the musket, and athletic prowess with foot-races and jumping matches.

The Thanksgiving feast did not become an annual event. The only other Thanksgiving occurred in 1623, to celebrate the end of a drought. Harvest festivals certainly continued throughout the colonial period, but actual "thanksgivings" were saved for major events, like the one in 1789 proclaimed by George Washington to commemorate the new Constitution. It was around this time that the term *Pilgrim* came into use. The Puritans referred to themselves as First Settlers, or First Comers. They eventually became known as the Forefathers, but during the American revolution, *Pilgrim* became an alternative.

We have our modern holiday thanks to the dogged efforts of one woman, Sarah Josepha Hale. Hale was the influential editor of the popular woman's magazine *Godey's Lady's Book*. With over a hundred and fifty thousand subscribers, she used her editorials to promote a national day of Thanksgiving, and wrote letters to presidents, governors, and other high-profile people. She espoused a day to "offer to God our tribute of joy and gratitude for the blessings of the year." The magazine did much to romanticize the Pilgrim as a steadfast, hardworking, religious model of American perseverance. After years of grandstanding, she finally got the support of President Abraham Lincoln, who declared Thursday, November 23, 1863, a national holiday. Over the years, Thanksgiving was always an excuse for unabashed feasting and fun. Staid New Englanders considered Christmas a religious holiday, and hardly "celebrated" it at all.

(It wasn't until German immigrants brought their customs to America in the late 1880s that Christmas got a makeover.)

Until 1941, it was up to the President to declare the holiday each year, which usually occurred on the last Thursday of November. In 1939, President Franklin D. Roosevelt, who felt Thanksgiving was too close to Christmas and diluted the effect of the later holiday, moved the date to the third Thursday of that year. The country responded bitterly, and a lot of people took off the fourth Thursday anyway. The next year, emotions ran even higher. The only people who liked the change were the merchants, who saw a longer Christmas buying season. Finally, in December 1941, a joint resolution of Congress specified the fourth Thursday in November (which is sometimes, but not always, the last Thursday) as Thanksgiving.

The first Thanksgiving Day parade was marched in Philadelphia in 1923, sponsored by Gimbel's Department Store. Macy's first parade occurred the next year, in New York City. The first professional Thanksgiving football game was played by the Detroit Lions and the Chicago Bears in 1934.

Thanksgiving has never enjoyed the same literary attention as Christmas. Few Thanksgiving songs, movies, or books have established themselves like "Jingle Bells," *It's a Wonderful Life,* or *A Visit from St. Nicholas*. My favorite Thanksgiving story is "The Thanksgiving Visitor" by Truman Capote, and I don't like to let a Thanksgiving go by without playing my old LP of Arlo Guthrie's "Alice's Restaurant." "Over the River and Through the Woods" just doesn't stand up to Arlo. Also, while the turkey scenes in *Home for the Holidays* are hilarious, don't expect the movie to make you feel like phoning your family.

game. When people come to my house for Thanksgiving, they come for a good meal, and the television never gets turned on (except to keep the kids occupied). Perhaps you should try my friend Monica's tactic. She decided that she wasn't going to let the football schedule call the shots. So, she roasted a turkey, but only served it with fixings for fresh sliced turkey sandwiches. It has become her family's annual Thanksgiving meal.

Help!

Another Thanksgiving Rule:

Let your friends help you . . . kinda.

There are times when being a control freak can come in handy . . . like the fourth Thursday of November. The first few times I made Thanksgiving dinner, people asked if they could bring something, and I was glad to let them pitch in. But, I couldn't help noticing a few recurring trends. One friend always brought something different from what she'd said she would. If she'd said she'd bring cranberry sauce, she'd bring green bean bake . . . but only when I already had four other green bean bakes, and no cranberry sauce. Another friend considered it a crime to follow a recipe, and always got "creative" with his contribution. The problem was, that his experiments never turned out. (Like the year he substituted honey for sugar in the pumpkin pie and the filling wouldn't set.) I considered having a sampler saying "No More Potlucks . . . Ever!" made to hang in the kitchen. It's much better to be in complete charge of the menu.

It's not that I'm ungrateful, it's just that there are other ways that my friends can help. My favorite friend is the one who comes over on Wednesday night to keep me company while I prep. Even if he isn't a good cook, he can run to the store if I left something off the list, clean up the dirty dishes, pour us a glass of wine, order pizza (Who has time to make dinner?), set the dining room table for the big dinner. Of course, on Thanksgiving Day, anyone who offers to wash dishes is my best friend for life.

If you must have a potluck, here's a strategy that has worked for me. I designed my menu from clipped newspaper and magazine recipes, and assigned them according to the person's cooking skills. I knew exactly what everyone was going to bring, and that it was all going to fit together. My friends were relieved, because they didn't have to fret about what they were going to bring.

When the going gets rough, remember that at the first Thanksgiving, only six women had to prepare all the food for ninety-one Indians and fifty-six settlers, and that the party lasted three days.

Setting the Scene

I know caterer-types who seem to have hot glue guns at the ready. Not me. I prefer to spend my creative time in the kitchen. When it comes time to decorate, I subscribe to the philosophy "less is more."

You can do very simple things that say "Thanksgiving." Roll up napkins, rolling an autumn leaf around the center, and tie with a piece of raffia straw. Put a foil-wrapped chocolate turkey at each place setting. One of my favorite settings wasn't especially elegant, but it was fun. Each setting had a lighted kitschy candle (Pilgrims, Indians, and turkeys) that I had collected from different department stores. They looked great, all grinning and blazing away. And everyone took a candle home.

Remember that centerpieces for a dining table must be low enough for people to see over. Pumpkins are always a great start. Large hollowed-out ones can serve as vases. Mini-pumpkins or apples can hold candles (remove the stems and carve a hole in the center). Another simple centerpiece is a floating candle in a glass bowl, with cranberries added to the water. Sometimes I do nothing more complicated than a basket filled with autumn foods (persimmons, grapes, apples, and nuts), entwined with a length of French wired ribbon. Of course, the food can be eaten at the end of the dinner, so it doesn't go to waste.

At formal table settings, place cards are appropriate, and they look great taped to the side of a mini-pumpkin at each plate. I have also baked large turkey- or leaf-shaped cookies and decorated them with my guests' names inscribed in icing. (They rarely get eaten that evening, because people like to take them home as a memento. To each their own. I eat *mine.*) To try this, just use your favorite rolled sugar or gingerbread cookie recipe.

The Kids' Table

When kids are a part of your Thanksgiving guest list, be sure that you have activities that don't just keep them busy, but let them contribute to the festivities.

My young friends love helping in the kitchen. Sometimes I let them do easy chores like peeling vegetables or whipping cream. But, they really love it when they can create something to share with the whole group. The day before the dinner, bake turkey-shaped cookies. On Thanksgiving, set up a corner in the kitchen with icing and colored sugar, and let them decorate the cookies to serve with coffee for dessert.

If there is just too much activity in the kitchen for small bodies to be around, I provide crayons, construction paper, paste, and scissors for them to create placecards. I'll get them going by making turkey-shaped cut-outs—it's their job to cut out and paste colorful paper feathers onto the tail and write the guests' names on the bodies. (Some craft stores sell inexpensive small, real feathers that can also be used.)

When you've set up a kids' table, make it something special. Don't make them feel like they're in Siberia. Once, when up in the country, we sent the youngsters out to collect the best-looking autumn leaves. When they returned, they washed and dried the gathered leaves well. I covered the kids' table with a piece of white butcher paper and they glued the leaves all over the paper as a tablecloth. It looked so great that the adults were envious. Another time, we simply stenciled outlines of turkeys all over the butcher paper and put out crayons to color the turkeys during dinner.

Of course, there's the time-honored tradition of the touch-football game to help the kids let off steam. But I wonder if it's really to keep the kids occupied or to help the adults burn off calories.

Appetizers and Beverages

Just a Little Something to Keep the Edge Off

The concept of "make-ahead cuisine" is of paramount importance at Thanksgiving, but even more so when planning your appetizer and beverage strategy. Serve tasty goodies that will take the edge off everyone's hunger, but nothing that needs last-minute preparation or warming up. Little hors d'oeuvres that need to be baked are definitely out, if for no other reason than that the oven will probably be in use cooking the main event. The best tactic is to set out foods that need no attention other than an occasional refill. Spiced nuts, hot or cold dips, cheese balls and cheese boards, savory cookies—all of these can be prepared well ahead of time.

Foods such as marinated olives, pâtés, and pickles, which *must* be prepared ahead to allow their flavors to mellow, are among my favorites because they allow me to scratch an item off my preparation list days in advance. The only time of year I serve a relish tray is at Thanksgiving. (When I was growing up, all of us kids would stick pitted black olives on our fingers and eat them off, one by one.) If I have home-preserved pickles from my summer canning, they get place of honor. Otherwise I buy high-quality goods like pickled okra, Italian giardinera, and stuffed olives from a specialty food market. And at least two kinds of pickles, one sweet and one sour.

Visual appeal is really important. Here are a few ideas I learned from my days as a Manhattan caterer:

- Choose crackers for their shape as well as their flavor.

- Pick crudité vegetables that have contrasting colors and textures. Place contrasting vegetables next to each other, i.e., the broccoli next to the carrots, next to the cauliflower, next to the green beans, next to the cherry tomatoes. Don't put the green broccoli next to the green beans.

- Line serving baskets with colorful napkins. Tie bunches of dried berries around the handles with raffia to give a harvest look.

- Garnish platters with bunches of tiny Indian corn or small gourds or line them with leaves of curly kale or collard greens.

- Serve dips in hollowed-out cabbages (look for curly varieties with the outer leaves attached) or winter squash (the larger and more exotically colored, the better).

Don't forget incidental details. Put cocktail napkins on your shopping list. If you are serving a warm dip in a mini-electric slow cooker, be sure you have a long enough extension cord and that it can be plugged in where no one will trip over it. If you are using a fondue pot or chafing dish to keep the dip warm, purchase a supply of the appropriate liquid fuel.

When it comes to beverages, remember that you are under no obligation to have a fully stocked bar. If you have narrowed down your menu choices to make an intelligent, balanced meal, you can do the same with the drinks. Remember your obligation to your guests' well-being, and don't encourage overdrinking, especially by anyone who will be driving. If you offer homemade nonalcoholic beverages, it doesn't make abstainers feel like they are cursed to an evening of club soda. Always offer one beverage that is just as tasty spiked as it is without alcohol, such as Bloody (or Virgin) Marys or Autumn Glow Punch (pages 11 and 12). If someone who isn't driving wants to add a splash of vodka or rum, he can go ahead. Sparkling apple cider, such as Martinelli's, is a great choice—I like to serve it in champagne flutes to make the drinkers feel that their drinks are just as important as the alcoholic ones. Set up the bar outside of the kitchen, and in a manner so that everyone can help themselves.

Glittering Spiced Walnuts

Makes 4 cups 6 to 8 servings

Make Ahead: The walnuts can be prepared up to 1 week ahead.

It makes no difference how many of these I make, they always seem to be gone by the end of the evening. They have many irresistible qualities. The unusual deep-frying procedure gives them a delectably thin glaze, and the seasoning mixture is so much better and fresher than any Asian five-spice powder you can buy in a jar. Walnut halves, not pieces, give the best results, and can be found at specialty food stores and many candy and nut shops.

Asian Spices

1 whole star anise (or use 6 or 7 "points" if pods
   are broken)

$1/2$ teaspoon ground cinnamon

$1/2$ teaspoon coriander seeds

$1/2$ teaspoon Szechwan peppercorns

$1/4$ teaspoon fennel seeds

4 whole cloves

$1/8$ teaspoon cayenne pepper

Vegetable oil for deep-frying

1 pound walnut halves

$1/2$ cup sugar

Salt for sprinkling (fine sea, or iodized)

Special Equipment

A deep-frying thermometer

A large wire skimmer

1. To make the spice mixture, finely grind the spices in a spice or electric coffee grinder. Set aside.

2. Place a baking sheet next to the stove. Line a second baking sheet with paper towels. In a deep Dutch oven over high heat, heat enough vegetable oil to come 3 inches up the sides to 365°F.

3. Meanwhile, bring a medium saucepan of water to a boil over high heat. Add the walnuts and cook for 1 minute; the water does not have to return to a boil. (This warms the walnuts and removes excess bitterness.) Drain in a large colander. Do not rinse. Immediately toss the walnuts in the colander with the sugar until the hot water clinging to the walnuts melts the sugar to form a thin glaze.

4. In two batches, deep-fry the walnuts until golden, about 3 minutes. Using a large skimmer, transfer the walnuts to the unlined baking sheet (the hot walnuts would stick to paper towels) and cool completely. When cooled, transfer the walnuts to the paper towels to drain excess oil.

5. Place the walnuts in a bowl. While tossing the nuts, sift the spice mixture through a fine-meshed wire sieve over them. Discard the hulls in the sieve. Season with salt. (The walnuts can be prepared up to 1 week ahead and stored in an airtight container at room temperature.)

Note: If you want to make more than one batch, have extra oil on hand. The sugar on the nuts "caramelizes" the oil after deep-frying a pound or two and makes it necessary to use fresh oil.

Buttered Cajun Pecans

Makes about 12 servings

Make Ahead: The pecans can be prepared up to 2 days ahead.

These are tossed together in a flash to make a nibble that everyone will love. The secret is making your own Cajun seasoning. There are many Cajun/Creole spice mixtures on the market, but they can be salty, and it's easy to make a batch from the spices in your kitchen cabinet. Use any leftover to season grilled poultry, fish, or pork, or sprinkle on popcorn.

3 tablespoons unsalted butter

1 pound pecan halves

1 tablespoon Cajun Seasoning (recipe follows)

2 teaspoons sugar

In a large nonstick skillet, melt the butter over medium heat. Add the pecans and cook, stirring often, until heated through, about 2 minutes. Sprinkle with the Cajun Seasoning and sugar and stir until the sugar melts, about 1 more minute. (The pecans can be prepared up to 2 days ahead of serving and stored in an airtight container at room temperature.) Serve warm or at room temperature.

Cajun Seasoning: In a small bowl, combine 2 tablespoons sweet paprika (preferably Hungarian), 1 tablespoon each dried thyme and dried basil, 1 teaspoon each garlic powder and onion powder, $1/2$ teaspoon freshly milled black pepper, and $1/8$ teaspoon cayenne pepper.

Spicy Cheddar and Pecan Balls

Makes 2 "cannonballs"; 8 to 12 servings each

Make Ahead: The cheese balls can be prepared up to 3 days ahead.

Most of us who grew up in the fifties and sixties remember those party animals, nut-covered cheese balls. Here's an updated, zesty cheese ball for today's tastes, chunky with roasted red pepper, green olives, capers, and pickled jalapeños. It's a great recipe for large gatherings. The mixture can be rolled into one large ball, but two smaller balls make for easier serving, as they can be placed in different spots within reach of more people.

Two 8-ounce packages cream cheese, at room temperature

1 pound extra-sharp Cheddar cheese, shredded

1 medium red bell pepper, roasted (see Note) and cut into $1/4$-inch dice

$1/2$ cup pitted Mediterranean green olives

2 tablespoons nonpareil capers, rinsed

2 tablespoons chopped pickled or seeded fresh jalapeños

1 to 2 teaspoons chili powder

2 teaspoons Worcestershire sauce

2 garlic cloves, crushed through a press

$1/4$ teaspoon hot red pepper sauce

1 cup coarsely chopped pecans

Assorted crackers for serving

1. The day before serving, in a large bowl, using a rubber spatula, mash the cream cheese and Cheddar cheese together until combined. Using a rubber spatula, work in the remaining ingredients except the pecans.

2. Transfer half of the cheese mixture to an 18-

inch-long piece of plastic wrap. Bring up the edges of the plastic wrap and twist them to form the mixture into a ball. Repeat with the remaining cheese mixture. Refrigerate until chilled and firm, at least 4 hours. (The cheese balls can be prepared up to 3 days ahead.)

3. Before serving, roll the cheese balls in the pecans to cover completely. Let stand at room temperature for 1 hour. Serve with crackers.

Note: It's easiest to roast bell peppers in the broiler. Position the broiler pan about 4 inches from the source of heat and preheat the broiler. Cut the top and bottom from one or more red bell peppers, discarding the green stem (pop it out from the cut top). Slice each bell pepper open vertically and open it up into a long strip. Remove and discard the ribs and seeds. Place the bell pepper pieces, including the top and bottom, skin sides up, on the broiler rack. Broil until the skin is blackened and blistered, about 5 minutes. Transfer to a paper bag, close, and let stand until cooled, about 10 minutes. Scrape off the blackened skin. If you need to rinse the peppers, do so briefly under cold water. Bell peppers can be roasted up to 2 days ahead, covered, and refrigerated.

The Famous Disappearing Spinach Dip

Makes about 5 1/2 cups; 20 servings

Make Ahead: The dip and crudités can be prepared up to 2 days ahead.

A colorful selection of crudités with a tasty dip is just enough to tide some folks over until the big meal. It's always hard to decide which dip to serve, but this creamy, green-flecked mixture often makes my final cut. It makes a huge bowl, but on the rare occasion when leftovers occur, I make it into a great salad dressing by blending the dip with buttermilk and a dash of vinegar. This recipe is from my dear friend Diane Kniss, who insists that its secret lies in store-bought ingredients.

One 10-ounce box chopped frozen spinach
One 15-ounce container sour cream
2 cups mayonnaise
$1/2$ cup chopped scallions
$1/2$ cup chopped fresh parsley
$1/2$ cup chopped fresh dill
One 1.8-ounce package leek-vegetable soup
 mix, such as Knorr's
1 tablespoon cheese-based salad seasoning,
 such as Salad Supreme
Assorted crudités for serving

1. Put the spinach in a wire sieve and run under lukewarm water until thawed. A handful at a time, squeeze the moisture out of the spinach, and transfer the spinach to a large bowl.

2. Add the sour cream, mayonnaise, scallions, parsley, dill, leek soup mix, and salad seasoning and mix well. Cover and refrigerate until ready to serve. Serve with crudités.

The Crudités Garden

Crudités (the French word for raw vegetables) are always a welcome addition to the appetizer spread. Crudités should be thought of as an appetite-teasing, color-filled, crunchy, delicious cornucopia, not just a few carrot sticks in a bowl. Of course, the vegetables should be fresh and appealing, but choose them with an eye to contrasting colors, shapes, and textures to make the selection interesting to the eye and the palate. To set them off, place the crudités in a basket lined with curly kale leaves.

Some vegetables are fine raw, but others benefit from a quick blanching to set their color or make them less crunchy, such as asparagus spears, carrot sticks, green beans, and broccoli and cauliflower florets. Cherry tomatoes, cucumber rounds, celery sticks, mushroom caps, bell pepper (green, yellow, red, and/or orange) strips, and zucchini sticks should be served raw.

To parboil crudités, cut the vegetables into the desired shape—florets, spears, or sticks. Bring a large pot of lightly salted water to a boil over high heat. In separate batches, cook the vegetables just until crisp-tender, about 1 to 2 minutes, no longer. Drain the vegetables and rinse well under cold running water to stop the cooking and set the color. Some cooks plunge the crudités into bowls of ice water, but that is a huge bother, and you can easily run out of ice—something to be avoided during a holiday. (If you are cooking a variety of vegetables, start with the mildest-tasting vegetable first, as each vegetable will leach some flavor into the cooking water. Using a large wire skimmer, transfer them from the water to a colander, and keep the water boiling to cook subsequent batches.) Drain the vegetables well. Pat them completely dry with paper towels, wrap in paper towels, and store in self-sealing plastic bags for up to 1 day.

Shrimp Cocktail Dip

Makes 8 to 12 servings

Make Ahead: The cocktail sauce can be prepared up to 2 days ahead.

For years, my family's Thanksgiving dinner began with a little glass of shrimp cocktail for each of us. Even though they were the supermarket variety, my brothers and I understood that shrimp cocktail was reserved for very classy occasions, and that serious eating was ahead. The shrimp cocktail is back, reestablishing itself on the menus of tony restaurants from coast to coast. This is shrimp cocktail for a crowd.

1 cup American-style chili sauce

1 medium celery rib with leaves, finely chopped

1 scallion (white and green parts) finely
   chopped

1 tablespoon chopped fresh parsley

1 tablespoon fresh lemon juice

1 tablespoon bottled horseradish

Hot red pepper sauce

8 ounces cooked, peeled, deveined, and finely
   chopped shrimp

One 8-ounce package cream cheese, at room
   temperature

Crackers, baguette slices, or celery sticks for
   serving

1. In a medium bowl, mix the chili sauce, celery, scallion, parsley, lemon juice, horseradish, and hot pepper sauce to taste. Cover and refrigerate for 2 hours to allow the flavors to blend. (The cocktail sauce can be prepared up to 2 days ahead.)

2. Stir the shrimp into the cocktail sauce. Place the cream cheese on a serving platter, and pour the shrimp mixture over the top. Serve immediately, with crackers.

Hot Crab Salsa Dip

Makes 12 to 16 servings

Make Ahead: The dip can be prepared up to 8 hours ahead.

Here's another update of an old favorite that my guests can't get enough of. This recipe makes a large amount, but it always disappears. If your appetizer menu is long, the recipe is easily halved. It's a natural for tortilla chips, but try it with fresh crudités like broccoli and cauliflower florets, sweet red pepper strips, and cherry tomatoes. There are a number of options for keeping the dip warm. I use a mini-slow cooker, but fondue pots or electric warming plates also work. For the best flavor, use fresh crabmeat instead of pasteurized or canned.

1 cup chunky tomato salsa

Two 8-ounce packages cream cheese, at room
   temperature

$1/2$ cup mayonnaise

1 teaspoon Worcestershire sauce

1 pound fresh lump crabmeat, picked over to
   remove shells and cartilage and flaked

Hot red pepper sauce

$1/3$ cup fresh bread crumbs, preferably from
   day-old French or Italian bread

Tortilla chips and assorted fresh vegetables for
   serving

1. Position a rack in the center of the oven and preheat to 350°F. Lightly butter a round 1-quart baking dish.

2. Drain the salsa in a sieve to remove excess liquid. Place the drained salsa in a medium bowl and add the cream cheese, mayonnaise, and Worcestershire sauce. Using a rubber spatula, work the ingredients until combined. Stir in the crabmeat. Season with the hot pepper sauce to taste. Spread evenly in the baking dish. (The dip can be prepared up to 8 hours ahead, covered tightly with plastic wrap, and refrigerated.)

3. Sprinkle the bread crumbs over the dip. Bake until the dip is bubbling, about 30 minutes. Serve hot, with tortilla chips and vegetables.

Savory Cheddar and Jalapeño Jelly Cookies

Makes about 4 1/2 dozen

Make Ahead: The cookies can be baked up to 2 days ahead.

My friend Ruth Henderson owns The Silo, a kitchen shop, art gallery, and cooking school nestled in the gorgeous Litchfield Hills in Connecticut. (In fact, many of these recipes debuted at my annual Thanksgiving classes there.) Ruth often serves these delectable appetizer cookies at their gallery opening parties. The dough is easiest to make in a food processor, but the butter and cheese mixture could be creamed by hand, if necessary, if you shred the cheese as finely as possible (use the smallest holes you can on a box grater). If you don't have jalapeño jelly, use apple butter or your favorite chutney instead.

8 ounces extra-sharp Cheddar cheese, shredded (about 2¹/₂ cups)

6 tablespoons (³/₄ stick) unsalted butter, softened

1 cup all-purpose flour

¹/₃ cup jalapeño jelly, apple butter, or chutney

1. Place the cheese and butter in a food processor and pulse a few times to combine. Add the flour and process until the mixture forms a soft dough. Gather up the dough and divide into two flat disks. Wrap in wax paper and freeze until chilled, about 45 minutes.

2. Position two racks in the center and top third of the oven and preheat to 400°F. Line two baking sheets with parchment cooking paper, or use nonstick cookie sheets.

3. Using 1 teaspoon dough for each, roll the dough into small balls and place 1 inch apart on the prepared baking sheets. Bake for 5 minutes. Remove from the oven. Using the handle of a wooden spoon or a ¹/₂-inch-thick dowel, poke an indentation in each cookie. Place the jelly in a small plastic bag and force it down into one corner. Snip off the corner of the bag to make a small hole. Pipe the jelly into the indentations.

4. Return to the oven and bake, switching the positions of the sheets from top to bottom halfway through baking, until the tops are very lightly browned, about 10 minutes (the cookies will continue to crisp as they cool). Transfer to wire cake racks and cool completely. (The cookies can be baked up to 2 days ahead. Store in an airtight container, separating the layers with waxed paper, at room temperature.)

Potato Tortilla with Smoked Salmon

Makes about 48 squares 8 to 12 servings

Make Ahead: The tortilla can be prepared up to 4 hours ahead.

In America, tortilla means one thing, and it is made from corn or wheat and used in Mexican cooking. In Spain, however, a tortilla is a thick omelet that resembles an Italian frittata. It occurred to me to slice up a potato tortilla and use the golden squares as the beginning of the perfect Thanksgiving bite, topped with sour cream and smoked salmon. When guests are arriving in the late morning, these give a brunch-like feel to the appetizer menu. These could also be garnished with black or red caviar, using whatever type fits into the budget.

2 tablespoons olive oil

$1/2$ teaspoon salt

$1/4$ teaspoon freshly milled black pepper

1 pound (3 small) russet or Idaho potatoes, peeled and sliced into $1/8$-inch-thick rounds

5 large eggs, at room temperature

Hot red pepper sauce

Approximately $1/2$ cup sour cream

6 ounces smoked salmon, cut into 1 × $1/4$-inch strips

Minced chives or scallion greens for garnish

1. In a 9-inch nonstick skillet, heat the oil over medium-low heat. In a small bowl, combine $1/4$ teaspoon each of salt and pepper. In four additions, spread the potatoes in the skillet, seasoning each layer with some of the salt and pepper mixture. Stir each addition well to coat with the oil and prevent sticking. Cook, stirring often, until the potatoes begin to soften, about 3 minutes. Cover and cook, stirring often to keep the potatoes from sticking to each other, until the potatoes are just tender, 20 to 25 minutes.

2. In a large bowl, beat the eggs with the remaining $1/4$ teaspoon salt and the hot pepper sauce to taste. Using a slotted spoon, stir the potato slices into the eggs, leaving any oil in the pan.

3. Position the broiler rack 6 inches from the source of heat, and preheat the broiler. Reheat the skillet over medium-low heat. Pour in the egg mixture and spread out the potatoes to make an evenly thick cake. Using a rubber spatula, lift up the cooked part of the tortilla and tilt the skillet so the uncooked eggs run underneath. Continue cooking, occasionally lifting the tortilla and tilting the skillet as described, until the top is almost set, 4 to 5 minutes.

4. Broil the tortilla until the top is puffed and lightly browned, about 1 minute. Place a plate over the top of the skillet and invert the frittata onto the plate. Cool completely. (The tortilla can be prepared up to 4 hours ahead, covered, and refrigerated. Return to room temperature before serving.)

5. Cut the tortilla into 1-inch squares (you will have a few odd-shaped trimmings that you can serve if you wish, or eat as the cook's treat). Top each square with a small dab of sour cream, then a strip of salmon, curled into a decorative shape. Sprinkle with chives and serve.

Pork and Veal Pâté with Dried Cranberries

Makes 8 to 12 servings

Make Ahead: The pâté must be prepared 1 day ahead; it can be refrigerated for up to 3 days.

Pâté is the kind of indulgence that only seems to appear at special occasions. This is a favorite, scented with brandy and studded with sweet-sour cranberries. A pâté is a boon to the busy cook—it's as easy to make as meat loaf, homey and sophisticated at the same time, and, *because it must be made at least a day or two ahead for the flavors to mellow, it allows one more thing to be checked off the prep list well ahead of time. Serve it with thin slices of French bread or crackers, a crock of grainy mustard, and maybe some tiny pickles (cornichons) or picked onions.*

$^1/_2$ cup dried cranberries

$^1/_3$ cup cognac or brandy

1 tablespoon unsalted butter

$^1/_2$ cup finely chopped shallots

2 garlic cloves, minced

$^1/_2$ cup fresh bread crumbs, preferably
   from day-old French or Italian bread

$^1/_3$ cup heavy cream

2 large eggs

$^1/_4$ cup chopped fresh parsley

$^1/_2$ teaspoon dried thyme

$^1/_2$ teaspoon dried rosemary

$^1/_4$ teaspoon ground allspice

2 teaspoons salt

$^1/_4$ teaspoon freshly milled black pepper

1 pound ground veal

1 pound ground pork

4 ounces smoked or boiled ham, sliced $^1/_4$ inch
   thick and cut into $^1/_4$-inch cubes

1. Start the pâté at least 1 day before serving. In a small bowl, plump the cranberries in the cognac for about 1 hour. (Or, place in a small microwave-safe bowl, cover with plastic wrap, and microwave on High for 30 seconds. Stir and let stand for 10 minutes.)

2. Position a rack in the center of the oven and preheat to 350°F. Lightly oil an 8 $^1/_2$ × 4 $^1/_2$ × 2 $^1/_2$-inch loaf pan.

3. In a medium skillet, melt the butter over medium heat. Add the shallots and garlic and cook, stirring often, until softened, about 2 minutes. Set aside.

4. In a large bowl, mix the bread crumbs, heavy cream, eggs, parsley, thyme, rosemary, allspice, salt, and pepper. Let stand for 5 minutes. Add the ground veal and ground pork and mix well (your hands work best). Stir in the ham. Pack into the prepared loaf pan and cover tightly with a double thickness of aluminum foil.

5. Place the loaf pan in a roasting pan. Transfer to the oven. Pull out the oven rack slightly and pour enough hot water into the roasting pan to come $^1/_2$ inch up the sides. Bake until an instant-read thermometer inserted in the center of the pâté (right through the foil) reads 160°F, about 1 $^1/_4$ hours.

6. Remove the loaf pan from the water and place on a wire cake rack. Cool to room temperature.

7. Run a knife around the inside of the pan. Invert to unmold the pâté, wiping away any congealed juices with paper towels. Wrap tightly in plastic wrap. Refrigerate for at least overnight before serving. (The pâté can be prepared up to 3 days ahead.) Serve the pâté chilled or at room temperature.

Tossing Crumbs

Few kitchens are without a box of dried bread crumbs stashed in a cabinet corner. These have their place (to bind some meat loaves and meatballs), but I use fresh bread crumbs more often. The lighter texture and superior flavor of freshly prepared bread crumbs make them much more versatile than the sandy, store-bought kind. Whenever I have leftover bread, I make bread crumbs and freeze them to have when needed.

For the best results, use firm, day-old bread, such as French, Italian, or a high-quality sandwich loaf. English muffins or sandwich rolls also work well, as long as they aren't sweetened. Don't bother to trim off the crusts—they'll add texture and color. With the machine running, drop the bread crumbs through the feed tube of a food processor and process until finely ground and fluffy. (The crumbs can also be prepared in a blender, in small batches.) The crumbs can be frozen in a self-sealing plastic bag for up to 2 months. There's no need to defrost the crumbs before using.

A Pitcher of Bloody Marys

Makes 8 servings

Make Ahead: The tomato mix can be prepared up to 1 day ahead.

When I worked at Teacher's, a popular New York restaurant that was home away from home for many Upper West Siders, the owner was a world championship vodka drinker. Murray wouldn't have dreamed of serving canned Bloody Mary mix, so we made ours according to this blue-ribbon recipe. So that guests can have Virgin Marys too, leave the vodka out of the pitcher and serve it on the side. The perfect formula is three quarters of a cup Bloody Mary mix plus one jigger (1 1/2 ounces, or 3 tablespoons) vodka.

One 48-ounce can tomato-and-vegetable juice cocktail, such as V-8
1/3 cup bottled horseradish
1/3 cup fresh lime juice
2 tablespoons Worcestershire sauce
1 1/2 teaspoons ground celery seeds or celery salt
1 teaspoon hot red pepper sauce, or more to taste
Vodka, as needed
Celery sticks for garnish

1. In a large pitcher, stir the tomato-and-vegetable juice, horseradish, lime juice, Worcestershire sauce, celery seeds, and hot pepper sauce. (The tomato juice mix can be prepared up to 1 day ahead, covered, and refrigerated.)

2. To serve, pour 3/4 cup of the tomato juice mix into each ice-filled glass. Add vodka and stir. Garnish with celery sticks.

A Blender of Ramos Fizzes

Makes 4 servings

Make Ahead: The fizzes are best prepared just before serving.

This is my extended family's Thanksgiving cocktail of choice. Most of us are from San Francisco, where Ramos Fizzes are the ne plus ultra of brunch drinks, and we drink them every year as a toast to our beloved hometown. (New Orleans, the birthplace of the Fizz, is the only other city where it is commonly served at bars and restaurants. I suspect that San Francisco's Fairmont Hotel may have gotten the recipe from the Crescent City's Fairmont Hotel, and popularized the Fizz on the West Coast.) The most important thing to know about these potent drinks is that they may taste like grownup milk shakes, but they aren't as innocent as they look.

1 cup gin
$1/2$ cup half-and-half
$1/2$ cup fresh lime juice
$1 1/2$ teaspoons orange blossom water (available at specialty food stores and many liquor stores and supermarkets)
$1/4$ cup superfine sugar
4 large ice cubes
4 egg whites, 2 large eggs, or $1/2$ cup liquid egg substitute
Approximately $1/2$ cup club soda

1. In a blender, combine the gin, half-and-half, lime juice, orange blossom water, sugar, ice cubes, and egg whites. Blend at high speed until well mixed.

2. Pour into glasses and top off each with approximately 2 tablespoons club soda to provide the "fizz." Serve immediately.

Autumn Glow Punch

Makes 12 to 16 servings

Make Ahead: The punch can be prepared up to 4 hours ahead.

There are two kitchen aromas guaranteed to make your guests feel all warm and fuzzy. One belongs to a roasting turkey, and the other comes from a simmering pot of mulled cider. So your friends don't get too warm and fuzzy, make the punch without any alcohol, but have a bottle of dark rum available for those who wish to spike their cup.

1 teaspoon allspice berries
$1/2$ teaspoon whole cloves
Two 3- to 4-inch cinnamon sticks, broken
2 quarts apple juice
One 32-ounce bottle cranberry juice cocktail
2 large oranges, sliced into rounds
Dark rum, optional

1. Place the allspice, cloves, and cinnamon sticks in a tea ball, or tie into a bundle with cheesecloth and kitchen string. In a large saucepan over medium-low heat, heat the apple juice, cranberry juice, orange slices, and spices just until simmering. (The punch can be prepared up to 4 hours ahead of serving and kept at room temperature. Reheat gently before serving.)

2. To keep the punch warm, transfer to a slow cooker or place the saucepan on a hot plate. Serve hot, allowing each guest to add rum as desired.

Soups and Salads

Who's On First?

Y ou can be sure that there will always be a lot of last-minute activity when it's time to put the main course on the Thanksgiving table. So, I want a first course that is as carefree as possible. Again, make-ahead is the order of the day. Soups that just need a quick reheating or a marinating salad that only needs to be spooned onto a plate are my two standbys, and they have never done me wrong. To decide whether I serve soup or salad, I toss a coin. No matter which one wins, these first courses celebrate the season's bounty with winter squash, sweet potatoes, fennel, celery root, pears, and other seasonal ingredients that say autumn.

More important, a first course acts as a diversion while the side dishes are finishing cooking. Here's the game plan: When the turkey is done, remove it from the oven. It needs to stand for at least twenty minutes before carving anyway, and will stay piping hot for at least one hour. Place the other side dishes that need baking in the oven. Finish the first course (reheat the soup or spoon out the salad), and serve. It will take about fifteen minutes to enjoy the first courses, and you have started your dinner on a leisurely, relaxed note.

Soup is always best prepared with homemade stock. If necessary, a good reduced-sodium canned broth is fine, but a homemade version can be prepared with very little effort and frozen for weeks or months before using. If you only want to make one big batch of all-purpose stock, make turkey instead of chicken. Its deeper flavor will heighten the taste of most of these soups. (Many of my chef friends tell me turkey has replaced veal stock at their restaurants because it's lighter, yet more flavorful and versatile.)

There is a tradition of shellfish soup at many Thanksgiving tables, especially in New England. Overcooked shellfish is tough and rubbery, so always heat up the soup without the shellfish, then add it at the last minute, just to heat through.

To serve the soup at its piping-hot point of perfection, serve it from a warmed soup tureen. If an empty oven is available, place the tureen in a 200°F oven for a few minutes. Otherwise, fill the tureen with very hot water and let stand until warmed. Then pour out the water and dry the tureen. If you have enough space at the back of the stove, warm the tureen there. Try to warm the soup bowls, too. (I know you're not running a restaurant, but who wants lukewarm soup?) Garnishes that are usually chilled, such as sour cream, should be at room temperature so they don't cool down the soup.

At my parents' Thanksgiving dinner, as at millions of other households, a fruity gelatin salad is always the first course of choice. I usually serve savory salads and relegate the gelatin mold to the side-dish category. My Thanksgiving salads are all made in advance, so their flavors can mingle and improve. If any greens are called for, they have been washed early in the day (or even the night before), and are waiting in the refrigerator to be dressed with the (made-ahead) vinaigrette. The salads all feature a mixture of ingredients that are as delicious as they are eye-catching. If possible, serve the salads on large dinner plates—they'll look more attractive and dramatic. Chilled plates are really an affectation, and aren't as necessary as warmed soup bowls.

New England Oyster Stew

Makes 8 servings

Make Ahead: The stew should be prepared just before serving.

In New England, oyster stew is a Thanksgiving must-have. Oysters are at their best during cold weather and are a fine example of how autumn's bounty can be celebrated. Simplicity is the name of the game here—use the finest, freshest oysters, the best cream (go to a natural food store for a brand that hasn't been ultrapasteurized), and a gentle hand with the seasoning.

2 tablespoons unsalted butter
1 scallion (white and green parts), finely
   chopped
2^1/$_2$ cups milk
2 cups heavy cream, preferably not
   ultrapasteurized
3 dozen large oysters, shucked, with their juices
Salt
^{1}/$_8$ teaspoon freshly milled white pepper
Sweet Hungarian paprika (see Note)

1. In a Dutch oven or soup pot, melt the butter over medium heat. Add the scallion and cook, stirring constantly, until wilted, about 1 minute. Add the milk, cream, and the oyster juices. Cook, stirring often, just until small bubbles appear around the edges, about 5 minutes.

2. Add the oysters and cook just until they curl at the edges, about 2 minutes. Season with salt and pepper. (The oysters are already briny, so add salt with caution.) Transfer to a warmed soup tureen and serve immediately in warm soup bowls, sprinkling each serving with a dash of paprika.

Note: Hungarian paprika has more flavor than other varieties, so it does more than just act as a garnish. If you like spicy seasonings, use hot paprika.

Celery Root and Oyster Chowder

Makes 8 servings

Make Ahead: The chowder vegetables can be prepared up to 4 hours ahead.

This is my gussied-up version of standard oyster stew, bolstered with celery root and red bell pepper. If you aren't familiar with celery root (also called celeriac or knob celery), give it a try. This gnarly tuber doesn't look at all like celery, but it has a delicious mild celery flavor that makes it a superior addition to cold-weather soups and chowders.

Juice of 1 lemon
1 pound celery root (2 medium or 1 large)
2 tablespoons unsalted butter
1 medium red bell pepper, cored, seeded, and
   chopped into ^{1}/$_4$-inch dice
^{1}/$_2$ cup chopped leeks
4 cups half-and-half
2 dozen oysters, shucked, with their juices
^{1}/$_2$ teaspoon salt
^{1}/$_8$ teaspoon freshly milled white pepper
2 tablespoons chopped fresh parsley

1. In a bowl, stir the lemon juice into 2 quarts of cold water. Cut off the gnarly parts of the celery root (it is too much trouble to pare all the nooks and crannies). Using a sharp knife, peel the celery root. Cut in half, and remove any soft, spongy center parts. Remove any skin still in the crevices with the tip of the knife. Cut into ½-inch cubes and place in the lemon water.

2. Bring a large pot of lightly salted water to a boil over high heat. Drain the celery root and add it to the boiling water. Return to a boil and reduce the heat to medium. Cook the celery root until tender when pierced with the tip of a knife, about 7 minutes. Drain and rinse under cold running water. Transfer to a bowl, cover, and set aside. (The celery root can be prepared up to 4 hours ahead and stored at room temperature.)

3. In a Dutch oven or soup kettle, melt the butter over medium-low heat. Add the red pepper and leeks, cover, and cook, stirring occasionally, until the red pepper softens, 5 to 7 minutes. (The leek/red pepper mixture can be prepared up to 4 hours ahead and kept at room temperature. Reheat over low heat before proceeding.)

4. Pour the half-and-half and oyster juices into the Dutch oven and increase the heat to high. Cook just until small bubbles appear around the edges, about 5 minutes. Add the oysters and celery root and cook just until the oysters curl around the edges and are heated through, about 2 minutes. Season with the salt and pepper. Transfer to a warmed soup tureen and serve immediately in warmed soup bowls, garnished with the parsley.

Clam and Mushroom Soup

Makes 8 servings

Make Ahead: The clams and the soup base can be prepared up to 8 hours ahead.

This recipe is based on one that I first enjoyed years ago at the Stanford Court Hotel in San Francisco. While it is an excellent Thanksgiving soup, you'll want to keep it in mind for other occasions too. If they're available, use flavorful brown cremini mushrooms.

3 dozen littleneck clams, well scrubbed

¹/₂ cup dry white wine

3 tablespoons unsalted butter

1¹/₂ pounds brown cremini or white button
   mushrooms, thinly sliced

¹/₂ cup finely chopped shallots

3 tablespoons all-purpose flour

3¹/₂ cups Homemade Turkey or Chicken Stock
   (page 22 or 24) or reduced-sodium chicken
   canned broth

1 teaspoon dried marjoram or thyme

³/₄ cup heavy cream

¹/₄ teaspoon salt

¹/₄ teaspoon freshly milled black pepper

¹/₂ cup sour cream, at room temperature

2 tablespoons chopped fresh parsley

1. Place the clams and wine in a Dutch oven or soup pot. Cover tightly and bring to a boil over high heat. Cook, occasionally checking the progress of the clams, until the clams open, about 5 minutes. As the clams open, use kitchen tongs to transfer them to a large bowl. When the clams are cool, working over the bowl, remove the clam meat. Transfer the meat to a small bowl. Cover tightly and refrigerate until ready to use. (The clams can be prepared up to 8 hours ahead.)

2. Line a wire sieve with moistened cheesecloth (or paper towels that have been moistened with water and wrung out). Strain the clam juices from the bowl and the Dutch oven through the sieve into a small bowl and set aside.

3. Rinse and wipe out the Dutch oven and return to the stove. Add the butter and melt over medium heat. Add the mushrooms, cover, and cook, stirring occasionally, until the mushrooms give off their juices, about 3 minutes. Uncover and cook until the juices

have evaporated and the mushrooms are beginning to brown. Add the shallots and stir until the shallots soften, about 2 minutes. Sprinkle with the flour and stir until the mushrooms are well coated with the flour, about 1 minute.

4. Add the stock, strained clam juice, and marjoram. Reduce the heat to low and simmer for 10 minutes. (The soup can be prepared to this point up to 8 hours before serving, cooled, covered, and refrigerated. Reheat to simmering before proceeding.)

5. Add the heavy cream and clams and heat until very hot but not boiling. Season with the salt (be careful, as the clams could have added enough salt of their own) and pepper.

6. Transfer to a warmed soup tureen. Ladle the soup into warmed soup bowls, topping each serving with a dollop of sour cream and a sprinkling of parsley. Serve immediately.

Leeking Information

Leeks are grown in sandy soil and need to be cleaned thoroughly. They are best cleaned after chopping, as the sand often hides between the layers of the leek. To clean leeks, trim off the roots. Chop the leeks, using only the white part and about 1 inch of the pale green top and discarding the tops. (Some cooks use the dark green leek tops in stock, but I find it makes the stock too dark.) Place the chopped leeks in a wire sieve and place under cold running water, tossing the leeks with your hand to be sure all that the surfaces are rinsed well. You will be able to tell by touch if the leeks are sandy. Drain completely.

Aw Shucks

Large- to medium-sized oysters make the best stew, as they give off more delicious, briny juices than smaller specimens. There are many varieties on the East Coast, usually named for the place they were raised, such as Malpeque (Prince Edward Island) or Pemmaquid (Maine). Pacific (also called Japanese) or European flat oysters, both of which have distinctly different flavor characteristics from Eastern oysters, can also be used. Small oysters such as Kumamoto and Olympia are too tiny to give off enough juice to make a proper stew.

Freshly shucked oysters have better flavor and texture than prepacked, shucked ones. Unfortunately, oyster shucking is one of the most challenging jobs in the home kitchen. New Englanders usually know someone who is proud to be known as a master oyster-shucker, and if you can enlist that person, you're home free. Otherwise, place an order with the fish store for freshly shucked oysters (instructing them to save the oyster juices) to be picked up on Wednesday afternoon. They'll charge extra for opening the oysters, but it's worth it.

Sometimes you'll have no choice but to open the oysters yourself. There are two methods. Use the first technique when serving oysters that must remain raw and uncooked, such as oysters on the half-shell. The second method can be used if the oysters are going to be cooked in stuffings or stews.

To shuck raw oysters, try Julia Child's technique, taught to her by a oyster fisherman. Instead of an oyster knife (with a sturdy blade and pointed, somewhat blunt tip), use an old-fashioned can opener, the kind some people call a church key. Scrub the oysters well with a stiff brush under cold running water. Place an oyster, curved side down, on a folded kitchen towel. Oysters are usually teardrop-shaped. Locate the spot where the top shell meets the bottom shell at the pointed tip of the "teardrop." Pointed end up, wedge the tip of the can opener into the crack about ¼ inch below the pointed tip of the shell. Push the end of the can opener down, and the shell should pop open from the leverage. If the shell crumbles, you'll have to use an oyster knife to wedge open the crack farther down the shell. Holding the oyster over a wire sieve placed over a bowl to catch and strain any bits of shell from the juices, run a small sharp knife around the top shell to release it. Slip the knife under the flat top shell to cut the oyster free, and discard the top shell. Run the knife underneath the oyster to loosen it from the curved bottom shell. If you are serving the oysters on the half-shell, leave the oyster in the shell and place the shell on a bed of ice in the refrigerator until ready to serve, within 2 hours. If you are going to cook the oysters, place the oysters in a small bowl, add the strained oyster juices, and cover tightly. Refrigerate until ready to use them, up to 24 hours.

If the oysters are going to be cooked in a soup or stuffing, they can be baked in a very hot oven until the shells open. The oysters will be slightly cooked, but not enough to overcook them in the finished dish. This is the method I use most often, as I rarely serve raw oysters at my Thanksgiving table, while oyster stew and oyster stuffing often show up.

Preheat the oven to 500°F. Choose a roasting pan or baking dish large enough to hold the oysters in a single layer, and fill the pan with a thick layer of rock or coarse (kosher) salt (or crumpled aluminum foil). Place the pan in the oven to heat for 10 minutes. Remove the pan from the oven and nestle the oysters, curved sides down, in the salt to keep them from rocking. Bake until the oyster shells gap open, 7 to 20 minutes, depending on the size of the oysters (they never open all at once). Discard any oysters that do not open after 20 minutes of baking. (The oysters can also be opened in the microwave. Microwave six oysters at a time on High until they open, 1 to 2 minutes.) When all of the oysters are open, and have cooled enough to handle, remove the oyster meat from the shells and place in a small bowl. Pour the strained oyster juices in the large bowl over the oysters, cover, and refrigerate. Use the partially cooked oysters within 2 hours.

Pumpkin Tortellini in Chicken Broth

Makes 8 to 10 servings

Make Ahead: The broth can be prepared ahead and refrigerated for up to 3 days or frozen for up to 2 months; the tortellini can be prepared up to 1 day ahead.

Pumpkin tortellini are very popular in Northern Italy, although the authentic filling can be on the sweet side, flavored with amaretti cookie crumbs and an unusual fruit relish called mostarda. *This version, made with round wonton wrappers and with Parmesan cheese in the filling, gets no points for authenticity, but it is delicious. When serving tortellini* en brodo *(in broth), it is important to use an excellent homemade broth.*

Pumpkin Tortellini

1 cup pumpkin puree, canned or freshly
   prepared (see page 128)

¹/₃ cup freshly grated Parmesan cheese

3 tablespoons dried bread crumbs

1 large egg, separated

A few gratings of nutmeg

¹/₈ teaspoon salt

¹/₈ teaspoon freshly milled black pepper

40 round wonton (gyoza) wrappers

8 cups Homemade Chicken Stock (page 24)

¹/₂ cup freshly grated Parmesan cheese, for
   serving

2 tablespoons finely chopped fresh rosemary

1. To make the tortellini, line a baking sheet with wax paper and dust it with cornstarch. In a medium bowl, mix the pumpkin, Parmesan cheese, bread crumbs, egg yolk, nutmeg, salt, and pepper. Place the egg white in a small bowl and beat until foamy. Using a small pastry brush, lightly brush the edges of one wonton wrapper with egg white. Place a teaspoon of the pumpkin filling in the center of the wrapper. Fold the wrapper over, making a half-moon-shaped dumpling, and firmly press the edges to seal. Place a dab of egg white on one corner of the tortellini. Curve the tortellini around your index finger so the two corners meet, and press them together. Place the tortellini on the prepared baking sheet and cover with a large sheet of plastic wrap. Repeat the procedure with the remaining filling and wrappers. (The tortellini can be prepared up to 1 day ahead, covered tightly with plastic wrap, and refrigerated.)

2. In a large Dutch oven or soup pot, bring the stock to a boil over high heat, then reduce the heat to very low. Fill another Dutch oven or large pot with lightly salted water and bring to a boil over high heat.

3. One at a time, quickly drop the tortellini into the boiling water (don't dump the tortellini into the water, or you'll get too much cornstarch in the cooking water). Reduce the heat to medium and gently cook the tortellini until the pasta is tender and the filling is heated through, 3 to 5 minutes. Using a slotted spoon, transfer the tortellini to a warmed soup tureen. Pour the hot broth into the tureen.

4. Ladle the tortellini and broth into warmed soup bowls, sprinkling each serving with Parmesan cheese and rosemary. Serve immediately.

Winter Squash Soup with Prosciutto and Sage

Makes 8 servings

Make Ahead: The soup can be prepared up to 2 days ahead.

This bright-orange soup seems rich and creamy, without a drop of cream in sight. You have many choices, from sugar or cheese pumpkins to butternut, Hubbard, or calabaza squash. Because each squash has a different moisture content, you may find that you need to adjust the consistency of the finished soup. If it is too thick, just thin it with more broth. If it is too thin, dissolve one tablespoon cornstarch in a quarter cup of cold water. Bring the soup to a boil, and stir in enough of the cornstarch mixture to thicken to your taste. (Remember that the soup must be boiling for the cornstarch thickening to work.)

2 pounds winter squash (see above)

2 tablespoons unsalted butter

1 medium onion, chopped

1 medium carrot, chopped

1 medium celery rib, chopped

2 garlic cloves, minced

3 cups Homemade Chicken Stock (page 24) or reduced-sodium canned chicken broth, or as needed

3 ounces sliced ($1/4$-inch-thick) prosciutto, chopped (about $1/2$ cup; see Note)

1 tablespoon finely chopped fresh sage or
   $1^1/2$ teaspoons dried sage

$1/4$ teaspoon salt

$1/4$ teaspoon freshly milled white pepper

1. Using a large sharp knife, cut the squash into large pieces. Using a large spoon, scrape away and discard any fibers and seeds. Cut the squash into 1-inch pieces. Using a small sharp knife, pare away the thick skin. Set the squash aside.

2. In a Dutch oven or soup pot, melt the butter over medium heat. Add the onion, carrot, and celery, cover, and cook, stirring often, until the vegetables soften, about 5 minutes. Add the garlic and cook for 1 minute. Add the squash and chicken stock. Bring to a boil. Reduce the heat to medium-low and simmer, covered, until the squash is tender when pierced with the tip of knife, about 15 minutes.

3. In batches, transfer the soup to a blender and puree. Return the puréed soup to the Dutch oven and add the prosciutto and sage. Cook over low heat for 5 minutes to blend the flavors. Season with the salt and pepper. (The soup can be prepared up to 2 days ahead, cooled, covered, and refrigerated. The soup will thicken when chilled. Reheat over medium-low heat, stirring often and thinning the soup as needed with additional chicken broth.)

4. Transfer the soup to a warmed soup tureen. Ladle into warmed soup bowls and serve immediately.

Winter Squash and Sage Soup: Delete the prosciutto.

Note: When you order prosciutto from the delicatessen counter, be sure to ask for it sliced $1/4$ inch thick, not paper-thin. Any leftover prosciutto can be double-wrapped in aluminum foil and frozen for up to 2 months.

Sweet Potato and Peanut Soup

Makes 8 to 10 servings

Make Ahead: The soup can be prepared up to 2 days ahead.

Two Southern favorites, sweet potatoes and peanuts, blend beautifully in this elegant soup made with humble ingredients. With just a few seasoning vegetables (and a little zip from jalapeño pepper and garlic), the soup has a depth of flavor that belies its simplicity.

2 tablespoons unsalted butter

$^1/_2$ cup chopped shallots

1 medium carrot, chopped

1 medium celery rib, chopped

1 jalapeño pepper, seeded and minced

2 garlic cloves, crushed under a knife

2 pounds sweet potatoes (yams), peeled and
    cut into 1-inch cubes

$3^1/_2$ cups Homemade Turkey or Chicken Stock
    (page 22 or 24), or canned reduced-sodium
    chicken broth

$^1/_2$ cup smooth peanut butter (not natural)

1 tablespoon fresh lime juice

$^3/_4$ teaspoon salt

$^1/_4$ teaspoon freshly milled white pepper

Approximately 2 tablespoons heavy cream

Chopped fresh cilantro optional

1. In a Dutch oven or soup pot, melt the butter over medium heat. Add the shallots, carrot, celery, jalapeño, and garlic. Cover and cook, stirring often, until the vegetables soften, about 5 minutes. Add the sweet potatoes, stock, and 1 $^1/_2$ cups water. Bring to a boil. Reduce the heat to medium-low and simmer, covered, until the sweet potatoes are ten-

der when pierced with the tip of knife, about 15 minutes.

2. In batches, transfer the soup to a blender and purée. Return the puréed soup to the Dutch oven and stir in the peanut butter and lime juice. Cook over low heat, stirring constantly, until very hot but not simmering. Season with the salt and white pepper. (The soup can be prepared up to 2 days ahead, cooled, covered, and refrigerated. Reheat over very low heat, stirring often.)

3. Transfer to a warmed soup tureen. Ladle the soup into individual soup bowls, drizzle each serving with heavy cream, and sprinkle with the cilantro.

Homemade Turkey Stock 101

Makes about 2 1/2 quarts

Make Ahead: The stock can be prepared and refrigerated for up to 3 days ahead or frozen for up to 3 months.

Every Thanksgiving Eve, I put on a big pot of stock to simmer overnight. Then I use it all Thanksgiving Day long. It is one of the secrets to a moist, beautifully colored roast bird with wonderful gravy, as in Perfect Roast Turkey on page 43. Some of the stock also goes into the stuffing, some usually gets turned into soup, and I often use it in my side dishes as well. The recipe is easily doubled or even tripled, assuming you have a stockpot big enough to hold the ingredients. If you want a smaller amount of stock, make the Small-Batch Turkey Stock variation on page 24. But don't worry about having too much stock. Any leftovers can be frozen, or used the next day to make a terrific soup.

• *Turkey parts with lots of bone, like wings and backs, make the best stock. Use the turkey neck, heart, and gizzard in the stock, but not the liver. (Liver makes the stock bitter.) When the stock is strained, you can retrieve the neck and giblets to use in giblet gravy. If you want to use the liver in the gravy, add it to the stock during the last 15 minutes of simmering, and poach it just until cooked through.*

• *Browning the turkey parts first give the stock a rich color that will make a dark gravy. Cooking the vegetables brings out their flavor. Too many cooks throw some giblets in a pot with some water to boil up a weak, pale stock that doesn't have much flavor.*

• *Never let stock come to a rolling boil, or it will become cloudy and have a less refined flavor. Cook the stock uncovered.*

• *Add the herbs to the stock after you've skimmed it. If you add them at the beginning, they will rise to the surface and be skimmed off with the foam. The foam isn't anything unwholesome—it's just the coagulating proteins in the bones. They are removed to make the stock clearer.*

• *The longer a stock simmers, the better, up to 12 hours. Replace the water as needed as it evaporates. While I trust my stove to simmer the stock overnight, some of my students have been shocked at the idea. A great alternative is to make the stock in a 5 ½-quart slow cooker. Transfer the browned turkey and vegetable mixture to the cooker, add the herbs, and pour in enough cold water to cover generously. Cook on Low, and the stock will barely simmer all night long, to make a clear, delicious stock.*

• *If time is a factor, just simmer the stock for an hour or two—it will still be better than using water or canned broth to make your gravy. Or, make a pot well ahead of Thanksgiving and freeze it.*

• *Don't add salt to your stock. The stock is often used in recipes where it must be reduced, and the final dish could end up too salty. To check the stock's flavor, ladle some into a cup and season lightly with*

salt before tasting. Without the salt, it may taste deceptively weak.

3 pounds turkey wings

Turkey neck and giblets (liver reserved, if desired; see above)

2 tablespoons vegetable oil

1 medium onion, chopped

1 medium carrot, chopped

1 medium celery rib with leaves, chopped

6 parsley sprigs

¹/₂ teaspoon dried thyme

¹/₄ teaspoon black peppercorns

1 bay leaf

1. Using a heavy cleaver, chop the wings and neck into 2-inch pieces. (If necessary, ask the butcher to do this for you.) Using a sharp knife, trim away any membranes from the giblets.

2. In a large pot, heat the oil over medium-high heat. In batches, add the turkey wings, neck, and giblets and cook, turning occasionally, until browned on all sides, about 8 to 10 minutes. Transfer to a plate. Add the onion, carrot, and celery to the pot and cook, stirring often, until softened, about 6 minutes.

3. Return the turkey to the pot. Add enough cold water to cover the turkey by 2 inches. Bring to a boil, skimming off the foam that rises to the surface. Add the parsley, thyme, peppercorns, and bay leaf. Reduce the heat to low. Cook at a bare simmer for at least 2 and up to 12 hours. As needed, add more water to the pot to keep the bones covered.

4. Strain the stock through a colander into a large bowl. Let stand for 5 minutes, then skim off the clear yellow fat that rises to the surface. If desired, remove the giblets, cool, finely chop, and refrigerate for use in gravy. The neck meat can be removed in strips, chopped, and reserved as well. Cool the stock completely before refrigerating or freezing. (Turkey stock can be prepared up to 3 days ahead, cooled, covered, and refrigerated. It can also be frozen in airtight containers for up to 3 months.)

Small-Batch Turkey Stock: A smaller amount of stock can be prepared with just the turkey neck and giblets. As this relatively small amount of turkey won't give a very full flavored stock, use chicken broth (homemade or canned) as a booster. Following the instructions above, brown the neck and giblets from 1 turkey in 1 tablespoon oil. Add 1 small onion, 1 small carrot, and 1 small celery rib, all chopped, and cook until softened. Add 1 quart water and one 13¾-ounce can low-sodium chicken broth and bring to a simmer. Add 3 parsley sprigs, ¼ teaspoon dried thyme, 6 peppercorns, and 1 small bay leaf. Simmer for 2½ to 3 hours (the smaller amount of liquid would evaporate away if cooked longer). Makes about 1 quart.

Homemade Chicken Stock: Substitute 3 pounds chicken wings, cut into 2-inch pieces, for the turkey wings. Delete the turkey neck and giblets.

Cranberry Waldorf Salad

Makes 16 to 20 servings

Make Ahead: The salad must be prepared at least 8 hours ahead; it can be refrigerated for up to 2 days.

This magenta-colored mold can be served as a side dish, but it really shines as a special first-course salad. I love it just as it is, but if you like, serve it the way my grandma would: Mix equal portions of mayonnaise and sour cream, and place a dollop alongside each serving. The recipe is easily doubled to fit a nine-cup mold.

1 tablespoon (1½ envelopes) unflavored gelatin

2 cups bottled apple juice

One 12-ounce bag fresh cranberries, rinsed and picked over

²/₃ cup sugar

1 Granny Smith apple, peeled, cored, and chopped into ½-inch pieces

1 medium celery rib, chopped

¹/₃ cup coarsely chopped walnuts

1. In a small bowl, sprinkle the gelatin over ½ cup of the apple juice; set aside. In a large saucepan, mix the cranberries, the remaining 1½ cups apple juice, and the sugar. Bring to a boil over medium-high heat, stirring often to dissolve the sugar. Cook until all the cranberries have popped, about 5 minutes. Reduce the heat to very low. Stir in the gelatin and continue stirring until the gelatin is completely dissolved, 1 to 2 minutes. Transfer the cranberry mixture to a large bowl. Refrigerate until cool and partially thickened (a spoon drawn through the mixture will leave a definite impression), about 2 hours. Or, place the bowl in a larger bowl filled with ice water. Let stand, stirring often and adding more ice to the water as it melts, until the mixture is cool and partially thickened, about 45 minutes.

2. Lightly oil a 5-cup mold. Stir the apple, celery, and walnuts into the cranberry mixture. Pour into the prepared mold and cover with plastic wrap. Refrigerate until the mixture is completely set, at least 8 hours, or overnight. (The salad can be prepared up to 2 days ahead.)

3. To unmold, fill a sink or a large bowl with hot tap water. Dip the mold, just to the top edge, into the water and hold for 5 seconds. Remove from the water and dry the outside of the mold. Remove the plastic wrap. Invert the mold onto a serving platter. Holding the mold and the platter firmly together, shake them until the salad releases from the mold. Cut the salad into wedges and serve chilled.

Spinach and Persimmon Salad with Ginger Vinaigrette

Makes 8 servings

Make Ahead: The ginger dressing and spinach can be prepared up to 1 day ahead; the persimmons can be prepared up to 4 hours ahead.

This unusual but absolutely mouthwatering salad will generate a conversation on the merits of persimmons. Be sure to use Fuyu (sometimes called Israeli) persimmons, which can be eaten while crisp-ripe. (Other varieties, such as Hachiya, need to be ripened until very soft, or they will be inedibly tannic, and they don't make the best salads.) Also, buy fresh, plump ginger with smooth, unwrinkled skin—it will yield the most juice.

Ginger Vinaigrette

6 ounces firm ginger

¹/₃ cup cider vinegar

1 tablespoon sugar

³/₄ teaspoon salt

¹/₂ teaspoon freshly milled black pepper

1 cup vegetable oil

1 tablespoon dark Asian sesame oil

2 tablespoons finely chopped shallots

Three 12-ounce bunches spinach (see Note)

3 firm Fuyu persimmons

1 tablespoon plus 1 teaspoon sesame seeds

1. To make the vinaigrette, shred the unpeeled ginger on the large holes of a box grater. Wrap half of the shredded ginger in the corner of a clean kitchen towel. Wring the towel over a small bowl to extract the juice. Discard the juiced ginger. Repeat with the remaining ginger. You should have about ¹/₄ cup of juice.

2. In a medium bowl, whisk the vinegar, ginger juice, sugar, salt, and pepper. Gradually whisk in both oils. Stir in the shallots. Cover tightly and refrigerate until ready to serve; whisk the vinaigrette well before using. (The dressing can be prepared up to 1 day ahead.)

3. Remove the tough stems from the spinach. Fill a sink with cold water. Place the spinach leaves in the water and agitate well to loosen any sand and grit. In batches, lift the spinach out of the water (leaving the grit to sink to the bottom of the sink), and spin dry in a salad spinner. Wrap the spinach loosely in paper towels and place in a large plastic bag (a grocery bag is perfect). Refrigerate until ready to serve. (The spinach can be prepared up to 1 day ahead.)

4. Using a small sharp knife, cut out the green calyx from the top of each persimmon. Using a vegetable peeler, peel the persimmons, moving the peeler vertically around the outside of each persimmon to remove the peel in a long strip. Cut the peeled persimmons into ¹/₄-inch-thick wedges. Place in a small bowl, cover tightly, and refrigerate until ready to serve. (The persimmons can be prepared up to 4 hours ahead.)

5. To serve, toss the persimmons with 2 tablespoons of the ginger vinaigrette. In a large bowl, toss the spinach with the remaining vinaigrette. Divide the spinach equally among chilled salad plates. Top with the persimmon wedges and sprinkle with the sesame seeds.

Note: Use young, tender, flat-leaf spinach for this salad, not the crinkled packaged, variety. The best spinach can usually found at Asian markets.

Roasted Beet, Endive, and Blue Cheese Salad with Walnuts

Makes 8 servings

Make Ahead: The beets can be prepared up to 1 day ahead.

I'm not suggesting that this salad will be a hit at the kids' table. But, it will be welcome at an "adults only" Thanksgiving, especially one with other European-inspired dishes on the menu. Roasting works wonders with beets, bringing out their sweetness and maintaining their color better than boiling or steaming. Use a high-quality balsamic vinegar, which is less acidic than inexpensive versions. If the dressing is too tart, balance it with a little brown sugar.

9 medium beets (about 2¹/₄ pounds)

3 heads Belgian endive, wiped with a moist paper towel (do not rinse)

¹/₃ cup balsamic vinegar

¹/₂ teaspoon salt

¹/₄ teaspoon freshly milled black pepper

¹/₃ cup walnut oil (see Note)

4 ounces blue cheese, such as Roquefort, crumbled

¹/₂ cup toasted and coarsely chopped walnuts (2 ounces)

1. Preheat the oven to 400°F.

2. If the beets have their greens attached, trim the greens, leaving about 1 inch of the stems attached to the beets. Scrub the beets under cold running water. Wrap each beet in aluminum foil and place on a baking sheet. Bake until the beets are tender when pierced with the tip of a long sharp knife, about 1 hour, depending on the size of the beets. Cool completely, without unwrapping the beets.

3. Unwrap the beets and peel them. Cut into ¹/₂-inch cubes. Place in self-sealing plastic bags and refrigerate until chilled, at least 2 hours. (The beets can be prepared up to 1 day ahead.)

4. Using a sharp knife, cut the endive crosswise into ¹/₂-inch-wide pieces. Separate the endive pieces into strips, discarding any tough, solid center pieces. Set the endive aside.

5. In a large bowl, whisk the vinegar with the salt and pepper. Gradually whisk in the oil. Add the beets, endive, blue cheese, and walnuts and toss well. Spoon onto chilled salad plates and serve immediately.

Note: Walnut oil can be found in specialty food stores, many supermarkets, and some natural food stores. Imported French walnut oil has the richest flavor. If you can't find it, you can make an excellent substitute: In a blender, blend ¹/₂ cup coarsely chopped toasted walnuts with ¹/₂ cup vegetable oil until the walnuts are very finely chopped. Let stand for 2 minutes, then strain through a fine-mesh sieve.

Fennel, Pear, and Hazelnut Salad in Radicchio Cups

Makes 8 servings

Make Ahead: The salad can be prepared up to 6 hours ahead.

Fennel is another one of those winter vegetables that deserves to be better known by American cooks. European cooks love it for its crisp texture and mild anise flavor. The interplay of the crunchy fennel and hazelnuts with sweet and tender pears makes this an exceptional salad. It's also just lightly dressed—a perfect choice when the menu requires a first course that isn't filling.

1 large bulb fennel (about 1¹/₄ pounds)

3 tablespoons fresh lemon juice

3 ripe red Bartlett or Comice pears, or a
   combination

3 tablespoons extra virgin olive oil

¹/₈ teaspoon salt

¹/₄ teaspoon freshly milled black pepper

1 large or 2 medium heads radicchio

³/₄ cup (3 ounces) toasted, skinned, and
   coarsely chopped hazelnuts

1. Using a large sharp knife, trim the fennel of any bruises. If the feathery green fronds are still attached, trim them off. (If you want the salad to have a more pronounced anise flavor, chop the fronds and stir into the salad to taste.) Cut the fennel lengthwise in half. Remove the tough, solid "heart" that grows up from the bottom of each half by cutting it out in a wedge. Place the fennel cut side down on the work surface and cut crosswise into ¹/₂-inch-thick strips. Transfer the fennel to a large bowl and toss with 2 tablespoons of the lemon juice.

2. Rinse the pears well, but do not peel. Cut each pear lengthwise into quarters and trim away the core. Cut the pears into ¹/₂-inch-thick wedges. Add to the bowl and toss with the remaining 1 tablespoon of lemon juice. While tossing gently, drizzle with the olive oil and season with the salt and pepper. (The salad can be prepared 6 hours ahead, covered tightly, and refrigerated.)

3. To serve, separate the radicchio leaves into 8 separate "cups." (Save any leftover radicchio for another use.) Mix the hazelnuts into the salad. Place the radicchio on individual plates, spoon equal amounts of the salad into the radicchio cups, and serve immediately.

Shrimp Salad on Mesclun with Saffron Vinaigrette

Makes 6 to 8 servings

Make Ahead: The salad and the dressing can be prepared up to 1 day ahead.

Mesclun, the colorful combination of baby salad greens that can be found in just about every supermarket these days, is a great timesaver, as the greens have already been washed. This attractive salad, with firm, pink shrimp in a bright yellow saffron dressing, is a fine first course—its bright combination of flavors really perks the appetite. The problem is, it's so delicious that guests could easily fill up on it—so this recipe makes modest servings.

Saffron Vinaigrette

1 tablespoon boiling water

¹/₂ teaspoon crumbled saffron threads

¹/₃ cup fresh lemon juice

1 tablespoon honey

2 garlic cloves, crushed through a press

¹/₂ teaspoon salt

¹/₄ teaspoon freshly milled black pepper

1 cup olive oil (not extra virgin, which is too
strong for this recipe)

2 pounds medium shrimp

1 large red bell pepper, cored, seeded, and finely
chopped

2 tablespoons chopped fresh parsley

12 ounces mesclun or other mixed salad greens

1. To make the vinaigrette, combine the boiling water and the saffron in a medium bowl and let stand for 5 minutes. Add the lemon juice, honey, garlic, salt,

and pepper. Gradually whisk in the olive oil. Set the vinaigrette aside.

2. Bring a large pot of lightly salted water to a boil over high heat. Add the shrimp and cook until the shrimp turn pink and firm, 2 to 3 minutes (the water does not have to return to a boil). Drain and rinse under cold running water until cool enough to handle. Peel and devein the shrimp.

3. Transfer the shrimp to a medium bowl. Add ¹/₂ cup of the saffron vinaigrette, the red pepper, and the parsley and toss well. Cover tightly with plastic wrap and refrigerate for at least 2 hours and up to 1 day.

4. When ready to serve, in a large bowl, toss the mesclun with the remaining dressing. Spoon an equal amount of the shrimp salad onto one side of each chilled dinner plate. Heap the mesclun on the other side. Serve immediately.

Toasting Nuts

I always try to take the time to toast nuts for cooking, especially in salads and desserts. The difference in flavor is dramatic and well worth the trouble. In the case of hazelnuts, they must be toasted in order to remove their skins. Toasted nuts can be prepared up to 2 days ahead and stored airtight at room temperature.

To toast almonds, pecans, walnuts, and hazelnuts, place the shelled nuts in a single layer on a baking sheet. Bake them in a preheated 350°F oven, stirring occasionally (the ones on the edges

toast more quickly and need to be incorporated into the center so they don't burn), until lightly browned and fragrant, 8 to 10 minutes. (Toast the hazelnuts until the skins are peeling.) Let the nuts cool completely before chopping them.

To skin hazelnuts, wrap the still-warm toasted nuts in a clean kitchen towel and let them stand for about 10 minutes. Using the towel, rub off as much of the skins as possible. (You can rarely get all of the skin off, so don't try. Besides, a little skin will add flavor.)

Turkey and Friends

The Main Event

Everyone wants a perfect, moist, golden brown bird on the Thanksgiving table. Over the years, I have listened to friends and students relate their special, secret, ultimate, best-ever ways to roast the bird. I've tried them all, and just when I thought I was finished, along came even more techniques. In the last few years alone, these included roasting in a very hot oven, deep-frying outside in a huge pot of fat, and soaking overnight in a big pot of brine before cooking. Each absolutely guaranteed the best turkey ever. While I have my favorite method (see Perfect Roast Turkey on page 43), there are certainly reasons to consider the other recipes. For example, you may be cooking against the clock, so the high-temperature method will save valuable time (if you don't factor in the cleaning of the oven before and after roasting). Or, maybe this year you have an itch to smoke the bird outside on the grill, and need to know how to pull it off. So I offer the other recipes, but with my frank evaluations and detailed instructions based on my experience.

Turkey is not always the only game in town on Thanksgiving Day. Ham often makes a guest appearance. For many of my Italian friends, it isn't Thanksgiving if there isn't lasagna on the table, so I give a classic version of that beloved dish. There's also a special squash and rice dish for vegetarian guests.

But, regardless of how you plan to cook your turkey, there are general questions to be answered first.

Types of Turkeys

Other than gender, are there any differences between hen and tom turkeys? Is one more tender than the other?

Hens are female turkeys, weighing from 8 to 16 pounds. Male toms, bred to yield a high proportion of the white breast meat that most Americans prefer, weigh 14 to 26 pounds. The size of the bird relates to its age. Turkeys are often labeled "young," because no commercial turkey is much older than 26 weeks. Thanks to modern animal husbandry methods, there is no difference in flavor or tenderness between toms and hens. In the old days, a younger bird meant a more tender one, and while an old tom had plenty of flavor, it was also tougher. Unlike beef, turkeys are hormone- and steroid-free.

What are the differences between fresh and frozen turkeys?

There are actually three designations for fresh and frozen turkeys.

• "Frozen" turkeys have been deep-chilled at 0°F or below. They are at their best if defrosted and cooked within one year of purchase. (If you've ever wondered how your supermarket can give away free frozen turkeys as premiums at Thanksgiving time, it's probably because they are using up last year's surplus.)

• "Fresh" birds have never been chilled below 26°F, and have a correspondingly short shelf life. (Turkey freezes at eight degrees lower than water does.) Fresh turkeys are readily available at super-markets or butchers. You rarely have to special-order them anymore, unless your butcher requires that you do so or you are concerned about getting a certain size. Buy fresh turkey no earlier than two days before roasting, even if the "sell-by" date on the label is later. (Home refrigerators are warmer than the commercial walk-in refrigerators.) I always buy a fresh turkey.

• Kept at temperatures between 0° and 26°F, the turkey is considered "hard-chilled." You won't see turkeys labeled hard-chilled, though, as each turkey producer is allowed to create its own name for this designation, as long as it isn't misleading. Holding turkey at this temperature range prolongs shelf life and has little effect on quality. In 1996, about forty-five million turkeys were consumed at Thanksgiving (and twenty-two million at Christmas, and nineteen million at Easter). In order to get that many holiday turkeys to market and sold within a reasonable time, the hard-chilled method is necessary. Sometimes hard-chilled turkeys feel soft on the outside but the giblets are frozen inside. If that happens, just run cold water into the body cavity until the giblets thaw enough to remove them.

What about frozen turkeys?

Frozen turkeys are the least expensive, but freezing dries out the meat, and more moisture is lost down the drain during defrosting. Good turkey producers always inject the birds with a moistening solution to replace the lost liquid. The best frozen turkeys have been injected only with wholesome ingredients like broth, vegetable oil, and seasonings. I don't like birds that have been pumped with artificial flavorings and lubricants. (On the other hand, it's not a good idea to freeze a fresh bird that hasn't been injected with some moisteners.) Also, frozen birds require advance planning to defrost. I hardly have enough room in my refrigerator at holiday time as it is, without a huge turkey taking up all the space while it thaws for three to five days. Considering the minor difference in price between frozen and fresh (or hard-chilled, which is almost as good as fresh) turkeys, why not get the best you can afford?

I don't recommend frozen stuffed turkeys. To say the stuffing isn't as good as homemade is about the kindest thing I can say for them.

I have to get a frozen bird because I can only shop on weekends. How do I defrost it?

First and foremost, never defrost a turkey at room temperature.

Allow enough time for the turkey to thaw. It takes *a full 24 hours to defrost each 5 pounds of turkey in the refrigerator.* So, if you want a 25-pound turkey to be thoroughly defrosted by Thanksgiving morning, you must buy it by the preceding Sunday at the latest. (I'd buy it on Saturday, just to be sure.)

If you are in a hurry, a second-best option is to defrost the bird in a large sink of cold water, allowing 30 minutes per pound, changing the water and turning the turkey often. Do *not* add warm water to hasten the process.

Don't defrost a turkey in the microwave oven. The turkey is irregularly shaped, and some parts of the bird will cook while others are still defrosting. Besides, most microwave ovens won't hold a bird larger than 12 pounds.

What about self-basting birds?

Self-basting birds, available fresh and frozen, have been "enhanced" (in the eyes of the producer) with flavorings, some natural and some artificial. They purport to make the turkey moist—I say these make the turkey soggy and wet, and predisposed to fall apart when lifting it from the pan. They say the basting liquid makes the turkey taste better—I say a

turkey tastes good enough without fake flavorings. I want to promote turkeys that taste like turkey, not canned soup. And, I like to baste the bird, so the concept of "self-basting" leaves me cold. Not only does opening the oven and basting give the cook an idea of the turkey's progress, but the hot basting liquid helps to brown and seal the skin and hold in the juices.

My farmers' market has organic, free-range birds. Are they worth the price?

The terms *organic* and *free-range* are not recognized by the USDA. Butchers, farmers, and restaurants can use them as marketing terms, but they cannot use them in labeling (although they can be written on signs advertising the product). Generally, "organic poultry" has been raised on organically grown, antibiotic-free feed. "Free-range" turkeys, which are often organic, have been raised in a relatively spacious environment that gives them access to open spaces. Many turkeys that are not called free-range may have been raised in henhouses with the same amount of space. The term free-range may make you think of wide-open skies, but it's no guarantee that the birds have ever been outside—it just means that the door to the henhouse is open and they can go out if they want to. These birds can be excellent, but again, they still need to be cooked carefully for fine results. They are significantly more expensive than ordinary fresh turkeys, and whether they are worth it or not is up to you. If your guests are all adults who love eating out at fancy restaurants, try an organic bird.

My specialty butcher carries wild turkeys. What are they like?

Today, most wild turkeys are actually farm-raised. They are very full flavored, but not gamy like hunter-bagged wild turkeys. (Most true, wild turkeys are so tough that cooks roast only the tender breast, and stew the dark meat.) I like to say they are to regular turkeys what sourdough bread is to white bread. Some people just like the complex flavor of the former better than the latter.

Wild turkeys look much different from regular ones, with a high, humped breastbone and freckled white skin. The freckling comes from the pigmentation in the feather quills—regular turkeys are bred with white feathers that leave no colored freckle when plucked. While wild turkeys may look meaty, they actually have a very low meat-to-bone ratio. Their weight ranges from only 6 to 12 pounds. Allow about 1 ½ pounds per person. Because of supply-and-demand problems, you may not get the exact size bird you ordered. More than once I have had to supplement a wild turkey with a small ham or another main dish because the butcher only had tiny birds available. Wild turkeys are very lean and should be roasted only to 170° to 175°F, or the meat will dry out. The dark meat may be a little pink, but it is safe to eat. If you prefer your dark meat more well done, just pop the sliced meat back into a 400°F oven for a few minutes—it will probably be cooked by the time you get around to serving the mashed potatoes.

My neighbor swears by kosher turkeys. What makes them different?

Kosher turkeys are raised free-range in a manner similar to organic turkeys and are fed antibiotic-free feed. They are slaughtered and salted according to Jewish dietary laws. Some cooks feel that the method of slaughtering gives the birds a fresher, cleaner taste. The salting seasons the turkeys and makes their meat somewhat firmer than that of regular birds. These extra steps are labor-intensive, so kosher turkeys always cost more. Many kosher turkeys are frozen, so be sure to defrost them properly to protect your investment.

Getting Ready

How much turkey should I buy?

Estimate 1 pound per person, which allows for seconds or leftovers. Larger toms are very chesty with lots of breast meat, so you will get more servings from a big bird.

My family likes white meat and we never have enough to go around. Any solutions?

Thanks to the year-round popularity of turkey, it's easy to buy individual parts to roast for extra servings. Most packaged parts have cooking instructions, but here are some general guidelines.

For extra white meat, buy turkey breast halves. (Turkey breast halves, with the skin and bone, are tastier than boneless, skinless breasts and cook more quickly than whole breasts.) Place them in an oiled roasting pan, rub with softened butter, and season with salt and pepper. Add ½ cup broth or water to the pan. Roast in a preheated 350°F oven, basting occasionally, until a meat thermometer reads 170°F, 20 to 25 minutes per pound.

If you need extra drumsticks or wings, always a favorite with kids, they can be roasted in the same manner, allowing 1 ½ to 2 hours at 350°F to cook until tender.

I have a huge crowd coming, but I can't handle roasting and carving two turkeys. Now what?

You will need two ovens. In the first oven, roast a large tom to present as a centerpiece; it can be carved as everyone admires it. In the second oven, roast turkey parts as directed above. The turkey parts will only take an hour or two to roast. When done, cover them loosely with aluminum foil and keep them in a warm place until ready to serve. (The USDA advises not holding cooked poultry for longer than 1 hour.) The second oven will now be empty and available to bake all the side dishes.

What are the essential tools for roasting the perfect turkey?

You'll need a high-quality roasting pan, a roasting rack, a meat thermometer, an oven thermometer, and a bulb baster.

A *high-quality roasting pan* makes all the difference in the world. A heavy dark metal pan allows the drippings to brown beautifully and turns gravy making into a snap. Buy the best roasting pan you can afford. Some of them cost over a hundred dollars, but you will probably never need to buy another one again. My favorite roasting pan is nonstick and measures $18 \times 14 \times 3$ inches. A turkey roasting pan should be fairly shallow so the air can circulate around the bird and promote browning. But choose the largest pan that fits your oven and accommodates the turkey size you roast most often. (I've heard many a tale about the turkey that wouldn't fit into the pan, or the pan that wouldn't fit into the oven.) Unlined heavy aluminum roasting pans have a porous surface that soaks up the drippings, so don't get an aluminum pan unless it has a stainless steel or nonstick lining. Old-fashioned blue enamel turkey roasters do a fair job. Those grooves in the bottom of the pan don't serve much purpose and are an obstacle at gravy-making time. If you have a covered turkey roaster, don't use the lid—uncovered turkeys brown best.

I am no fan of disposable aluminum foil roasting pans. They buckle under the weight of most turkeys, and are impossible to make gravy in. The bright metal allows the oven heat to bounce off the pan's surface and discourages browning. And they're too high to allow for proper heat and air distribution. Don't tell me that you want to buy the aluminum foil pan over a good roasting pan because you only do a turkey once a year! Once you have a beautiful heavy pan, you'll find lots of uses for it all year long. If you *absolutely* have to use an aluminum foil pan, at least put it on a large baking sheet to make it easier to take in and out of the oven. Better yet, buy two pans and insert one inside of the other for increased stability. (You may even be able to pull off making gravy in a double-thick aluminum pan.)

Turkey should always be baked on a *roasting rack*. If the turkey is placed on the bottom of the pan, it can stick. Also, the back of the bird will simmer in the juices, so when you lift the bird out the pan, the wings usually fall off (after all, they have been stewing in liquid for hours). Even though the turkey is roasted on a flat rack, an adjustable roasting rack is more versatile, as it can be folded up into a V shape for cooking cylindrical meat roasts.

The best way to tell when a turkey (or any poultry or meat) is done is with a *meat thermometer*. An old-fashioned meat thermometer is inserted into the meat before you put it into the oven and stays there throughout roasting. Its thick stem can make a large hole in the meat that releases juices. Most cooks prefer instant-read thermometers, which have thin stems and are only used when actually checking the temperature. Never leave an instant-read thermometer in the oven, or the plastic top will melt. The newest thermometers come with probes that are attached to monitors outside the stove so you can easily check the progress without opening the oven door. *Pop-up thermometers* are good indicators of doneness, but not always reliable. It's not that they don't work, but sometimes they get glued shut by the basting juices. Always back up the pop-up with a reliable meat thermometer.

An *oven thermometer* is the only way to determine your oven's true temperature. A turkey is one of the largest things that you will ever cook in your oven, and a few degrees' discrepancy can make a big difference. Never trust your thermostat dial. I have gotten in the habit of bringing my own oven thermometer with me when I cook at a friend's or even a cooking school, because every oven is off to some degree. Mercury thermometers are the most accurate, but spring thermometers, which are less expensive, work well too.

Basting helps to brown the bird, sealing the skin and holding in juices. A *bulb baster* makes the job easy. The basters with metal syringes aren't worth the money, as the fat lubricates the metal and the rubber bulb slides off. Just get a good, inexpensive plastic baster.

Any other goodies that I can pick up at the kitchenware store?

I use a *bamboo skewer* or a *thin metal skewer* to close the neck cavity. Just in case you have to tie the drumsticks together, get a ball of *cotton kitchen twine*. Many cooks like *turkey lifters* that make it easier to remove the turkey from the pan. Be sure you have a *serving platter* big enough to hold the bird. And, if you don't have a good *carving set,* with a long thin-bladed sharp knife and a meat fork, now's the time to get one.

How do I get the bird ready for roasting?

Take the bird out of its plastic wrapper and rinse it well, inside and out, under cold running water. Place the bird on a work surface and pat it completely dry with paper towels. Remove the neck from the body cavity, and *don't forget the package of giblets in the neck cavity!* (But, if you ever do leave them in—and we all know people who have— don't worry, as they are usually packed in oven-safe materials and the cooked giblets won't hurt any-

one.) Pull out the lumps of pale yellow fat from either side of the tail area. Reserve the fat: It can be tossed into the roasting pan to increase the amount of drippings, or added to the stockpot.

After preparing the bird, be sure to wash the cutting board, your hands, and any utensils well with soap and hot water.

What about that metal clip in the tail area?

Some poultry producers provide a metal or plastic clip, called a "hock lock," that secures the drumsticks in place. Don't remove it! It will save you the trouble of having to tie the drumsticks together with kitchen string. Sometimes the producers cut a slit into the skin near the vent, which also acts to hold the drumsticks.

Cooking the Turkey

Sometimes my turkey breast turns out dry. Why?

Dry turkey is caused by overcooking. Admittedly, roasting a whole turkey is problematic. When was the last time you roasted *anything* that was twenty-five pounds? But the main problem is the turkey itself. The white meat is done to perfection at 170°F, and above that temperature, it begins to dry out and get stringy. On the other hand, the dark meat isn't tender until 180°F. It burns me up to see recipes in magazines suggest cooking the turkey only to 170°F. Granted, the white meat is cooked just right, but at that temperature, the dark meat still looks pink and rare and hasn't developed a roasted flavor. (The meat is safe to eat, it just looks and tastes undercooked.) Luckily, there are ways to "trick" the white meat into staying moist for the extra time it takes for the dark meat to cook that extra ten degrees.

There are so many ways to roast a bird, it's hard to decide what's the best method for me. What are your favorites?

My Favorite Method: The Perfect Roast Turkey on page 43 is my adaptation of the traditional method that uses a moderately low oven temperature of 325°F. Temperatures above that tend to shrink the turkey, and anything below that is unsafe. My secret for avoiding dried-out meat? I tightly cover (not just tent) the breast area with aluminum foil, which traps the steam and keeps the breast moist. During the last hour of roasting, I remove the foil to allow the skin to brown.

Bottom Line: This time-tested method doesn't call for any special skills, and it roasts a wonderful, juicy turkey with an old-fashioned flavor. It also makes a picture-perfect bird that looks like a Norman Rockwell magazine cover. The only drawback is that it takes time, but sometimes patience is its own reward.

High-Temperature Method: The turkey is roasted in a very hot oven, sealing the skin and holding in the juices. This method gives a richly colored, moist bird with a deep, roasted flavor in just a couple of hours. You'll find it detailed in Oven-Blasted Turkey on page 44. Be sure your oven is impeccably clean before roasting, and be warned that it will certainly need to be cleaned afterwards. You must use a heavy roasting pan and a fresh bird that hasn't been injected with any moistening agents. The hot turkey must be turned from side to side to get it evenly roasted—this calls for an agile, strong cook. The drippings can be burned beyond repair, leaving you to make a sauce on the side.

Bottom Line: The bird is delicious and cooks in record time, but it's a method for experienced cooks with self-cleaning ovens, or lots of oven cleaner, or hired help.

Brine Method: Proponents of the brine method (Herb-Brined Roast Turkey on page 46) report that soaking the turkey in salted water makes it juicer and better seasoned. You must have a large receptacle (such as a stockpot) to soak the bird, and a place to keep it chilled overnight. Most people don't have a refrigerator big enough to hold a huge stockpot. I live in a cold climate, so my turkey soaks outdoors. The brining does increase juiciness, but it also firms and seasons the flesh in a way that some people may not like.

Bottom Line: If your goal is a juicy bird, this is a worthwhile effort, once you can surmount the logistical problems of chilling the soaking bird.

Grilled Turkey: Fast becoming the preferred method of Thanksgiving cooks who live in warm climates. It gives you a smoke-scented bird with a deep brown skin. This method (Smoke-Grilled Cider-Basted Turkey on page 47) works best with birds no larger than 12 pounds. The drippings may be too smoky to make gravy, so plan to serve a sauce or salsa on the side.

Bottom Line: If the weather is good, and your family and friends enjoy nontraditional flavors, grill your bird.

Deep-fried Turkey: A contender for the "What a great turkey, but..." award. A favorite of Cajun cooks (see Bayou Deep-fried Turkey on page 50), the turkey is deep-fried in only 45 minutes. The skin turns out golden and crispy, and the meat deliciously juicy. If you have a 10-gallon stockpot with a deep-frying basket, a 125,000-BTU propane ring burner, a full tank of propane, and 5 gallons of cooking oil handy, this could be the bird for you—but only if you have nerves of steel, as well as an old set of clothes that you are willing to get oil-splattered, and are willing to forgo the stuffing and gravy. The method works best with smaller birds, so don't plan to feed a crowd, or plan to cook two turkeys.

Bottom Line: I'm not saying it isn't good, I'm only saying it's more work than most of us are willing to do, and definitely not the safest way of cooking a bird, especially if you have kids running around.

What are some of your least-favorite turkey methods?

I am almost loathe to mention these methods, because if it's your mom's turkey that's criticized, I'm asking for trouble. But, remember that I cook turkeys all year long, not just one day a year. I have taken a good hard objective look at roasting turkeys, and I think it's best to steer you away from potential problems.

Upside-down Turkey: Some cooks believe that roasting the bird upside down allows the juices to run into the breast and keep it moist. During the last hour of roasting, the bird is turned right side up. I remember the year that my friend Michelle tried this method. The person who gave her the instructions forgot to mention putting the bird on a rack, and when she tried to turn the bird right side up, about half of the breast stuck to the pan. In subsequent, nonholiday kitchen tests, the turning always made for some kind of disaster (usually the skin tears around the drumsticks) and the bird ended up looking as if it had been in an accident. If you have ever tried to turn a hot, greasy 25-pound turkey right side up, especially after a Bloody Mary, you know it is a job not to be taken lightly. There are easier ways to keep the breast moist.

Cheesecloth Turkey: The oiled turkey is covered with cheesecloth dipped in melted butter. I have no idea what advantage it provides. The cheesecloth is pulled off during the last hour of roasting, but mine always seems to stick to the skin.

Paper Bag Turkey: I haven't been able to try this method recently, even though it was popular when I was growing up. These days, it's hard to find large-enough paper bags, since most supermarkets have converted to plastic bags. And I wouldn't advise roasting a turkey in today's chemical-loaded recycled paper bags anyway.

Roasting Bag Turkey: The concept of the paper bag turkey has generally been replaced by the modern roasting bag. The bird turns out steamed, not roasted, and a pale steamed turkey isn't my idea of a terrific Thanksgiving centerpiece. The turkey tends to fall apart when you take it out of the bag (that is, when the bag doesn't stick to the bird). If you decide to try this method, and it is a timesaver, note that the instructions with the bag do not say to season the turkey. When I asked the company's consumer hot line about this, they said they assume that most people who use their product will be using defrosted frozen self-basting turkeys that are already seasoned. Season birds that aren't self-basting.

Foil-Wrapped Turkey: Again, the bird ends up steamed, not roasted, and lacks flavor and color. But, again, it saves time.

Overnight Turkey: Never try to roast a turkey overnight at low temperatures. It is a very unsafe method, and a sure way to turn the inside of your turkey into a Petri dish. And never try to partially roast the turkey, refrigerate it, and finish the cooking later. It is equally dangerous.

What about stuffing the bird?

In recent years, this issue has become quite a hot potato, as some cooks are concerned about the stuffing encouraging dangerous bacterial growth inside the bird. If you follow the guidelines on page 65 on how to stuff the bird safely, you'll have no problems. The only time I consider not stuffing the bird is when I want to save time. An unstuffed turkey weighs less and cooks more rapidly. The bird is just as tasty without the stuffing. (Whether the stuffing is as tasty cooked outside of the bird is a matter of personal taste.)

If you choose not to stuff the turkey, there are two excellent ways to add flavor to the bird and drippings. I usually replace the stuffing with a vegetable seasoning: Chop 1 large onion, 1 large carrot, and 1 large celery rib with leaves. Mix with 2 tablespoons chopped fresh parsley, 1 tablespoon poultry seasoning (preferably homemade, see Note, page 56), 1 teaspoon salt, and ¼ teaspoon freshly milled black pepper. The vegetables are only a seasoning—don't serve them as a side dish.

Or, stuff the neck and body cavities with fresh herbs which, again, are only seasonings, and are not to be served. I use about 2 packed cups of mixed fresh thyme, sage, rosemary, parsley, and marjoram sprigs for a 20-pound bird. This potpourri adds an incredible scent to the turkey and makes the gravy terrific.

If I stuff the bird, do I have to sew up the openings to hold it in?

It is unnecessary to sew up a bird. To hold the neck stuffing in place, skewer the neck skin to the back skin with a bamboo or thin metal skewer. To protect the exposed stuffing in the cavity from overbrowning, just cover it loosely with a small piece of foil. But, if your grandma taught you to sew up the stuffing, and you have good tailoring skills, go right ahead. If you are looking for a strong needle to do the job, go to a sewing store and buy a mattress or sailing canvas needle. These also have eyes big enough to thread thick kitchen twine.

Do you have to truss a turkey with string?

A trussed bird is more evenly roasted and holds its shape. Most cooks truss their birds with string, but I never tie up my bird unless necessary. To secure the wings, fold them back (akimbo) behind the turkey's shoulders. If the wings are too big to be folded back, then tie them alongside the body with string. To hold the drumsticks, insert them into the hock lock. If the bird doesn't have a hock lock or a strap of skin to hold the drumsticks, tie them together with string. If you are out of string, use unwaxed dental floss (I don't have to say "unflavored," do I?).

With the Oven-Blasted Turkey (page 44), the bird is easier to turn if it is trussed in the classic French manner, so instructions are included with that recipe.

What do you put on the outside of your turkey?

Not much—butter, salt, and pepper. I massage the bird with softened unsalted butter, but you can also brush it with melted butter. The butter promotes browning and melts to ensure drippings for basting and the gravy. Vegetable oil or margarine does not work as well. I season the bird with salt and pepper, nothing else. If the bird is seasoned on the outside with herbs, they often scorch during the long roasting period. Some cooks slip fresh herbs or an herb butter under the breast skin to add flavor. That it does, but during roasting, the herbs turn dark and look unappetizing. Paprika, which some people use on the bird as a browning agent, is particularly extraneous. When the correct oven temperature is used, your bird will be a gorgeous golden brown, even without paprika.

Generally, I don't glaze the bird, as some of the glaze always drips into the roasting pan and ends up in the gravy.

Do you baste the turkey?

Basting is one of the secrets to my Perfect Roast Turkey, page 43. Basting promotes browning, and the hot drippings help seal the skin and hold in the juices. (Other methods do not call for basting.) Baste every 40 minutes or so, and do it quickly so the temperature doesn't fall too much while the oven door is open.

At the beginning of roasting, I pour turkey stock into the roasting pan. The stock adds moisture to the oven interior (again, helping keep that turkey moist), and gives me something to baste *with*. Experienced cooks know that it takes quite a while for a turkey to release enough juices and rendered fat to create enough drippings for basting. As the stock evaporates, its flavor concentrates and enriches the drippings.

My mom always tents the bird with aluminum foil. What does that do?

Tenting is another Great Thanksgiving Myth. Loosely tenting the bird at the beginning of roasting doesn't do much. If you want to keep the turkey from drying out, the breast area must be *tightly* covered with foil, as directed in Perfect Roast Turkey, page 43. Some cooks tent the turkey if it seems to be browning too much. But, if your oven is at the right temperature (325°F), the turkey will brown properly and not need tenting.

Why are turkey roasting times always approximate?

There are a number of factors that determine how turkeys cook.

• The bigger the bird, the more meat on the bones. It takes less time for oven heat to pass through soft flesh than hard bone. Therefore, it takes more time per pound to roast a small hen than a large tom. Factor in the various conformations of the birds, and you can see why a certain leeway is needed.

• The differences in oven temperatures. Use an oven thermometer!

• Sporadic heat loss from opening the oven door. Don't baste more often than every 30 to 40 minutes.

• The exact temperature of the turkey when it goes in the oven. Unless the recipe says otherwise, the timings in this book are always for refrigerator-temperature turkeys.

When you estimate your cooking time, err on the long side, because if the turkey is done early, it will stay warm for up to an hour. In fact, turkey *should* rest for at least 20 minutes before carving anyway.

Start testing your bird for doneness about 30 minutes before the end of your estimated roasting time, just to be sure the turkey doesn't overcook. Remember, an overcooked bird is a dry bird.

How can you tell when the turkey is done?

The best way to tell is with a meat thermometer. Inserted into the thickest part of the thigh, but not touching a bone (which conducts heat and would give an incorrect reading), it should register 180° to 185°F. Also, the thigh and drumstick will feel tender when pressed with a finger. Do not cook the turkey until the drumstick "jiggles," which indicates that the bird is overcooked. When it's ready, the turkey will have released a lot of juices into the bottom of the pan that probably weren't there the last time you looked.

Don't trust the "pop-up" thermometers inserted into many turkeys. Sometimes they don't spring up because they have been glued closed by the basting liquid.

Serving the Turkey

What kind of wine should I serve with turkey?

Turkey can be served with just about any wine, and it really boils down to personal preference. If I want to serve the same wine throughout the meal, my favorite white is a full-bodied chardonnay, because it also complements many soups and salads. If your first course is creamy, you may want a crisp, slightly sharp sauvignon blanc to balance the richness. For a red wine, I usually choose a light type, maybe one of that year's Beaujolais Nouveau, which have just arrived in early November. To my taste, full-bodied reds are just too much to handle at the typical Thanksgiving spread with lots of contrasting flavors. But with a deep-flavored wild turkey, I'd pour a pinot noir. One of my favorite Thanksgiving dinner beverages is a dry hard cider. Served well chilled, it is very refreshing.

Are there any special ways to garnish the turkey?

Usually, a beautiful serving platter is all that a turkey needs. If you don't have one, you'll have to improvise. One year, when visiting friends, I forgot to bring my turkey platter, so we used a broiler pan—heavily garnished, but it worked.

Even with an heirloom platter, you may want to gild the lily. Dark curly kale makes an attractive bed for nestling the golden brown bird. Surround the turkey with small gourds, tiny ears of dried Indian corn, bouquets of fresh herbs, or nuts in the shell. Many fresh fruits make beautiful decorations. Try clusters of grapes or kumquats, miniature lady apples or Seckel or Forelle pears, or a scattering of fresh cranberries, all of which are in season during holiday time. If you plan to carve the bird at the table, have an empty bowl handy to hold the garnishes—while they look lovely, they can get in the way of carving.

I'm nervous about carving the bird. Help!

Let the turkey stand for at least 20 minutes before carving. The bird will stay perfectly hot for up to 1 hour. You can cover the turkey with aluminum foil and a kitchen towel to help retain the heat, but I find this is unnecessary, and it softens the skin. (Once I timed a hot-out-of-the-oven, 180°F 25-pound turkey to when it cooled off, and it took 3 hours.) This short rest period allows the hot juices to be drawn back into the meat, helping the turkey retain moisture and firming the meat for easy carving. Most people are so thrilled to have the turkey done that they rush it to the table for carving. The juices run out of the turkey and all over the tablecloth.

Carving is simple with a long thin very sharp knife and a sturdy meat fork. An electric knife is a very good investment, even if you only use it on holidays. As odd as it seems, think of the turkey in terms of human anatomy—i.e., the leg is connected to the thigh; the turkey's wing is its arm, which connects to the shoulder joint; and so on—and it will help you figure out what you're doing.

Have an empty platter nearby to hold the sliced meat. If you are carving for a crowd, you may want two platters, one for dark and one for white. Try to avoid carving for each individual, as you will have to alternate carving the light and dark meat, and that gets crazy. Carve the entire bird, then serve it. Before you get started, scoop all of the stuffing out of the cavity and place it in a serving dish.

1. Remove the drumsticks to make the breast easier to reach and carve. Cut off each drumstick at the knee joint. If the turkey is properly cooked (that is, to at least 180°F), they will pull away without any trouble, making the joints easy to sever. Do not remove the thighs at this point, or the bird will roll around on the platter while you try to carve it. Transfer the drumsticks to a platter. To allow more people to enjoy the dark meat, tilt each drumstick, holding it from the foot end, and cut down along the bone to slice the meat.

2. Hold the breast firmly with the meat fork. One side at a time, make a deep incision, cutting parallel to the table, down near the wing.

3. Cut down along the side of breast to carve it into thin slices. Every slice will stop at the parallel cut. Transfer the sliced breast to the platter. Turn the turkey around to carve the other side.

4. Pry the thighs away from the hips to reveal the ball joints, and sever at the joints. Transfer the thighs to the platter. To carve each thigh, hold the thigh with a meat fork and carve the meat by slicing parallel to the bone.

5. Pry the wings away from the shoulder joints and sever at the joints. Transfer to the platter.

If you still feel nervous about carving in front of your guests, present the whole roast bird at the table in all its glory, then, hightail it back into the kitchen and carve the meat where no one is looking.

After Thanksgiving dinner, I need a nap. Is there something in turkey that makes me tired?

If you are so full after dinner that you need to lie down, don't blame the turkey! Recent studies show that a carbohydrate-rich Thanksgiving dinner is the culprit, as the carbs increase the number of tryptophans in the brain. (It's not a normal meal that includes mashed potatoes, sweet potatoes, stuffing, and gravy, not to mention pie and rolls.)

Estimated Turkey Roasting Times

(Oven Temperature 325°F)

Roast until a meat thermometer inserted into the thickest part of the thigh reads 180°F to 185°F.

Unstuffed Turkey		Stuffed Turkey	
8 to 12 pounds	2 3/4 to 3 hours	8 to 12 pounds	3 to 3 1/2 hours
12 to 14 pounds	3 to 3 3/4 hours	12 to 14 pounds	3 1/2 to 4 hours
14 to 18 pounds	3 3/4 to 4 1/4 hours	14 to 18 pounds	4 to 4 1/4 hours
18 to 20 pounds	4 1/4 to 4 1/2 hours	18 to 20 pounds	4 1/4 to 4 3/4 hours
20 to 24 pounds	4 1/2 to 5 hours	20 to 24 pounds	4 3/4 to 5 1/4 hours

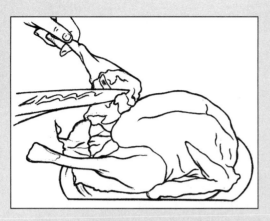

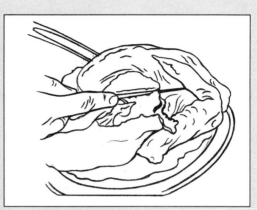

1. Cut off each drumstick at the knee joint. If the turkey is thoroughly cooked (to at least 180°F), they will pull away without any trouble, making it easy to sever the joints. Do not remove the thighs, or the bird will roll around on the platter while you try to carve it.

2. Hold the breast firmly with the meat fork. One side at a time, make a deep incision, cutting parallel to the table, down near the wing.

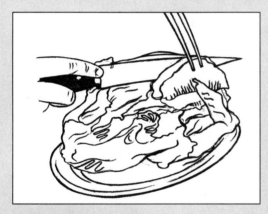

3. Cut down along the side of breast to carve into thin slices, stopping at the parallel cut.

4. Pry the thighs away from the hips to reveal the ball joints, and sever at the joints.

5. Pry the wings away from the shoulder joints and sever at the joints.

It Wouldn't Be Thanksgiving Without . . . Turkey

It is only assumed that wild turkeys were served at that first Thanksgiving in 1621. The firsthand accounts of the menu simply mention "fowl." We do know that the Pilgrims had venison, cod, and lobster on the table, so why don't we have surf and turf or fish cakes instead of turkey?

The turkey is an impressive bird, with its bronze feathers, unusual head markings, and showy tail. Even a hardened critic like Brilliat-Savarin (a French gourmand who, in 1825, uttered the phrase, "Tell me what you eat and I will tell you what you are") said, "The turkey is certainly one of the handsomest gifts the New World made to the Old World. . . . [It] is the largest and, if not the most subtle, at least the most tasty of our domestic birds." Just looking at its corpulent figure it gives one a feeling of abundance and well-being.

The wild turkey is native to North and Central America, and was domesticated by the Aztecs. No one knows when the first turkeys traveled to Europe, but they seem to have been brought to Spain by conquistadors in the early 1500s. The turkey quickly established itself as *the* bird to serve at festive occasions, especially in Italy, France, and England, and was bred into a plumper version. This new improved turkey was brought back to the Americas, where it was crossbred with its wild cousin to make the breed we know today. The turkey was not a strange bird to the Pilgrims— they were well acquainted with it, and must have been relieved to find a familiar food in this strange land.

No one really knows how the turkey got its name. There are many explanations, none definitive. Some think that early explorers, believing they were close to India, misidentified the bird and called it *tuki,* an Indian name for peacock. Because it also resembled the guinea fowl, which came from Africa via Turkish merchants, it could have picked up the name by another misappropriation of origin. (Guinea fowls were also called turkeys.) Or, it could have gotten its name from one of its calls, which sounds like "turk, turk, turk."

Because turkeys were so abundant in Colonial America, they were a major source of nourishment for our country's forefathers. In a well-known letter to his daughter, Benjamin Franklin expressed his dismay over the eagle's being chosen as the official United States bird. Referring to the eagle's "bad moral character," he went on to say, "I wish that the bald eagle had not been chosen as the representative of our country! The turkey is a much more respectable bird, and withal a true original native of America."

While about six hundred and seventy-five million pounds of turkey are served each Thanksgiving, in recent years, its healthy profile and versatility have changed the turkey from a holiday bird to one that competes with other meat and poultry on a year-round basis. Surprisingly, Americans do not eat the most turkey. In 1997, it was estimated that Israelis ate about 25.7 pounds per capita, while we weighed in at 18.7 pounds. Runner-up was France, at 13.4 pounds.

Most turkeys are of the White Holland variety, which have a lot of the white breast meat that more than seventy percent of Americans prefer. In fact, farm-raised turkeys are so chest-heavy that they cannot get close enough to mate. All farm-raised female turkeys are artificially inseminated.

Perfect Roast Turkey with Best-Ever Gravy

Makes about 18 servings, with about
7 cups gravy

After trying every turkey roasting method under the sun, this is the one I come back to, and the one I always teach at my cooking classes. Instructions here are for an average-sized eighteen-pound turkey, but this recipe can be adapted to the size of your bird. Read the information on stuffing and gravy on pages 63–65 and 96–99. If you prefer to roast an unstuffed turkey, use the vegetable or herb seasonings on page 46.

One 18-pound fresh turkey

About 12 cups of your favorite stuffing

8 tablespoons (1 stick) unsalted butter, at room temperature

Salt and freshly milled black pepper

2¹/₂ quarts Homemade Turkey Stock (page 22), or as needed

Melted unsalted butter, if needed

³/₄ cup all-purpose flour

¹/₃ cup bourbon, port, or dry sherry, optional

1. Position a rack in the lowest position of the oven and preheat to 325°F.

2. Reserve the turkey neck and giblets to use in gravy or stock. Rinse the turkey inside and out with cold water. Pat the turkey skin dry. Turn the turkey on its breast. Loosely fill the neck cavity with stuffing. Using a thin wooden or metal skewer, pin the neck skin to the back. Fold the turkey's wings akimbo behind the back or tie to the body with kitchen string. Loosely fill the large body cavity with stuffing. Place any remaining stuffing in a lightly buttered casserole, cover, and refrigerate to bake as a side dish. Place the drumsticks in the hock lock or tie together with kitchen string.

3. Place the turkey, breast side up, on a rack in the roasting pan. Rub all over with the softened butter. Season with salt and pepper. Tightly cover the breast area with aluminum foil. Pour 2 cups of the turkey stock into the bottom of the pan.

4. Roast the turkey, basting all over every 30 minutes with the juices on the bottom of the pan (lift up the foil to reach the breast area), until a meat thermometer inserted in the meaty part of the thigh (but not touching a bone) reads 180°F and the stuffing is at least 160°F, about 4 ¹/₄ hours. (See Estimated Roasting Times on page 40.) Whenever the drippings evaporate, add stock to moisten them, about 1 ¹/₂ cups at a time. Remove the foil during the last hour to allow the breast skin to brown.

5. Transfer the turkey to a large serving platter and let it stand for at least 20 minutes before carving. Increase the oven temperature to 350°F. Drizzle ¹/₂ cup turkey stock over the stuffing in the casserole, cover, and bake until heated through, about 30 minutes.

6. Meanwhile, pour the drippings from the roasting pan into a heatproof glass bowl or large measuring cup. Let stand for 5 minutes, then skim off and reserve the clear yellow fat that has risen to the top. Measure ³/₄ cup fat, adding melted butter if needed. Add enough turkey stock to the skimmed drippings to make 8 cups total.

7. Place the roasting pan in two stove burners over low heat and add the turkey fat. Whisk in the flour, scraping up the browned bits on the bottom of the pan, and cook until lightly browned, about 2 minutes. Whisk in the turkey stock and the optional bourbon. Cook, whisking often, until the gravy has thickened and no trace of raw flour taste remains, about 5 minutes. Transfer the gravy to a warmed gravy boat. Carve the turkey and serve the gravy and the stuffing alongside.

Oven-Blasted Turkey

Makes 10 to 12 servings

My friend cookbook author Steven Schmidt taught me the beauties of a high-roast turkey. The method was popularized by Barbara Kafka in her book Roasting: A Simple Art *but both Steve and I prefer a lower (but still darned hot) oven temperature than Kafka. It is the opposite end of the roasting spectrum from my Perfect Roast Turkey, page 43, which uses a relatively low temperature to discourage shrinkage.*

The high-temperature method blasts the outside of the bird to seal the skin and hold in juices. As good as it is, even Steve admits there are things to look out for.

- *Unless you have an good oven ventilation system, you won't want to try this recipe, as there will be some smoke no matter what you do. The oven must be very clean before roasting, as any old splatters will burn and really smoke up the kitchen.*
- *Use a heavy high-quality dark metal (or stainless steel–lined) roasting pan. Do not use an unlined aluminum pan, even if it is a heavy one.*
- *All of the recipes I have seen for this method say a rack is unnecessary. But every time I tried it, even in a nonstick pan, the turkey stuck to the pan, so now I use a rack, regardless of conflicting advice.*
- *The bird should be at around room temperature to cook most quickly. However, I don't like letting a bird stand out of the refrigerator for longer than 1 hour. To bring up the temperature, I rinse the refrigerator-cold bird under lukewarm water for about 15 minutes.*
- *Because the bird must be turned, you may want to use a smaller (12- to 14-pound) turkey and even they can make for awkward turning. If you aren't an agile cook, move on to another recipe. If you are strong, you can use as big a bird as you like, allowing about 10 minutes per pound for a stuffed bird, or*

8 minutes per pound for an unstuffed bird. Turning also requires a string-trussed turkey with the body vents sewn shut.

- *It's difficult to predict whether the drippings will be too dark to use for gravy or will be fine. As a safety precaution against burned drippings, prepare 4 cups Head Start Gravy. If the drippings taste fine, stir the gravy base into the degreased drippings and reheat in the pan. If they have burned, discard them and reheat the gravy base without the drippings to serve instead. Either way, you won't be left with an empty gravy boat.*

One 12- to 14-pound fresh turkey

About 8 cups of your favorite stuffing

4 tablespoons ($^1/_2$ stick) unsalted butter, melted

1 teaspoon salt

$^1/_4$ teaspoon freshly milled black pepper

$^1/_2$ cup Homemade Turkey Stock (page 22)

4 cups Head Start Gravy (page 99)

Special Equipment

High-quality heavy-duty roasting pan, just large enough to hold the turkey comfortably

Adjustable roasting rack

Thin metal skewers

Kitchen twine

Oven mitts

1. Position a rack in the lowest position of the oven and preheat to 425°F.

2. Reserve the turkey neck and giblets to use in gravy or stock. Rinse the turkey inside and out with *lukewarm* water. Place the turkey in a large bowl and place in the sink, directly under a thin stream of lukewarm water. Let the water run over the turkey for about 15 minutes.

3. Drain the turkey and pat the skin dry. Turn the turkey on its breast. Loosely fill the neck cavity with stuffing. Using a thin metal skewer, pin the neck skin to the back. Loosely fill the large body cavity with stuffing. Place any remaining stuffing in a lightly buttered casserole, cover, and refrigerate to bake as a side dish.

4. Holding the skin over the body cavity closed, pierce 4 or 5 metal skewers down the opening. Loop the middle of a piece of kitchen twine around the top skewer, then lace it, shoestring-style, around the skewers, pulling the string tight to close the opening; knot and trim the string. To truss the bird, place a 4-foot length of string under the shoulders of the turkey. Cross the string over the breast and pull tight, securing the wings to the body. Bring the string down to the ends of the drumsticks. (See illustration 1.) Wrap the ends of the string around the drumstick knobs. Pull the ends of the string together, bringing the drumsticks together, and knot. (Illustration 2.)

5. Adjust a roasting rack in a V to hold the bird on its side (with a drumstick facing up), and place the rack in the roasting pan. Brush the turkey with the butter, then season with the salt and pepper. Roast for 30 minutes, basting with the butter in the pan after 15 minutes.

6. Protecting your hands with oven mitts or wads of paper towels, turn the turkey onto its other side. Roast for another 30 minutes, basting after 15 minutes.

7. Turn the turkey back to the first side, and roast for 30 minutes more, basting after 15 minutes. Then, turn it once again to the second side, and roast for another 30 minutes, basting again, for a total roasting time of 2 hours.

8. Remove the turkey from the rack, and adjust the rack to the flat position. Return the turkey to the rack. Continue roasting until a meat thermometer inserted in the thickest part of the thigh reads 180°F, 10 to 30 minutes. Drizzle the refrigerated stuffing with the stock and cover. Bake at 350°F until heated through while the turkey is resting, about 30 minutes.

9. Transfer the turkey to a serving platter and let stand for at least 20 minutes before carving. If the drippings taste burned, discard them, and serve the turkey with the reheated gravy. If the drippings taste fine, pour them into a glass bowl, leaving the browned bits in the bottom of the pan. Let stand for 5 minutes, then skim off and discard the layer of clear fat that has risen to the surface. Return the drippings to the pan and place the pan on two burners over medium-high heat. Add the gravy and bring to a boil, scraping up the browned bits in the pan with a wooden spatula. Simmer until the gravy thickens. Strain and transfer to a warmed gravy boat.

10. Remove the trussing strings. Carve the turkey and serve with the stuffing and gravy.

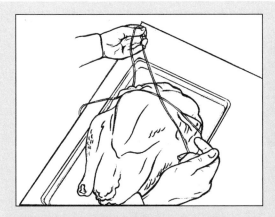

1. To truss, place a 4-foot length of string under the shoulders of the turkey. Cross the string over the breast and pull tight, securing the wings to the body. Bring the string down to the ends of the drumsticks.

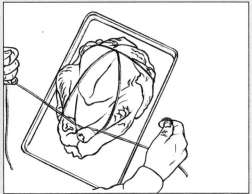

2. Wrap the ends of the string around the drumstick knobs. Pull the ends of the string together, bringing the drumsticks together, and knot.

Herb-Brined Roast Turkey

Makes 15 to 20 servings

Brined turkey first made a splash a few years ago, in the pages of Cook's Illustrated *magazine, whose authors, in turn, derived their recipe from a Portuguese version in Jean Anderson's* The Food of Portugal *(with a few tips from kosher butchers along the way). The brining idea is a good one, as the bird soaks up moisture and seasoning (I include herbs for added flavor), but the logistics can be daunting.*

• *This method only works with fresh turkeys—self-basting, frozen, and kosher turkeys have already been salted.*

• *You'll need a container big enough to hold your turkey in the brine. A 6-gallon stockpot will hold a 15- to 18-pound bird. If you don't have a big enough pot, use a new large, inexpensive plastic wastebasket, washed well before using.*

• *To estimate the amount of brine, place the turkey in the container and measure in enough cold water to cover the bird completely. The proportions in the recipe are for 2 gallons water, but the amount of brine can be adjusted as needed. For each 2 quarts water, use ¹/₂ cup kosher or ¹/₄ cup plain table salt (kosher salt is less salty than table salt), 1¹/₂ teaspoons each, dried rosemary, thyme, and sage, and ³/₄ teaspoon each dried marjoram, celery seeds, and peppercorns.*

• *The turkey must be chilled during brining. As few of use have refrigerator space to hold a large heavy stockpot, especially during the holidays, you may have to opt for outdoors or an unheated room, if the weather is cold enough (below 40°F).*

• *Don't run the risk of baking the stuffing in the turkey, as the salty juices could ruin it. Instead, loosely fill the cavities with seasoning vegetables and bake the stuffing on the side.*

One 15- to 20-pound fresh turkey
2 cups kosher salt or 1 cup plain (noniodized) table salt
2 tablespoons dried rosemary
2 tablespoons dried thyme
2 tablespoons dried sage
1 tablespoon dried marjoram
1 tablespoon celery seeds
1 tablespoon black peppercorns
1 medium onion, chopped
1 medium carrot, chopped
1 medium celery rib, chopped
6 tablespoons (³/₄ stick) unsalted butter, at room temperature
About 1¹/₂ quarts Homemade Turkey Stock (page 22), plus more as needed for gravy
Pan Gravy 101 (page 97), as needed

Special Equipment

Large (over 6-gallon) stockpot or other receptacle

1. The night before roasting, rinse the turkey inside and out with cold water. Reserve the turkey neck and giblets to use in gravy or stock.

2. In a very large stockpot, mix 2 gallons cold water with the salt, rosemary, thyme, sage, marjoram, celery seeds, and peppercorns, stirring until the salt dissolves. Place the turkey in the pot. Cover and place in a cold spot (lower than 40°F) or the refrigerator and let stand overnight.

3. Position a rack in the lower third of the oven and preheat to 325°F. In a small bowl, mix the onion, carrot, and celery.

4. Remove the turkey from the brine and rinse well, inside and out, under cold running water. Pat the skin and body cavities dry with paper towels. Turn the turkey on its breast. Loosely fill the neck cavity with the onion mixture. Using a thin wooden or metal skewer, pin the neck skin to the back. Fold the turkey's wings akimbo behind the back or tie to the body with kitchen string. Loosely fill the large body cavity with the remaining onion mixture. Place the drumsticks in the hock lock or tie together with kitchen string.

5. Place the turkey, breast side up, on a rack in the roasting pan. Rub all over with the butter. Tightly cover the breast area with aluminum foil. Pour 2 cups of the turkey stock into the bottom of the pan.

6. Roast the turkey, basting all over every 30 minutes with the juices on the bottom of the pan (lift up the foil to reach the breast area), until a meat thermometer inserted in the meaty part of the thigh (but not touching a bone) reads 180°F, about 4½ hours. (See Estimated Turkey Roasting Times, page 40.) Whenever the drippings evaporate, add stock to moisten them (about 1½ cups at a time). Remove the foil during the last hour to allow the breast skin to brown.

7. Transfer the turkey to a large serving platter and let it stand for at least 20 minutes before carving. Meanwhile, make the pan gravy according to the directions on page 97. Carve the turkey and serve the gravy alongside.

Smoke-Grilled Cider-Basted Turkey

Makes 12 to 14 servings

Smoking adds a robust flavor to turkey, and a zesty basting mixture keeps the breast moist without covering it with foil, which would block out the smoke. The turkey is cooked by the indirect method, meaning that it is cooked by the radiating heat supplied by banks of coals on either side of the bird. Of course, it can be cooked on a gas grill, but I prefer the deeper flavor provided by charcoal briquettes.

• *This method smokes the turkey in a standard 22½-inch charcoal grill. The turkey can also be smoked on a gas grill, but the recipe was not designed for a water smoker, which should be used according to the manufacturer's instructions.*

• *Two accessories, available to owners of Weber charcoal grills, will help make indirect cooking easier. A hinged cooking grate makes it easier to add the ignited coals to the grill. To hold the charcoal in mounds and concentrate their heat, use charcoal rails or basket-shaped fuel holders. If your grill didn't come with these accessories, you may want to mail-order them from Weber-Stephen Products at 1-847-934-5700, or call other manufacturers to see if they have similar products.*

• *Allow about 15 minutes per pound of turkey. If the grill temperature fluctuates, adjust the timing.*

• *Smoke the turkey in a disposable aluminum foil roasting pan. The smoke will discolor the pan, so you won't want to use your best roaster.*

• *Maintain a grill temperature of about 325°F. With a charcoal grill, you will need to add ignited coals every 40 minutes or so to keep up the heat. Light the charcoal briquets in a separate small grill, hibatchi, or metal chimney starter. Use long tongs to transfer the coals to the large grill.*

• *Even with a gas grill, it is a challenge to maintain an even temperature. The weather is a factor (cold breezes can chill the outside of the grill and affect the inner temperature too), as is the kind of charcoal used (briquettes burn more evenly and slowly, while hardwood charcoal burns very hot and quickly). If you can, cook the turkey in a grill that has a thermometer in the lid. Otherwise, place an inexpensive oven thermometer next to the turkey on the grill to monitor the temperature. Don't open the lid too often, because the heat will escape.*

• *Smaller 12- to 14-pound turkeys cook best on the average grill. It's risky to cook big turkeys outside, because the sides of the turkey are too close to the banked coals and can overcook. A big bird won't even fit onto a typical gas grill. (A Weber gas grill can cook a turkey of up to 18 pounds. Its unique design has burners set front-middle-back, instead of side-by-side, and those grills have more cooking space. To fit the burner configuration, choose a turkey with an elongated, not round, shape.) If you insist on grilling a large bird, cook it on the grill with plenty of wood chips for about 1 1/2 hours to get it nice and smoky. Then transfer it to a roasting rack and continue cooking it indoors in a preheated 325°F oven for the rest of the time.*

- *Smoke-cooking gives the turkey a very dark brown skin. If the bird is getting too dark, tent it with foil. When the turkey is done, there will be a thin layer of pink under the skin, also caused by the smoke, which is harmless and does not indicate that the turkey is undercooked.*

- *To my taste, regular stuffing gets oversmoked inside a grilled bird. I substitute a seasoning mixture of apples and onions. My favorite dressing for a grilled turkey, baked separately, is Southwestern Chorizo Stuffing (page 70).*

- *For real Western flavor, serve the turkey with Cranberry-Pineapple Salsa. If you want gravy, be flexible, as the condition of the pan drippings is unreliable. With a charcoal grill, ashes from the coals usually get blown into the drippings. Even if the drippings are clean, or you have cooked the bird in a gas grill, they can be too smoky. Make Head Start Gravy, on page 99. Pour out the drippings from the roasting pan, leaving the browned bits in the pan. Skim and discard the fat from the surface of the drippings, and taste them. If the drippings aren't too smoke-flavored or gritty with ashes, stir the hot gravy into the pan, scraping up the browned bits with a wooden spoon. (You won't be able to place the aluminum foil pan on the stove, so just scrape up what you can.) If the drippings aren't usable, just serve the Head Start Gravy.*

Cider Baste

4 tablespoons (1/2 stick) unsalted butter

1/3 cup finely chopped shallots or red onion

2 garlic cloves, minced

1 tablespoon chili powder

One 12-ounce bottle dry hard cider or 1 cup apple cider plus 1/2 cup dry white wine

1 teaspoon dried rosemary

1 teaspoon dried sage

1/2 teaspoon salt

One 12- to 14-pound turkey

1 medium apple, peeled, cored, and chopped

1 small onion, chopped

2 garlic cloves, minced

1 1/2 teaspoons chili powder

1/2 teaspoon dried rosemary

1/2 teaspoon dried sage

1/2 teaspoon salt

Cranberry-Pineapple Salsa (page 95)

6 cups mesquite chips, soaked in water for at least 30 minutes, drained

1. To make the cider baste, melt the butter in a medium saucepan over medium heat. Add the shallots and garlic and cook, stirring often, until softened, about 1 minute. Add the chili powder and stir for 30 seconds. Add the cider, rosemary, sage, and salt. Bring to a simmer and reduce the heat to very low. Simmer for 10 minutes. Cool completely.

2. If the turkey has a pop-up thermometer, remove it. Reserve the neck and giblets for another use. Rinse the turkey inside and out with cold water. Pat the turkey skin dry. In a small bowl, mix the apple, onion, garlic, chili powder, rosemary, sage, and salt. Turn the turkey on its breast. Loosely fill the neck cavity with the apple mixture. Using a thin wooden or metal skewer, pin the neck skin to the back. Fold the turkey's wings akimbo behind the back or tie to the body with kitchen string. Loosely fill the large body cavity with the remaining apple mixture. Place the drumsticks in the hock lock or tie together with kitchen string. Place the turkey on a roasting rack, breast-side up, in a large disposable aluminum foil pan. Cover the turkey loosely with plastic wrap and set aside while you light the grill.

3. *For a charcoal grill,* light 5 pounds of charcoal briquettes in the grill and let burn until covered with white ash, about 30 minutes. Using a garden spade (protect your hands with an oven mitt), bank equal amounts of the coals on either side of the grill. Place the roasting pan on the cooking grate in the center of the grill. Sprinkle a handful of drained chips over the coals. *For a gas grill,* preheat the grill on High. Place the wood chips in the chip box; or wrap the drained chips in aluminum foil, poke a few holes in the foil, and place the packet directly on the heat source. Turn one burner off, and turn the other(s) down to Medium. Place the roasting pan on the cooking grate in the center of the grill.

4. Pour 2 cups of water into the roasting pan. Baste the turkey with the cider mixture. Cover the grill and cook until a meat thermometer inserted in the thickest part of the thigh reads 180°F, 3 to 3½ hours. *For a charcoal grill,* add more hot coals and drained wood chips every 30 to 40 minutes to maintain a temperature of about 325°F, and baste the turkey. *For a gas grill:* To improve browning, 30 minutes before the turkey is cooked, remove the turkey from the roasting pan. Lightly oil the cooking grate and place the turkey directly on the grate over the turned-off burner. If your burners are side-by-side, turn the turkey around after 15 minutes, so both sides can be evenly browned by the heat coming from the Medium burner(s). *For both grills:* As the liquid in the pan evaporates, add more water to keep the drippings from burning. If the turkey is getting too brown, tent it with foil.

5. Transfer the turkey to a serving platter and let stand for 20 minutes before carving. Carve and serve with the salsa.

The Great Blackened-Turkey (Almost) Disaster

My mom and dad called me for a recipe for grilled turkey. While relating it, I warned them that a big bird really doesn't fit on a regular grill. Of course they listened politely, and then went right out and bought their usual bird—which is about the size of a '64 Volkswagen.

Dad got up early and stuffed the bird into his Weber. Like most California men over the age of eighteen, my father is a grilling expert, specializing in burgers and ribs (the barbecuing gene is part of our DNA makeup), but he didn't know what to expect from a whole turkey.

My folks's patio is right outside their dining room. Relaxing at the table, in the middle of sipping his Bloody Mary, Dad calmly glanced out to see that the grill had so much smoke coming out of it it looked like Mount Saint Helens. He ran outside to find that the sides of the bird, which were hanging over the coals, burned black.

Well, Dad wasn't about to throw out a turkey and start all over from scratch. So, after a consultation with Mom, they decided to protect the blackened parts of the bird with foil and finish roasting it in the oven. The rest of my family all took the situation in stride—after all, the prized breast meat was unscathed.

When the bird was served, everyone swore it was the best bird they'd ever had. And the wings? They were fought over by my relatives who like crispy skin. And they said they were the best wings they'd ever had.

Bayou Deep-Fried Turkey

Makes 10 to 12 servings

Every time I turned around, another person was telling me about how deep-fried turkey was the best method known to man. A quick Internet search revealed hundreds of deep-fried turkey sites, all with guaranteed recipes, some only a couple of paragraphs long to describe what is not a procedure for inexperienced cooks. (The most detailed was from my friend "Hoppin'" John Taylor, from his Fearless Frying Cookbook.) Some of my guests did love the crisp golden skin and moist tender meat, while others just could not get past the idea of deep-fried turkey. It certainly is the quickest way to cook a bird—about three minutes a pound.

For years it has been a staple at Cajun-country cookouts, where the idea does make sense. In Louisiana at church suppers where they are cooked outdoors in huge pots on propane burners with lots of lard from the local hogs, deep-fried turkeys are no hassle. Outside of the bayou, I have my reservations. In order to try this recipe, I had to buy two hundred dollars worth of equipment: a ten-gallon stockpot (my little ol' six-gallon pot was way too small), a deep-frying basket insert to fit into the pot, a twelve-inch propane gas burner (with at least 100,000 BTUs), a deep-frying thermometer (preferably with a long stem), and five gallons of vegetable oil. The turkey cost ten bucks. And disposing of the dirty cooking oil took some thought. The city health department told me to flush it away. Seriously, you may want to share the costs with your guests, unless you are sure you want to keep the equipment yourself.

• Of all the turkey cooking methods, this takes the most organization. You must keep your wits about you, so stay away from the Bloody Marys. Also, don't allow kids and pets to come near the pot.

• Place the propane burner on a level dirt or grass surface. Splattering oil will stain concrete driveways, and wood decks could catch fire. Do not fry turkeys in attached buildings, such as garages, or near bushes. Of course, in inclement weather, the area must be covered. Do not leave the burner, not for even a second. I made this mistake, and when I returned, found that some paper had blown onto the burner and started a scary fire. Have a fire extinguisher or a box of baking soda nearby.

• You will get oil on your clothes, so wear old ones. An apron is not enough protection.

• Many of those Internet recipes from pseudo-gourmets inject the bird with spicy liquid seasonings from a marinating syringe, although the herbs and spices in the recipe I tried wouldn't go through the tiny nozzle. Anyway, this seasoning detracts from the natural turkey flavor. It does absolutely no good to season the bird with salt, pepper, spice rubs, or the like, as they wash off into the oil. Allow your guests to season their own servings with salt, pepper, and hot red pepper sauce. A squeeze of fresh lemon juice is also an excellent accent.

• Buy the vegetable oil at a wholesale warehouse club or Asian grocer for the best price. While some cooks often use rendered lard, and many cooks suggest expensive peanut oil, regular vegetable oil works just as well. Save the oil container, as you will need it to dispose of the used oil. Cool the oil completely (let it stand overnight in the pot if necessary), and funnel it back into its container for disposal. (Do not even think about using the oil again. It is very easy for previously used oil to catch fire when reheated. You must factor the oil into your budget.)

• Heat the oil to 390°F. Watch it carefully, because if begins to smoke (usually at around 410°F), the turkey will have an off flavor. When the turkey is added to the hot oil, the temperature will drop. Adjust the heat as needed to keep the oil around 365°F.

• The amount of oil called for here works for a

10-pound turkey. To double-check the amount of oil needed, place the turkey in the pot and fill the pot with water until it reaches one to two inches above the turkey. (To allow for the inevitable oil bubbling, the pot must never be more than two-thirds full.) Remove the turkey and measure the amount of water. Dry the turkey and the pot very well to reduce splattering before adding the oil.

- *The frying basket keeps the turkey from touching the bottom of the pot, where it could burn. If you can't locate a basket, place a large collapsible metal vegetable steamer or colander in the pot before adding the oil. (Some deep-fried turkey equipment suppliers—yes, there are such companies!—sell turkey holders, but they have to be lowered into the oil with some kind of a hook, like a fireplace poker.)*

- *Small 10- to 14-pound turkeys work best. If you have a lot of guests, cook two birds. Cover the first bird loosely with aluminum foil to keep warm while the second bird fries.*

- *Do not stuff turkeys for deep-frying. Bake the Sausage Gumbo Stuffing (page 70) on the side for the perfect partner.*

- *If you want gravy, use Head Start Gravy on page 99, spiked with 1 tablespoon bourbon for every 1 cup of liquid and well seasoned with hot red pepper sauce.*

- *Be sure your propane tank is full. You don't want to run out of gas in the middle of frying.*

- *Propane burners are available at propane gas suppliers and outdoor furniture stores. Be sure the burner comes with hose and regulator units and an adapter that fits your propane tank. It is a good idea to take your tank to the store to be sure everything fits properly. The other equipment can be purchased at restaurant supply stores. There are many Web sites that have all the equipment for deep-frying turkeys— a site-search will reveal many sources. One supplier is The Cajun Shoppe, P.O. Box 168, Lake Charles, LA 70602; 1-800-434-2809.*

One 10- to 14-pound fresh turkey
5 gallons vegetable oil
Salt, hot red pepper sauce, and fresh lemon wedges for serving

Special Equipment
One 10- to 12-gallon stockpot
Large deep-frying basket insert for stockpot
A 12-inch propane gas burner with at least 100,000 BTUs (an electric hot plate will not work)
A deep-frying thermometer, attached to a long piece of flexible wire
Oven mitts
A large roasting pan

1. Reserve the turkey neck and giblets for another use. Rinse the turkey well, inside and out, with *barely warm* water to help remove the chill from the bird. Pat completely dry, inside and out, with lots of paper towels. You do not want any moisture at all on the turkey, or it will splatter dangerously when it goes into the oil. Fold the turkey wings akimbo behind the shoulders. Remove the hock lock and do not tie the drumsticks together. Place the turkey on a large wire rack and let stand while you heat the oil.

2. Place the stockpot on the burner and fill it with the oil. Attach the deep-frying thermometer to the pot handle with thin, flexible wire so its tip is submerged 1 to 2 inches into the oil. Light the fire and heat the oil to 390°F. This will take about 30 minutes, depending on the burner's efficiency. Be sure that flames are not licking the outside of the pot.

3. Place the well-dried turkey, breast first, in the basket. Wearing oven mitts, carefully lower the basket into the oil. The oil will bubble up dramatically, so don't be surprised. Lift up the turkey, and dip it again into the oil three or four times before leaving it in the pot. This allows the oil temperature to gradually adjust to the turkey and prevents the oil from boiling over. Fry the turkey, allowing about 3½ minutes per pound, until golden and a meat thermometer inserted in the thickest part of the thigh registers 175°F (the temperature will rise 5° to 10°F while the turkey stands), 40 to 49 minutes. Adjust the heat as needed to maintain the oil temperature at 365°F.

4. Lift the basket out of the oil and transfer to the roasting pan. Drain the turkey completely, especially the body cavity, allowing the oil to drain into the pan. Let the turkey stand for at least 20 minutes before carving. Carve and serve, letting each guest season the turkey with salt, hot pepper sauce, and lemon juice.

French Boned Turkey with Pâté Stuffing

Makes 8 to 10 servings

Make Ahead: The boned turkey and the stuffing can be prepared the night before, covered separately and refrigerated. (Don't stuff the turkey until just before roasting.)

One of the most elegant and flavorful ways to serve the holiday bird, this is the kind of turkey you would find on many French tables as Christmastime. It translates well to our Thanksgiving. Sure, it takes ingenuity to bone a turkey, but it's not really hard to do—given you have a good sharp boning knife. Some people may find the sauce, called demi-glace *by French cooks, easier to make than old-fashioned gravy. Because it is no more than concentrated stock, it must be made with the very best homemade variety.*

• *While boning the turkey, try keep the skin as intact as possible. If you do make a couple of holes, they* *can be sewn shut with kitchen twine. After the turkey is roasted and the twine pulled out, no one will know.*

• *Boned turkey gives you lots of turkey parts that should be turned into stock. Save the neck, giblets, wing tips, thigh bones, carcass, and any trimmings. Chop the neck and carcass into manageable pieces. Make Homemade Turkey Stock (page 22), substituting the turkey pieces for the turkey wings, and 1¾ cups canned reduced-sodium chicken broth for an equal amount of the water.*

Stuffing

½ cup diced (½-inch) pitted prunes

½ cup Madeira wine

2 tablespoons unsalted butter

½ cup finely chopped shallots

1 pound ground pork

1 pound ground turkey or veal

¾ cup fresh bread crumbs, preferably from
   day-old French or Italian bread

¼ cup chopped shelled pistachios (available at
   Indian grocers, or shell your own)

¼ cup chopped fresh parsley

1 large egg

1 large egg yolk

1 teaspoon dried thyme

2 teaspoons salt

½ teaspoon freshly milled black pepper

One 11-pound fresh turkey

2 tablespoons unsalted butter, melted

Salt and freshly milled black pepper

About 1½ quarts Homemade Turkey Stock
   (page 22)

Special Equipment

A sharp thin-bladed boning knife

Kitchen twine

A sturdy (mattress or sailing canvass) needle

1. To make the stuffing, place the prunes and Madeira in a small bowl and let stand for 1 hour. (Or, cover with plastic wrap and microwave on High for 1 minute, then let stand for 10 minutes.)

2. In a medium skillet, melt the butter over medium-low heat. Add the shallots and cook, stirring often, until softened, 1 to 2 minutes. Transfer to a large bowl and cool slightly. Add the ground pork, ground turkey, prunes and Madeira, bread crumbs, pistachios, parsley, egg, egg yolk, thyme, salt, and pepper. Mix well. (The stuffing can be prepared up to 1 day ahead, covered, and refrigerated.)

3. To bone the turkey, reserve the turkey neck and giblets (except the liver) to use in the stock. Use a heavy cleaver or large knife to chop off the first two joints of each wing (the tip and the center bone), and reserve for the stock. (See illustration 1, page 54.) Rinse the turkey well, inside and out, with cold water. Pat the turkey dry.

4. Place the turkey breast side down on the work surface. Using the boning knife, make an incision down the backbone. Keeping the point of the knife pointed toward the bones, make short slashes down one side of the rib cage until you reach the ridge of the breastbone. Repeat the procedure on the other side. (Illustration 2.) Cut the carcass away from the turkey at the breastbone (be careful, it's close to the skin). (Illustration 3.) To remove the thick silver tendon running down each breast, make a cut to reveal the wide end of the tendon. Pulling on the wide end of tendon, scrape it with the knife to release it from the flesh. (Illustration 4.)

5. Bend one thigh back to reveal the ball joint, and sever the ball joint. Holding the ball joint, scrape along the thigh bone to reach the drumstick joint. Sever the drumstick joint and remove the thigh bone, leaving the drumstick bone intact. (Illustration 5.) Repeat with the other thigh. Remove the spatula-shaped collarbone. Leave the wing joints intact. (The turkey can be boned up to 1 day ahead, covered tightly, and refrigerated.)

6. Position a rack in the center of the oven and preheat to 350°F.

7. Place the boned turkey, skin side down, on the work surface. Place the stuffing, forming into a loaf shape, down the center of the turkey. Using kitchen string and a mattress needle, sew up the turkey. Tie the turkey crosswise in several places to form into an elongated shape. (Illustration 6.)

8. Place the turkey on a long roasting rack (or use two overlapped wire cake racks) in a roasting pan. Brush with the melted butter and season with $1/2$ teaspoon salt and $1/4$ teaspoon pepper. Pour 2 cups of the stock into the pan.

9. Bake, basting occasionally, until a meat thermometer inserted in the thickest part of the turkey reads 175°F, about 3 hours. If the drippings evaporate and threaten to burn, moisten them with 2 cups additional stock. (With a boned turkey, the dark meat area will not look undercooked at this temperature, as it does with bone-in turkey.) Transfer the turkey to an oval serving platter and tent with foil to keep warm. Let the turkey stand for 15 minutes before slicing.

10. Pour the pan drippings into a heatproof glass bowl. Let stand for 5 minutes, then skim and discard the clear yellow fat that has risen to the surface. Place the roasting pan on two burners over high heat. Return the drippings to the pan. Pour in 1 quart stock. Bring to a boil, scraping up the browned bits in the pan with a wooden spoon. Boil until syrupy and reduced to $3/4$ cup, about 12 minutes. Season to taste with salt and pepper. Pour the sauce into a warmed sauceboat.

11. Remove the strings from the turkey. Carve the turkey crosswise into thick slices. Serve, drizzling a bit of sauce over each portion.

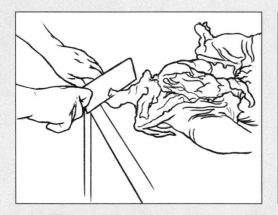

1. Use a heavy cleaver or large knife to chop off the first two joints of each wing (the tip and the center bone), and reserve for stock.

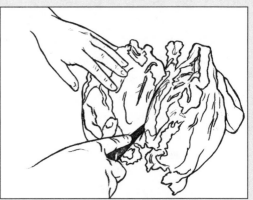

2. Keeping the point of the knife pointed toward the bones, make short slashes down one side of the rib cage until you reach the ridge of the breastbone. Repeat on the other side.

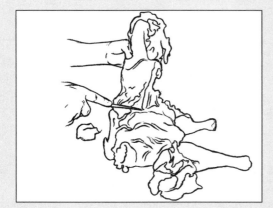

3. Cut the carcass away from the turkey at the breastbone (be careful, it's close to the skin).

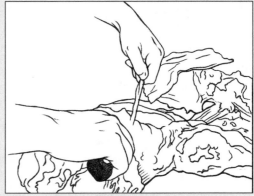

4. To remove the thick silver tendon running down each breast, make a cut to reveal the wide end of the tendon. Pulling on the wide end of the tendon, scrape it with the knife to release it from the flesh.

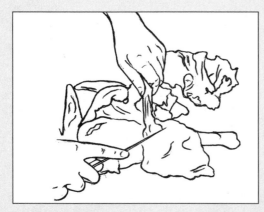

5. Holding the ball joint, scrape along the thigh bone to reach the drumstick joint. Sever the drumstick joint and re-move the thigh bone, leaving the drumstick bone intact.

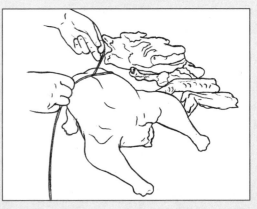

6. Tie the stuffed turkey crosswise in several places to form into an elongated shape.

Wild Turkey with Wild Rice and Dried Cherry Stuffing

Makes 6 to 8 servings

Make-Ahead: The wild turkey stock can be prepared up to 1 day ahead, cooled, covered, and refrigerated. Roast the turkey just before serving.

No, that's not a mistake. An eleven-pound wild turkey will only feed six to eight people. The meat a wild turkey does have is firm and full flavored, but don't expect it to come cheaply. If your investment is cooked beyond 175°F, it will dry out, so keep an eye on the meat thermometer. Be sure to special-order your wild turkey, and be prepared for it to be a different weight from your order; small-scale turkey farms cannot always supply exact orders. Adjust the timing as needed, allowing about fifteen minutes per pound for a stuffed turkey, twelve minutes per pound for unstuffed.

One 11-pound wild turkey, neck and giblets
   (except the liver) reserved

2 quarts Homemade Turkey Stock (page 22)

Wild Rice, Dried Cherry, and Almond Stuffing
   (page 72)

4 tablespoons (¹/₂ stick) unsalted butter,
   softened, plus 2 tablespoons unsalted butter

Salt and freshly milled black pepper

2 teaspoons cornstarch

¹/₃ cup tawny or ruby port

1. At least 2 hours before roasting the turkey, chop the turkey neck into 1-inch pieces. Place in a medium saucepan and add the turkey heart and gizzard. Add the stock and bring to a simmer over medium-high heat. Reduce the heat to very low and simmer for 2 hours. Strain the stock. You should have 1¹/₂ quarts

stock; add water to the stock, if needed. Set aside.

2. Position a rack in the lower third of the oven and preheat to 325°F.

3. Rinse the turkey inside and out with cold water. Pat the turkey skin dry. Turn the turkey on its breast. Loosely fill the neck cavity with stuffing. Using a thin wooden or metal skewer, pin the neck skin to the back. Fold the turkey's wings akimbo behind the back or tie to the body with kitchen string. Loosely fill the large body cavity with stuffing. Place any remaining stuffing in a lightly buttered casserole, cover, and refrigerate to bake as a side dish. Tie the drumsticks together with kitchen string.

4. Place the turkey, breast side up, on a rack in the roasting pan. Rub all over with the softened butter. Season with ¹/₂ teaspoon salt and ¹/₄ teaspoon pepper. Tightly cover the breast area with aluminum foil. Pour 2 cups of the stock into the bottom of the pan.

5. Roast the turkey, basting all over every 30 minutes with the juices on the bottom of the pan (lift up the foil to reach the breast area), until a meat thermometer inserted in the meaty part of the thigh (but not touching a bone) reads 170°F and the stuffing is at least 160°F, about 2³/₄ hours. Whenever the drippings evaporate, add water to moisten them (about 1¹/₂ cups at a time). Remove the foil during the last 45 minutes to allow the breast skin to brown.

6. Transfer the turkey to a large serving platter and let it stand for at least 20 minutes before carving. Increase the oven temperature to 350°F. Drizzle the reserved stuffing with ¹/₂ cup stock. Cover and bake the stuffing until heated through, about 20 minutes.

7. Meanwhile, pour the drippings from the roasting pan into a heatproof glass bowl or measuring cup. Let stand for 5 minutes; then skim off and reserve the clear yellow fat that has risen to the top. Return the drippings with the remaining stock to the roasting pan. Bring to a boil over high heat, scraping up the browned bits on the bottom of the pan with a wooden spatula. Boil until the liquid is reduced to 2 cups, 10 to 15 minutes.

8. In a small bowl, sprinkle the cornstarch into the port and stir to dissolve. Stir into the pan and cook until the sauce is slightly thickened. Remove from the heat. One tablespoon at a time, whisk in the remaining 2 tablespoons butter until melted. Season with salt and pepper. Pour the sauce into a warmed sauceboat.

9. Carve the turkey and serve with the stuffing and gravy.

Whole Turkey Breast with Walnut-Raisin Stuffing

Makes 6 to 8 servings

Make Ahead: Stuff and roast the turkey breast just before serving.

By no means are my Thanksgiving guest lists predictable. Sometimes it's dinner for twenty, sometimes for six. One year, I decided a whole bird wasn't necessary for our small gathering, and as I was leaving the next day on a trip, I didn't want to worry about a lot of leftovers. We had this whole turkey breast, stuffed under the skin with a walnut-raisin dressing. My guests loved its traditional flavors in a contemporary presentation and I appreciated its easy preparation.

Stuffing

12 tablespoons (1¹/₂ sticks) unsalted butter
¹/₂ cup finely chopped leeks (white and tender green parts)
1 medium carrot, finely chopped
1 medium celery rib, finely chopped
¹/₄ teaspoon salt
¹/₄ teaspoon freshly milled black pepper
6 cups seasoned bread stuffing cubes (about 11 ounces)

1¹/₂ cups Homemade Turkey Stock (page 22) or canned reduced-sodium chicken broth
¹/₂ cup raisins
¹/₂ cup toasted and coarsely chopped walnuts
1¹/₂ teaspoons poultry seasoning, preferably homemade (see Note, page 66)

One 7-pound whole turkey breast
2 tablespoons unsalted butter, melted, or as needed
Salt and freshly milled black pepper
About 3¹/₃ cups Homemade Turkey Stock (page 22) or canned reduced-sodium chicken broth
¹/₃ cup all-purpose flour

1. To make the stuffing, in a medium skillet, melt 2 tablespoons of the butter over medium-low heat. Add the leeks, carrot, and celery, cover, and cook, stirring occasionally, until tender, about 10 minutes. Season with the salt and pepper and transfer to a large bowl. Add the remaining 10 tablespoons butter to the skillet and melt. Pour into the bowl. Add the stuffing cubes, stock, raisins, walnuts, and poultry seasoning and mix well.

2. Position a rack in the center of the oven and preheat to 325°F.

3. Rinse the turkey breast under cold water and pat dry. Slip your fingers underneath the skin to loosen it from the breast without detaching it. Spread about one third of the stuffing mixture under the skin, smoothing it to an even thickness. Place the remaining stuffing in a buttered casserole, cover, and refrigerate to bake later as a side dish.

4. Place the turkey breast on a roasting rack in a roasting pan. Brush with the melted butter and season with ¹/₂ teaspoon salt and ¹/₄ teaspoon pepper. Pour 2 cups water into the pan. Roast, basting occasionally, until a meat thermometer inserted in the thickest part of the breast reads 170°F, about 2¹/₄ hours. Twenty minutes, before the turkey is done, drizzle the reserved stuffing with ⅓ cup stock and place in the oven to re-heat.

5. Transfer the turkey breast to a serving platter and set aside. Pour the drippings from the roasting pan into a heatproof glass bowl or large measuring cup. Let stand for 5 minutes; then skim off and reserve the clear yellow fat that rises to the top. Measure ⅓ cup fat, adding melted butter if needed. Add enough stock to the skimmed drippings (there won't be many) to make 3 cups total.

6. Place the roasting pan on a stove burner over low heat. Add the turkey fat. Whisk in the flour, scraping up the browned bits on the bottom of the pan, and cook until lightly browned, about 2 minutes. Whisk in the turkey stock. Cook, whisking often, until the gravy has thickened and no trace of raw flour taste remains, about 5 minutes. Season the gravy with salt and pepper. Transfer the gravy to a warmed gravy boat.

7. Carve the turkey and serve with the stuffing and gravy.

Turkey Breast with Wild Mushroom Stuffing and Marsala Sauce

Makes 8 to 10 servings

Make Ahead: The breasts can be stuffed up to 4 hours ahead.

Need a great low-fat Thanksgiving entrée? Look no further. A combination of fresh and dried mushrooms gives hearty flavor to the mild turkey breast meat, and it's further enhanced by a Marsala wine sauce. It meets the criteria for any good recipe, low-fat or not, and I serve it throughout the year at dinner parties.

Wild Mushroom Stuffing

1 cup boiling water

1 ounce (about 1 cup) dried porcini or Polish mushrooms

8 ounces cremini or white button mushrooms

1 tablespoon unsalted butter

¼ cup finely chopped shallots or white part of scallions

1 garlic clove, minced

1½ teaspoons chopped fresh rosemary or 1 teaspoon dried rosemary

½ teaspoon salt

¼ teaspoon freshly milled black pepper

½ cup fresh bread crumbs, preferably from day-old French or Italian bread

1 large egg white, beaten until foamy

Two 1½-pound boneless, skinless turkey breast roasts

Nonstick vegetable oil spray

Salt and freshly milled black pepper

1½ cups Homemade Turkey Stock (page 22) or canned reduced-sodium chicken broth

1 teaspoon cornstarch

¼ cup dry marsala

1 tablespoon unsalted butter, chilled

1. To make the stuffing, combine the boiling water and the dried mushrooms in a small bowl. Let stand until the mushrooms soften, about 30 minutes. Lift the mushrooms out of the water, rinse under cold running water, and coarsely chop. Strain the soaking liquid through a paper towel–lined sieve set over a small bowl. Reserve the liquid.

2. In a food processor, pulse the fresh mushrooms until finely chopped. Set aside.

3. In a large skillet, melt the butter over medium heat. Add the shallots and garlic and cook, stirring often, until softened, about 1 minute. Add the fresh mushrooms, soaked mushrooms, the reserved soaking liquid, the rosemary, salt, and pepper. Cover and cook for 3 minutes. Uncover and cook over high heat until the liquid evaporates, about 10 minutes. Transfer to a medium bowl and cool completely. Stir in the bread crumbs and egg white.

4. Place a turkey breast, skin side down, on a work surface. Using a sharp knife, cut a deep diagonal incision into the thickest part of the breast from the center of the roast almost to the edge, being careful not to cut completely through. Open this flap like a book. Make another cut in the other side, to butterfly the other side of the roast, and fold out in the other direction. Pound gently with a meat mallet, rolling pin, or empty wine bottle to flatten to an even thickness. Repeat with the other breast.

5. Spread half of the stuffing over one breast. Starting at a long side, roll up into a thick cylinder. Tie the breast crosswise in several places with kitchen string. Repeat with the remaining stuffing and breast. (The turkey breasts can be prepared to this point up 4 hours ahead, covered with plastic wrap, and refrigerated.)

6. Position a rack in the center of the oven and preheat to 350°F. Spray a flameproof baking dish large enough to comfortably hold the turkey breasts with nonstick spray.

7. Spray a large nonstick skillet with nonstick spray and heat over medium-high heat until very hot. Season the turkey with ¼ teaspoon salt and ⅛ teaspoon pepper. Add the turkey breasts to the skillet and cook, turning occasionally, until browned on all sides, about 6 minutes. Transfer the turkey to the prepared dish. Pour the stock into the dish and cover loosely with aluminum foil. Bake until a meat thermometer inserted in the centers of the breasts reads 165°F, about 40 minutes. Transfer the breasts to a serving platter and cover with foil to keep warm.

8. Place the baking dish on top of the stove and bring the liquid to a boil over high heat. Boil until reduced to about ½ cup, about 8 minutes. In a small bowl, sprinkle the cornstarch into the marsala and stir to dissolve. Pour into the dish and cook until the sauce

is slightly thickened. Remove from the heat and whisk in the butter until melted. Season with salt and pepper.

9. Discard the kitchen string. Slice the turkey into ½-inch-thick slices. Serve immediately, drizzling each serving with sauce.

Turkey Roulade with Prosciutto and Sage in Cranberry–Red Wine Sauce

Makes 4 servings

Make Ahead: The turkey cutlets can be prepared up to 1 day ahead.

There were only four of us for dinner that Thanksgiving. We had a full schedule of visiting friends, but we wanted to have dinner at home during a three-hour period between visits. Without any fuss, I prepared this spin on Italian saltimbocca, *usually made with veal cutlets. Saltimbocca means "jump in the mouth," which is exactly what these tender morsels will do.*

• *Some turkey cutlets are one beautiful slice of turkey of breast that is easy to roll. Others cutlets may look whole in the package, but separate into two or more pieces when taken out. Don't worry. Just overlap the slices in a cutlet shape on a piece of moistened wax paper. Top with another piece of moistened wax paper and lightly pound the edges together with a meat mallet or rolling pin to help them adhere. When the cutlets are rolled and cooked, any irregularities will disappear.*

• *Turkey cutlets are lean and should be cooked over moderate heat, for they toughen if browned over the high heat we typically use for other meats and poultry.*

- *If you want to double the recipe, use two 12-inch skillets—the cutlets should not be crowded in the pan.*

1½ cups dried cranberries (6 ounces)

½ cup hearty red wine, such as Chianti or zinfandel

8 turkey breast cutlets (about 2 pounds)

3 ounces thinly sliced prosciutto, cut into pieces (about 1 × 2 inches) to fit each cutlet

4 teaspoons chopped fresh sage or 2 teaspoons dried

1 tablespoon vegetable oil

¼ teaspoon salt

¼ teaspoon freshly milled black pepper

1 cup Homemade Turkey Stock (page 22) or canned reduced-sodium chicken broth

3 tablespoons unsalted butter

2 tablespoons finely chopped shallots

2 tablespoons balsamic vinegar

1 teaspoon light brown sugar

⅛ teaspoon crushed hot red pepper

Wooden toothpicks, to secure the roulades

1. Place the cranberries in a wire sieve and rinse well under hot water to remove excess sugar. Drain well, place in a small bowl, and add the wine. Let stand for 1 hour. (Or, cover with plastic wrap, microwave on High for 1 minute, and let stand for 10 minutes.)

2. Place a piece of prosciutto on each cutlet and sprinkle with ½ teaspoon fresh sage or ¼ teaspoon dried sage. Roll up each cutlet into a cylinder and secure with a wooden toothpick. Place the roulades on a wax paper–lined plate and cover with plastic wrap. Refrigerate until ready to cook. (The roulades can be prepared up to 1 day ahead.)

3. In a 12-inch nonstick skillet, heat the oil over medium heat until very hot but not smoking. Season the roulades with ¼ teaspoon salt and the pepper. Add the roulades to the pan and cook, turning once, until lightly browned on all sides, about 4 minutes. Add ¼ cup of the stock and cover tightly. Reduce the heat to medium-low. Cook gently until the roulades are cooked through and show no sign of pink when pierced in the center with the tip of a sharp knife, about 8 minutes. Transfer to a warmed serving platter and tent with aluminum foil to keep warm while making the sauce.

4. Discard the stock in the skillet. Return the skillet to medium heat and melt 1 tablespoon of the butter. Add the shallots and cook, stirring often, until softened, about 1 minute. Add the cranberries with the wine, the remaining ¾ cup stock, the balsamic vinegar, brown sugar, and hot pepper. Bring to a boil over high heat and cook until the liquid reduces by half, about 3 minutes. Remove from the heat and whisk in the remaining butter, 1 tablespoon at a time. Season with salt.

5. Remove the toothpicks. Serve the roulades immediately, spooning the sauce over each serving.

Smoked Ham with Zinfandel-Orange Glaze

Makes about 16 servings

Make Ahead: The ham must marinate for at least 8 hours, or overnight.

Sometimes you need to make your groaning board groan just a little more. A baked ham is a carefree and tasty way to feed a crowd, and it's a natural partner to turkey. A bone-in smoked ham has the best flavor, which can be improved upon by bringing it to a simmer in a large pot of water to extract excess salt. Basted with a not-too-sweet marinade, this ham gets a light glaze that goes with just about any menu. In fact, it has become one of my favorite recipes for any buffet, and from the amount of requests I get for this recipe, my friends must agree.

One 6¹/₂- to 7¹/₂-pound smoked ham
One 12-ounce jar bitter orange marmalade
¹/₂ cup hearty red wine, such as zinfandel
¹/₂ cup fresh orange juice
2 garlic cloves, crushed under a knife

1. Place the ham in a large kettle and add enough cold water to cover. Bring to a simmer over medium-high heat. (This could take up to 45 minutes.) Drain the ham and cool completely.

2. In a medium bowl, whisk the orange marmalade, wine, orange juice, and garlic. Place the ham in a large plastic bag (such as a small garbage bag), then pour in the marinade. Close the bag and place in a large bowl. Marinate for at least 8 hours, or overnight, turning occasionally.

3. Position a rack in the center of the oven and preheat to 350°F. Line a roasting pan with aluminum foil.

4. Remove the ham from the marinade, scraping off any bits of orange marmalade. Strain the marinade and set aside. Place the ham on a roasting rack in the pan. Bake, basting occasionally with the marinade, until a meat thermometer inserted in the thickest part of the ham (without touching a bone) registers 140°F, about 1¹/₂ hours (allow about 15 minutes per pound).

5. Transfer the ham to a carving board or platter. Let stand for 15 minutes before carving.

Holiday Meatball Lasagna

Makes 8 to 12 servings

Make Ahead: The sauce and meatballs can be prepared up to 2 days ahead and refrigerated; and the lasagna can be prepared up to 1 day ahead and refrigerated; both can be frozen for up to 1 month.

For Italian-American families, pasta must be a part of the Thanksgiving menu, and usually lasagna plays just as big a starring role as turkey. My neighbors rhapsodize about their family's version, where the meat for the sauce is rolled into little meatballs to make the dish extra-special. It's a simple process, and you don't have to brown the meatballs—just drop them into the simmering herb-scented tomato sauce.

Sauce and Meatballs
2 tablespoons olive oil
1 large onion, chopped
3 garlic cloves, minced
One 28-ounce can tomatoes in thick purée
Two 6-ounce cans tomato paste
One 8-ounce can tomato sauce
1 cup dry red wine

1¹/₂ teaspoons dried basil

1 teaspoon dried oregano

¹/₄ teaspoon crushed hot red pepper

1 pound ground beef round

1 pound ground pork

¹/₂ cup Italian-seasoned dried bread crumbs

2 large eggs, beaten

1¹/₂ teaspoons salt

¹/₂ teaspoon freshly milled black pepper

1 pound lasagna noodles

One 32-ounce container ricotta cheese

1¹/₂ cups freshly grated Parmesan cheese
  (about 6 ounces)

2 large eggs

¹/₃ cup chopped fresh basil or parsley

1 teaspoon salt

¹/₄ teaspoon freshly milled black pepper

1¹/₂ pounds mozzarella cheese, thinly sliced

1. In a large dutch oven, heat the oil over medium heat. Add the onion and cook, stirring often, until golden, about 5 minutes. Add the garlic and stir until fragrant, about 1 minute. Stir in the tomatoes with their purée, 1 cup water, the tomato paste, tomato sauce, wine, basil, oregano, and hot pepper. Bring to a boil, and reduce the heat to low. Simmer uncovered, stirring occasionally, until slightly thickened, about 10 minutes.

2. Meanwhile, in a large bowl, mix the ground round, ground pork, bread crumbs, eggs, salt, and pepper. Using about 1¹/₂ teaspoons for each, roll the mixture into small meatballs and place on a wax paper–lined baking sheet.

3. A few at a time, gently stir the meatballs into the simmering sauce. Return to a simmer and cook, stirring occasionally, until the sauce is thick and the meatballs show no sign of pink when pierced in the center, about 20 minutes. Set the sauce aside. (The sauce and meatballs can be prepared up to 2 days

ahead, cooled, covered, and refrigerated; they can also be frozen in airtight containers for up to 1 month.)

4. Meanwhile, bring a large pot of lightly salted water to a boil over high heat. Add the lasagna noodles, 2 or 3 at a time, and stir well. Boil, stirring occasionally to be sure the noodles don't stick to each other, just until tender, about 10 minutes. Drain and rinse under cold running water. (The noodles can be prepared up to 2 hours ahead, tossed with 1 tablespoon olive oil, and set aside at room temperature.)

5. Position a rack in the center of the oven and preheat to 375°F. Lightly oil a 10 × 15-inch baking dish.

6. In a medium bowl, mix the ricotta cheese, 1 cup of the Parmesan cheese, the eggs, basil, salt, and pepper. Set aside.

7. Using a large skimmer or a slotted spoon, transfer the meatballs to a large bowl. Coat the bottom of the prepared dish with ¹/₄ cup of the sauce. Arrange 5 lasagna noodles (4 horizontally and 1 vertically), slightly overlapping and cut to fit, in the dish. Spread half of the ricotta filling over the noodles. Cover with half of the mozzarella slices. Scatter half of the meatballs over the cheese, then top with one third of the tomato sauce. Arrange another 4 noodles in the dish. Cover with the remaining ricotta filling, mozzarella, and meatballs and then half of the remaining sauce. Top with the remaining noodles and spread with the remaining tomato sauce. Sprinkle with the remaining ¹/₂ cup Parmesan cheese. Cover with aluminum foil. (The lasagna can be prepared up to 1 day ahead, cooled, covered, and refrigerated; it can also be frozen, wrapped airtight, for up to 1 month.)

8. Bake for 30 minutes. Remove the foil and bake until the sauce is bubbling throughout, about 30 more minutes. (If baking frozen lasagna, increase the initial baking time to 45 minutes.) Let stand for 10 minutes before serving.

Butternut Squash and Rice Tian

Makes 8 to 12 servings

Make Ahead: The squash and sautéed vegetables can be prepared up to 1 day ahead.

Here's a terrific dish that serves two purposes. It's a substantial main course for vegetarians in the group, and it can be a savory side dish for turkey lovers. I used to serve a dramatic-looking rice-stuffed pumpkin, but now I make this casserole, based on a Provençal favorite. Large pumpkins, while great looking, have the least flavor, and there was a very fine line between the pumpkin being tender and falling apart. Keep this in mind for a supper or brunch main course when it isn't Thanksgiving.

3 pounds butternut squash (3 small squash)

$1/4$ cup extra virgin olive oil

1 large onion, chopped

1 large red bell pepper, cored, seeded, and
   chopped

2 garlic cloves, minced

$1^1/2$ cups long-grain rice

6 large eggs

$1^1/2$ cups shredded Gruyère cheese (6 ounces)

4 teaspoons chopped fresh sage or 2 teaspoons
   dried

$3/4$ teaspoon salt

$1/2$ teaspoon freshly milled black pepper

$1/2$ cup fresh bread crumbs, preferably from
   day-old Italian or French bread

$1/2$ cup freshly grated Parmesan cheese

1. Using a sturdy vegetable peeler, peel the squash. Cut off the neck of each squash where it meets the bulb. Quarter the bulb. Scoop out and discard the fibers and seeds. Cut the squash into pieces about $1/2$ inch wide and 1 inch long. You will have a variety of shapes, but as long as they are relatively the same size, it doesn't matter.

2. Bring a large pot of lightly salted water to a boil over high heat and add the squash. Cook until barely tender when pierced with the tip of a sharp knife, 10 to 15 minutes. Drain and rinse under cold running water. Set aside. (The squash can be prepared up to 1 day ahead, cooled, stored in self-sealing plastic bags, and refrigerated.)

3. In a large skillet, heat 3 tablespoons of the oil over medium-high heat. Add the onion and red pepper and cook, stirring often, until the onion is golden, about 5 minutes. Add the garlic and stir until softened, about 1 minute. Cool the vegetables until tepid, about 10 minutes. (The vegetables can be prepared up to 1 day ahead, cooled, stored in self-sealing bags, and refrigerated.)

4. Meanwhile, bring another pot of lightly salted water to a boil over high heat. Add the rice and cook until just tender, about 15 minutes. Drain, rinse under cold running water, and set aside.

5. Preheat the oven to 350°F. Lightly oil a 10 × 15-inch baking dish.

6. In a large bowl, beat the eggs. Add the rice, squash, sautéed vegetables, Swiss cheese, sage, salt, and pepper. Spread in the prepared dish. Mix the bread crumbs and Parmesan cheese and sprinkle over the top. Drizzle with the remaining 1 tablespoon oil.

7. Bake until the center feels set when pressed lightly, about 45 minutes. Serve hot, warm, or at room temperature.

Stuffings and Dressings

The Stuff That Dressings Are Made Of . . .

I f you live north of the Mason-Dixon line, you probably call the savory side dish baked inside a turkey stuffing. If you are a Southerner, you probably know it as dressing. (In classic cooking, such a mixture is called a forcemeat.) Until Victorian times, it was just called stuffing. Then all of a sudden, "stuffing" seemed a bit improper, and "dressing" took over, especially in the South, where morals in society were well defined.

Stuffings are most commonly made with bread. While white sandwich bread is probably the favorite choice, other breads can be used, usually depending on where the cook lives. On the West Coast, whole wheat or sourdough breads are used, while the Amish often use rye bread (often with potatoes). Of course, in the South, few native cooks would dream of making their dressing from anything other than corn bread. Cooked grains can be used for stuffing, and again, the regional preferences come into play. Rice stuffing is a favorite in Louisiana and Texas, both big rice-producing states. Wild rice is used in the Great Lakes region, where it is abundant. (For a full range of stuffing possibilities, see my book *50 Best Stuffings and Dressings,* Broadway Books.)

There is nothing wrong with packaged bread stuffing mix. In fact, the crisp texture of a mix ensures a moist, but not soggy, stuffing. If you want to use fresh bread (and I almost always do), it must be air-dried overnight. Use a firm sandwich bread like Pepperidge Farm or a high-quality unsweetened bakery loaf. Crusty French or Italian breads make fine stuffing too. With any bread, there is no need to cut off the crust. Don't use fluffy sandwich bread; it soaks up too much broth and makes soggy stuffing. Using a serrated knife, cut the bread into ½-inch cubes (or slightly large for crustier breads). If using corn bread, just crumble it. Let the bread stand at room temperature overnight to dry out. Or, bake the bread cubes in a 350°F oven, stirring occasionally, until they are dry and beginning to crisp, 20 to 30 minutes. Do not toast the bread cubes—they crisp slightly upon cooling.

The amount of stock needed for the stuffing is variable, depending on the dryness of the bread. Be flexible, and stir in just enough liquid to make a moist, not wet, mixture.

Allow about ¾ cup stuffing for every pound of turkey (and for each serving). Never pack the stuffing into the bird, as it will expand when heated, and I have heard of birds exploding because they were overstuffed. You do not have to sew up the openings. For the neck cavity, just pin the neck skin to the back with a thin wooden or metal skewer to enclose the stuffing. For the body cavity, cover the exposed stuffing with a small piece of aluminum foil.

You will rarely be able to stuff all of the dressing into the bird. Place the extra stuffing in a buttered shallow baking dish, cover, and refrigerate until ready to bake, up to 8 hours. To reheat, sprinkle the stuffing with about ½ cup turkey or chicken stock and bake in a preheated 350°F oven until heated to at least 160°F. The exact baking time, of course, depends on the amount of stuffing, but it generally takes about 30 minutes.

Playing Safe
with Stuffing

For years, roast turkey meant stuffed turkey. Then health concerns arose about whether or not stuffed birds were safe. While these concerns are real, they shouldn't affect sensible cooks who follow acknowledged food safety practices. Just follow these simple rules:

• Stuffing should always be cooked to at least 160°F in order to kill any potentially harmful bacteria. When the turkey is done, insert the meat thermometer deep into the center of the body cavity to check the temperature of the stuffing. If it isn't at least 160°F, scoop the stuffing out of the cavity and transfer to a casserole. Cover and bake at 350°F until the stuffing reaches 160°F.

• Always prepare your stuffing just before filling and roasting the bird. Never stuff a bird the night before roasting, as the turkey cavity provides the warm, moist environment that encourages bacterial growth. To save time on Thanksgiving morning, you can prepare the stuffing ingredients the night before—chop the vegetables, toast the nuts, and so on—and store them in self-sealing plastic bags in the refrigerator. If you are really pressed for time, you can cook, cool, and refrigerate the seasoning meat and vegetables the night before. But reheat them thoroughly in a large nonstick skillet before adding to the bread or grains.

• The stuffing should be warm when placed in the turkey. An ice-cold stuffing may not cook to 160°F by the time the turkey is ready.

• Never mix raw meat or vegetables into a stuffing. All meat and vegetables should be thoroughly cooked.

• To serve the stuffing, remove it from the turkey and place in a serving bowl. Do not allow the stuffing, or turkey, to stand at room temperature for longer than 2 hours. Refrigerate any leftover stuffing separately from the turkey and use within 2 days. Reheat leftover stuffing thoroughly before serving.

Bread Stuffing 101

Makes about 10 cups

Make Ahead: See suggestions on page 65.

Use this classic recipe, familiar in the best sense of the word, as the springboard for many equally classic variations. You can make your own variations by mixing and matching the different embellishments.

- *Most cooks use packaged cubed stuffing, which will give your stuffing a "just like Mom's" flavor. If you prefer crumb-texture prepared stuffing, use it. Skillet bread stuffings just aren't special enough for holiday meals and should only be used as a last resort.*
- *The directions on most stuffing bags recommend two sticks of butter, which is too rich for me. If you wish, however, melt an extra stick of butter, and stir it into this stuffing with the broth.*
- *Even though stuffing cubes are often label "seasoned," they can be bland. If you think it needs it, add poultry seasoning.*
- *Homemade turkey stock makes the best stuffing, so make an effort to use it. The amount of stock needed will vary, depending on the dryness of the bread cubes and the moisture provided by the other ingredients.*

8 tablespoons (1 stick) unsalted butter

1 large onion, chopped

3 medium celery ribs with leaves, chopped

One 15-ounce bag cubed seasoned stuffing or
   1 pound firm white sandwich bread, cut into
   1/2-inch cubes (10 cups) and dried overnight
   or in the oven (see page 64)

1/4 cup chopped fresh parsley

3 cups Homemade Turkey Stock (page 22) or
   canned reduced-sodium chicken broth, or as
   needed

2 teaspoons poultry seasoning, preferably
   homemade (see Note), optional

Salt and freshly milled black pepper

1. In a large skillet, melt the butter over medium heat. Add the onion and celery. Cook, stirring often, until the onion is golden, about 10 minutes.

2. Scrape the vegetables and butter into a large bowl. Add the stuffing and parsley. Stir in enough of the stock to moisten the stuffing, about 2½ cups. Season with the poultry seasoning, if desired, and salt and pepper to taste. Use to stuff the turkey, or place in a buttered baking dish, drizzle with an additional ½ cup stock, cover, and bake as a side dish.

Note: To make homemade poultry seasoning: Combine 1 teaspoon *each* crumbled dried rosemary, crumbled dried sage, dried thyme, dried marjoram, and celery salt with ¼ teaspoon freshly milled black pepper. Crush together in a mortar and pestle, mini-food processor, or spice grinder.

Giblet Stuffing: Use the giblets from your turkey. With a heavy cleaver or large knife, chop the turkey neck into 2- to 3-inch pieces. Trim the liver and refrigerate (if it is added to the broth too soon, the liver will overcook and make the broth bitter). In a large saucepan, heat 1 tablespoon vegetable oil over medium-high heat. Add the neck, heart, and gizzard and brown on all sides, about 10 minutes. Stir in 1 quartered small onion and 1 coarsely chopped small carrot. Add one 13¾-ounce can reduced-sodium chicken broth and enough cold water to cover the giblets by 1 inch. Bring to a simmer, skimming off the foam that rises to the surface. Add ¼ teaspoon dried thyme, ¼ teaspoon salt, and 8 peppercorns. Reduce the heat to low and simmer, partially covered, until the giblets are very tender, about 2 hours. Add the turkey liver and simmer until cooked through, 15 to 20 minutes. Strain, reserving the stock, if desired. Cool the giblets. Pull the meat off the neck. Chop the neck meat, heart, gizzard, and liver. Stir into Bread Stuffing 101 along with the bread cubes.

Sausage and Apple Stuffing: In a large non-stick skillet over medium heat, cook 1 pound bulk pork sausage, breaking up the meat with a spoon, until cooked through, about 10 minutes. Add to Bread Stuffing 101 along with 1 cup chopped dried apples (about 3 ounces).

Oyster Stuffing: Drain two 8-ounce containers of shucked oysters and reserve the juices. (Or shuck 24 oysters, opening them over a fine wire sieve placed over a bowl to catch the juices.) If the oysters are large, cut them into 2 or 3 pieces. Add to Bread Stuffing 101 along with the bread cubes. Add enough turkey broth to the reserved oyster juices to make 2½ cups and use to moisten the stuffing.

Mushroom Stuffing: In a large skillet, melt (an additional) 3 tablespoons unsalted butter over medium heat. Add 1 pound cremini or button mushrooms, sliced. Cook, stirring often, until the mushrooms are lightly browned, about 8 minutes. Transfer to a bowl. Stir into Bread Stuffing 101 along with the bread cubes.

Chestnut Stuffing: Preheat the oven to 400°F. Using a small sharp knife, cut a deep X in the flatter side of each chestnut. Place in a single layer on a baking sheet and bake until the outer skin is split and crisp, about 30 minutes. (They never seem to be done at the same time, so work with the ones that are ready and continue roasting the others.) Place the roasted chestnuts in a kitchen towel to keep them warm. Using a small sharp knife, peel off both the tough outer and thin inner skins. To loosen the peels on stubborn, hard-to-peel chestnuts, return to

the oven for an additional 5 to 10 minutes, or microwave on High for 1 minute. You can also use one 15-ounce jar vacuum-packed chestnuts, available at specialty food stores. (Avoid canned chestnuts, which don't have much flavor.) Coarsely chop the chestnuts and stir into Bread Stuffing 101. If desired, substitute ¼ cup cognac or brandy for an equal amount of the turkey stock.

Italian Stuffing with Sausage and Parmesan Cheese

Makes about 10 cups

Make Ahead: The stuffing should be made just before using.

When I asked my various Italian-American neighbors how they make their stuffing, they all shared what was essentially the same recipe. There's nothing subtle about this stuffing—Italian sausage, red bell pepper, Parmesan cheese, and lots of herbs give it a zesty Mediterranean flavor. Some cooks add one cup toasted pine nuts or one cup coarsely chopped black Mediterranean olives for even more flavor.

2 tablespoons extra virgin olive oil

1 medium onion, chopped

2 medium celery ribs with leaves, chopped

2 medium red bell peppers, cored, seeded, and chopped

2 garlic cloves, minced

1 pound sweet or hot Italian sausage, casings removed

1 teaspoon dried basil

1 teaspoon dried oregano

½ teaspoon salt

$^1/_2$ teaspoon crushed hot red pepper

12 ounces day-old crusty Italian bread, cut into
1-inch cubes (about 7 cups)

1 cup freshly grated Parmesan cheese (about 4
ounces)

8 tablespoons (1 stick) unsalted butter, melted

$^1/_2$ cup dry white wine

1$^1/_2$ cups Homemade Turkey Stock (page 22) or
canned reduced-sodium chicken broth, or as
needed

1. In a large skillet, heat the oil over medium heat.
Add the onion, celery, bell peppers, and garlic. Cook,
stirring often, until softened, about 5 minutes. Add the
sausage and cook, breaking up the meat with a spoon,
until it loses its pink color, 8 to 10 minutes. Stir in the
basil, oregano, salt, and crushed red pepper. Transfer
to a large bowl.

2. Add the bread and cheese and mix well. Stir
in the butter, wine, and enough of the stock to
moisten the dressing, about 1 cup. Use to stuff the
turkey, or place in a buttered baking dish, drizzle with
an additional ½ cup stock, cover, and bake as a side
dish.

Savory Sausage and Mushroom Bread Pudding

Makes 8 to 10 servings

Make Ahead: The vegetables and sausage can be
prepared up to 1 day ahead.

*If you aren't serving a stuffed turkey, this moist sa-
vory bread pudding will fill the bill. Seven cups of
cubed seasoned bread stuffing can be substituted for
the stale bread cubes.*

2 tablespoons unsalted butter

10 ounces fresh mushrooms, sliced

1 medium onion, chopped

1 medium celery rib with leaves, chopped

1 pound bulk pork sausage

3 cups milk

6 large eggs, beaten

3 tablespoons chopped fresh parsley

2 teaspoons poultry seasoning, preferably
homemade (see Note, page 66)

$^1/_2$ teaspoon salt

$^1/_4$ teaspoon freshly milled black pepper

12 ounces firm-textured white sandwich bread,
cut into $^1/_2$-inch cubes (about 7 cups) and
dried overnight or in the oven (see page 64)

1. Position a rack in the center of the oven and preheat to 350°F. Lightly butter a 9 × 13-inch baking
dish.

2. In a large skillet, melt the butter over medium
heat. Add the mushrooms and cook, stirring occasionally, until they give off their juices, about 3 minutes.
Add the onion and celery and cook, stirring occasionally, until the mushroom juices evaporate and the
onion softens, about 10 minutes. Transfer to a large
bowl.

3. In the same skillet, cook the sausage over
medium-high heat, breaking it up with a spoon, until
it loses its pink color, about 10 minutes. Transfer to the
bowl of vegetables. (The vegetables and sausage can
be prepared up to 1 day ahead, cooled, stored in self-
sealing plastic bags, and refrigerated.

4. Stir in the milk. Gradually beat in the eggs, then
add the parsley, poultry seasoning, salt, and pepper.
Stir in the bread cubes. Let stand for 5 minutes. Pour
into the prepared dish.

5. Bake until the top is browned and a knife inserted
in the center comes out clean, about 1 hour. Serve immediately.

"Tamale" Stuffing with Pork, Chiles, and Raisins

Makes 8 cups

Make Ahead: The cornmeal cubes can be prepared up to 1 day ahead.

Many Texan cooks told me that a tamale-stuffed roast turkey is right up there with the herb-and-bread stuffed kind—I tried their advice, and they were right. In the Lone Star State, it is easy to purchase a dozen or so slender, six-inch-long handmade pork tamales, mildly seasoned with chiles and dotted with dark raisins to complement the pork's sweetness. But, snagging tamales of high quality isn't so simple outside of the Southwest. So, I devised my own easy version that keeps all of the flavor of the original without the bother of making individual tamales.

1 teaspoon salt

2 cups white or yellow cornmeal, preferably stone-ground

1 tablespoon olive oil

1 large onion, chopped

1 small jalapeño or other hot green chile pepper, seeded and minced

2 garlic cloves, minced

1 pound ground pork

$^1/_2$ cup raisins

2 tablespoons chili powder

1 teaspoon salt

2 tablespoons tomato paste, dissolved in $^1/_4$ cup water

8 ounces stale crusty French or Italian bread, cut into $^1/_2$-inch cubes (4 cups)

$1^1/_2$ cups Homemade Turkey Stock (page 22) or canned reduced-sodium chicken broth, or as needed

1. Lightly oil a baking sheet. In a medium heavy-bottomed saucepan, bring 4 cups water and the salt to a boil over high heat. Whisking constantly, add the cornmeal in a steady stream. Reduce the heat to low and bring to a boil. Cook, whisking often, until very thick and smooth, about 3 minutes. Scrape onto the baking sheet. Using wet hands or an oiled metal spatula, pat or spread out the hot cornmeal into a $^1/_2$-inch-thick slab. Let stand until cool and firm, about 1 hour, then cut into $^1/_2$-inch cubes and set aside. (The cornmeal cubes can be prepared up to 1 day ahead, covered, and refrigerated.)

2. In a large skillet, heat the oil over medium heat. Add the onion, chile pepper, and garlic. Cook, stirring often, until softened, about 3 minutes. Add the ground pork and raisins. Cook, stirring often to break up the meat with a spoon, until the pork is cooked through, about 10 minutes. Drain off any fat. Stir in the chili powder and salt and cook for 30 seconds. Add the dissolved tomato paste and stir until it is absorbed by the meat, about 1 minute. Remove from the heat.

3. In a large bowl, toss the bread cubes and cornmeal cubes with the pork mixture, gradually adding enough of the stock to moisten to taste. Use to stuff the turkey, or place in a casserole, cover, and bake as a side dish.

Mason-Dixon Corn Bread Dressing 101

Makes about 10 cups

Make Ahead: See the suggestions on page 65.

Moist, golden brown corn bread dressing has as many variations as there are Southern cooks. This basic corn bread dressing recipe uses two equally popular Southern ingredients, ham and pecans.

• *This dressing is best made with homemade corn bread. Southern Corn Bread has the proper firm texture. While corn bread stuffing mix is an acceptable substitute, don't use corn bread baked from packaged mixes—these are usually very sweet and make okay muffins but lousy dressing.*

• *Bake the corn bread a day or two ahead, crumble it, and let it stand at room temperature to dry out. The corn bread can also be dried in the oven. Crumble the corn bread onto baking sheets and bake in a preheated 350°F oven, stirring occasionally, until dried out but not toasted, 20 to 30 minutes.*

• *As with Bread Stuffing 101, use homemade turkey stock for the best flavor, and be flexible about the amount of stock used to moisten the stuffing. Be sure the stock is cold (or at least cooled to lukewarm), as hot stock could scramble the eggs.*

8 tablespoons (1 stick) unsalted butter

8 ounces smoked ham, cut into $^1/_2$-inch cubes

2 medium celery ribs with leaves, chopped

1 cup chopped scallions (white and green parts)

10 cups coarsely crumbled Southern Corn Bread (page 106), dried overnight or in the oven

1 cup toasted and coarsely chopped pecans

2 large eggs, beaten

1 teaspoon poultry seasoning, preferably homemade (see Note, page 66)

$^1/_2$ teaspoon salt

$^1/_4$ teaspoon freshly milled black pepper

$2^1/_2$ cups Homemade Turkey Stock (page 22) or canned reduced-sodium chicken broth, or as needed

1. In a large skillet, melt the butter over medium heat. Add the ham and celery and cook until the celery softens, about 5 minutes. Add the scallions and cook until wilted, about 3 minutes.

2. Scrape the ham, vegetables, and butter into large bowl. Stir in the corn bread, pecans, eggs, poultry seasoning, salt, and pepper. Stir in enough of the stock to moisten the stuffing, about 2 cups. Use to stuff the bird, or place in a buttered baking dish, drizzle with an additional $^1/_2$ cup stock, cover, and bake as a side dish.

Dried Cranberry and Walnut Dressing: Substitute 1 cup toasted and chopped walnuts for the pecans. Soak 1 cup (4 ounces) dried cranberries in hot water until plump, about 20 minutes; drain. Stir into Mason-Dixon Corn Bread Dressing.

Sausage Gumbo Dressing: Substitute 1 pound andouille sausage, or pork kielbasa, cut into $^1/_2$-inch cubes, for the ham. Add 1 medium red bell pepper, cored, seeded, and chopped, to the pan with the sausage and celery. Add 2 garlic cloves, minced, to the mixture with the scallions. Substitute 1 tablespoon Cajun Seasoning (page 4) for the poultry seasoning. If desired, stir one 9-ounce box chopped frozen okra, thawed, into the dressing.

Southwestern Chorizo Dressing: Bake the Southwestern Chili and Cheese Corn Bread on page 107, and allow to dry out. Substitute 1 pound smoked chorizo sausage links, cut into $^1/_2$-inch cubes, for the ham. Add 1 medium red bell pepper, cored, seeded, and chopped, with the chorizo and celery. Add 2 garlic cloves, minced, to the mixture with the scallions. Stir 1½ cups frozen corn kernels, thawed, and ½ cup chopped fresh cilantro into the dressing.

Louisiana "Dirty" Giblet and Rice Dressing

Makes about 16 cups

Make Ahead: Although this dressing is best prepared just before using, it can be prepared up to 1 day ahead.

Louisiana is a leading rice-farming state, so there are lots of recipes for rice dressings. One of the most common is based on "dirty" rice, which is colored brown by a ground giblet and sausage mixture. Spicy andouille sausage, available at specialty food stores and many supermarkets and butchers, is the most authentic sausage, but pork kielbasa can be substituted, enlivened with a jolt of the Cajun Seasoning. It isn't the prettiest dressing in the Bayou, but it sure is good, with lots of flavor supplied by the meats, vegetables, herbs, and spices.

5 tablespoons vegetable oil

2 medium onions, chopped

3 medium celery ribs with leaves, chopped

1 large green or red bell pepper, cored, seeded, and chopped

2 garlic cloves, minced

1 pound chicken livers, rinsed and trimmed

8 ounces andouille sausage or pork kielbasa, cut into ½-inch slices

1 tablespoon Cajun Seasoning (page 4), if using kielbasa

3 cups long-grain rice

6 cups Homemade Turkey Stock (page 22) or canned reduced-sodium chicken broth

1 teaspoon salt

½ teaspoon freshly milled black pepper, if using kielbasa

1. In a large skillet, heat 3 tablespoons of the oil over medium heat. Add the onions, celery, bell pepper, and garlic and cover. Cook until the vegetables soften, about 6 minutes.

2. Meanwhile, in a food processor, process the chicken livers and andouille until smooth. Pour into the skillet and cook, stirring occasionally, until the meats are completely cooked and show no sign of pink, about 10 minutes. Stir in the Cajun seasoning, if using. Remove from the heat and set aside.

3. In a large Dutch oven, heat the remaining 2 tablespoons oil over medium heat. Add the rice and cook, stirring almost constantly, until most of the rice turns opaque, 2 to 3 minutes. Stir in the sausage mixture, stock, salt, and the pepper, if using. Bring to a boil over high heat. Reduce the heat to low and cover tightly. Cook until the rice is barely tender and has absorbed the stock, about 17 minutes. Remove from the heat and let stand for 5 minutes. Stir well. (The dressing can be prepared up to 1 day ahead, cooled, stored in self-sealing plastic bags, and refrigerated. Reheat in a large Dutch oven until warmed before using.)

4. Use to stuff the turkey. Place any remaining dressing in a buttered baking dish, cool, cover, and refrigerate. To reheat, drizzle with about ¼ cup water or additional broth and bake in a preheated 350°F oven for about 20 minutes.

Wild Rice, Dried Cherry, and Almond Stuffing

Makes about 10 cups

Make Ahead: The stuffing can be prepared up to 1 day ahead.

The deep, earthy flavors of this stuffing work especially well with wild turkey. Wild rice is really a grass, not a rice at all. Cooking times depend on the type of wild rice. The most expensive wild rice is hand-harvested from canoes, and takes the longest time to cook. Machine-harvested brands, often from California, cook more quickly.

1 cup (4 ounces) dried cherries

²/₃ cup tawny or ruby port

2 cups (11 ounces) wild rice, rinsed

2 tablespoons unsalted butter (plus 3 tablespoons butter if making ahead)

3 medium celery ribs, finely chopped, plus ¹/₃ cup finely chopped celery leaves

¹/₂ cup minced shallots

1 cup (4 ounces) toasted slivered almonds

4 teaspoons chopped fresh sage or 2 teaspoons dried

³/₄ teaspoon salt

¹/₂ teaspoon freshly milled black pepper

¹/₄ cup Homemade Turkey Stock (page 22) or canned reduced-sodium chicken broth, or as needed

1. In a small bowl, mix the dried cherries and port and let stand while preparing the stuffing.

2. Bring a large pot of lightly salted water to a boil over high heat. Add the wild rice and reduce the heat to medium. Cook until the wild rice is tender and most of the grains have burst, 45 to 60 minutes. Drain well and rinse under cold running water. Place the rice in a large bowl.

3. In a large skillet, melt the butter over medium heat. Add the chopped celery and cook until crisp-tender, about 5 minutes. Add the shallots and celery leaves and cook until softened, about 2 minutes. Add the cherries and their soaking liquid. Boil until the port has almost completely evaporated, about 3 minutes. Stir the mixture into the wild rice, along with the almonds, sage, salt, and pepper. (The stuffing can be prepared up to 1 day ahead, stored in self-sealing plastic bags, and refrigerated. To reheat the stuffing, melt 3 tablespoons unsalted butter over medium heat in a large skillet or Dutch oven. Add the stuffing and cook, stirring often, until warmed.)

4. Use to stuff the turkey. Place any remaining dressing in a buttered baking dish, cool, cover, and refrigerate. To reheat, drizzle with about ¹/₄ cup broth and bake in a preheated 350°F oven for about 20 minutes.

Side Dishes

And the Award for the Best Supporting
Side Dish Goes To . . .

As hard as I try to buck the concept of excess at the Thanksgiving table, I am as guilty as the next person when it comes to side dishes. How am I supposed to choose between mashed potatoes and sweet potatoes? Why not make both? Green beans or glazed carrots? Heck, green beans *and* glazed carrots! Most of the time, my menu is limited only by the amount of help I have in the kitchen and how many dishes I can fit on the table. There is no other holiday meal where side dishes are as important as the main course itself. No cranberry sauce? Unthinkable! Hold the gravy? I don't think so . . .

Thanksgiving side dishes are not known for their subtlety. They can usually be described in one word: Rich. When putting together a menu, balance it with some simply prepared sides like Green Beans and Portobello Mushrooms with Bacon (page 79). And try to include a brightly colored dish like Not-Your-Grandmother's Succotash (page 78).

In the midst of all the cream and marshmallows, I often long for the clean flavors of simply prepared vegetables. Often my side dishes are no more than sautéed vegetables sprinkled with nuts, seeds, or herbs. Parcook the vegetables in boiling salted water just until crisp-tender; drain, rinse under cold water, and drain again. Pat them completely dry with paper towels and store, wrapped loosely in more paper towels, in self-sealing plastic bags. When you're ready to serve, it's just a matter of sautéing in butter or oil until heated through. These don't need full recipes, just a few words to point you in the right direction and inspire you to come up with your own combinations.

Broccoli and Cauliflower with Almonds: In a large skillet, sauté parboiled broccoli and cauliflower florets in extra virgin olive oil. Sprinkle with toasted and chopped almonds. Season with salt and crushed hot red pepper.

Carrots with Tarragon: Cut carrots into ½ × 3-inch sticks, and parboil (and store) as directed above. In a large skillet, cook chopped shallots in butter until softened. Add the carrots and cook until heated through. Toss with chopped fresh tarragon. Season with salt and pepper.

Carrots with Sesame Seeds: Sauté the parboiled carrot sticks in butter and sprinkle with sesame seeds.

Green Beans with Hazelnuts: In a large skillet, cook chopped shallots in butter until softened. Add parboiled green beans and cook until heated through. Sprinkle with toasted, skinned, and chopped hazelnuts. Season with salt and pepper.

To be sure that your side dishes are served at their piping-hot best, follow these tips:
- Unless you plan accordingly, you could easily have a traffic jam in the oven trying to reheat all those sides. Be sure that at least one dish is prepared on top of the stove to lessen the load.
- Many side dishes can be prepared ahead and stored in the refrigerator until ready to serve. Increase the baking times by 10 to 15 minutes if the dishes have been chilled.
- Allow at least 20 minutes for the food to heat through in the oven. Cover the dishes with their lids or aluminum foil.

- Warm the serving dishes (in a preheated 200°F oven for a few minutes, or by filling with hot water) before adding the food.
- Have the serving utensils ready.
- If a hot dish is going to be served in the casserole or baking dish it was heated in, have pot holders and trivets at the table to make serving easier.

There are a lot of cranberry sauces in this chapter, but I just couldn't decide on which one to leave out, since every single one of them has been dubbed "the best one I ever had" by different friends and students over the years.

Broccoli with Roasted Garlic Butter

Makes 8 to 10 servings

Make Ahead: The roasted garlic butter can be prepared up to 3 days ahead; the broccoli can be cut up 1 day ahead.

Roasted garlic has become a classic American flavor—future cooks may regard it the same way we do the Pilgrims' pumpkin! Tossed with good old broccoli, roasted garlic butter turns that familiar vegetable into a side dish that will have everyone asking for seconds. The garlic butter can be made well ahead—it's a simple matter to cook the broccoli, drain, and mix with the butter just before serving.

2 large, plump heads garlic (about 3½ ounces each)
2 teaspoons extra virgin olive oil
Salt and freshly milled black pepper
8 tablespoons (1 stick) unsalted butter, at room temperature

2 large bunches broccoli (3 pounds)

1. To make the roasted garlic butter, preheat the oven to 400°F.

2. Cut each garlic head crosswise in half. Drizzle the cut surfaces with the oil, then season with a sprinkle of salt and pepper. Put the halves back together to reform into heads. Wrap each head in aluminum foil and place on a baking sheet. Bake until the garlic is tender when squeezed and the cut surfaces are deep beige (open up the foil to check), about 35 minutes. Cool completely.

3. Squeeze the soft garlic flesh out of the skin into a small bowl. Add the butter, 1/2 teaspoon salt, and 1/2 teaspoon pepper. Using a rubber spatula, mash the garlic and butter until well combined. Cover tightly and refrigerate until ready to use. (The garlic butter can be prepared up to 3 days ahead.) Bring to room temperature before using.

4. To prepare the broccoli, cut off the tops and separate into florets. Using a sharp paring knife, trim the thick skin off the stems. Cut the pared stems crosswise into 1/4-inch rounds. (The broccoli can be prepared up to 1 day ahead, stored in plastic bags, and refrigerated.)

5. Bring a large saucepan of lightly salted water to a boil over high heat. Add the broccoli stems and cook for 2 minutes. Add the florets and cook until the broccoli is crisp-tender, about 2 more minutes. Drain quickly, leaving some water clinging to the broccoli, and return to the warm cooking pot.

6. Add the softened garlic butter to the broccoli and mix gently, allowing the butter to melt and combine with the small amount of water in the pot to form a light sauce. Transfer to a warmed serving bowl and serve immediately.

Brussels Sprouts and Chestnuts, Italian Style

Makes 8 to 12 servings

Make Ahead: The chestnuts can be peeled and roasted up to 2 days ahead; the brussels sprouts can be parcooked up to 1 day ahead.

In many households, a mixture of brussels sprouts and chestnuts is considered the quintessential turkey side dish. These two ingredients are very full flavored, so serve in small portions.

1 1/2 pounds brussels sprouts, trimmed

2 tablespoons extra virgin olive oil

1/3 cup finely chopped (1/4-inch dice) prosciutto

1 pound chestnuts, roasted, peeled (see page 67), and coarsely chopped, or one 15-ounce jar vacuum-packed chestnuts

1/3 cup Homemade Turkey or Chicken Stock (page 22 or 24) or canned reduced-sodium chicken broth

1/4 teaspoon salt

1/4 teaspoon freshly milled black pepper

1. Using a small, sharp knife, cut a small, deep X in the bottom stem of each sprout. Bring a large pot of lightly salted water to a boil over high heat. Add the sprouts and cook until barely tender, about 8 minutes. Drain and rinse well under cold running water. Drain well, pat dry with paper towels, and cut the larger sprouts into halves or quarters. (The sprouts can be prepared up to 1 day ahead, wrapped in paper towels, stored in self-sealing plastic bags, and refrigerated.)

2. In a large skillet, heat the oil over medium heat. Add the prosciutto and cook until very lightly browned, about 3 minutes. Add the brussels sprouts, chestnuts, and stock and bring to a boil over high heat. Cook, stirring often, until the stock has evaporated, about 5 minutes. Season with the salt and pepper. Transfer to a warmed serving dish and serve hot.

Maple-Glazed Baby Carrots with Pecans

Makes 8 to 12 servings

Make Ahead: The carrots can be prepared up to 2 hours ahead.

Supermarkets now carry packages of regular carrots cut into shape to resemble baby carrots. Skillet size is especially important in this recipe, as a smaller skillet will not hold the large amount of carrots and liquid. If necessary, divide the recipe in half and cook in a nine-inch skillet.

2 tablespoon unsalted butter

2 pounds "baby-cut" carrots

1 ³/₄ cups reduced-sodium canned beef broth

¹/₂ cup maple syrup (see Note)

¹/₄ teaspoon salt

¹/₄ teaspoon freshly milled black pepper

¹/₂ cup toasted and coarsely chopped pecans

1. In a 12-inch nonstick skillet, melt the butter over medium heat. Add the carrots and stir to coat with the butter. Add the stock, maple syrup, salt, and pepper, increase the heat to high, and bring to a boil. Cover tightly and cook for 6 minutes.

2. Uncover and cook, stirring often, until the carrots are tender and the liquid has reduced to a glaze, 12 to 15 minutes. (The carrots can be prepared up to 2 hours ahead and kept at room temperature. To reheat, add ¹/₄ cup water and cook over medium heat, stirring occasionally, until the carrots are hot and the water has evaporated, about 5 minutes.) Stir in the pecans. Transfer to a warmed serving dish and serve immediately.

Port-Glazed Carrots: Substitute ¹/₃ cup tawny or ruby port for the maple syrup. Add ¹/₃ cup packed light brown sugar along with the broth to the skillet.

Note: I use real maple syrup here, which sweetens the carrots nicely without being cloying. Grade A maple syrup has a subtle maple flavor, which I prefer in this dish. Pancake syrup will make the carrots sweeter, and give more maple taste.

Tender Corn Pudding

Makes 8 to 12 servings

Make Ahead: Corn pudding is best prepared just before serving.

Dried corn played a large part in the Pilgrims' (and Indians') diet. They would probably appreciate the fact that this comforting dish is made with frozen corn, our modern method of food preservation. This is a mildly seasoned version, but it is easy to add Southwestern flavors to make a spicy variation. You can make the pudding with fresh corn kernels, but be prepared for it to be on the sweet side.

2 tablespoons unsalted butter

1 large green bell pepper, cored, seeded, and finely chopped

3 scallions (white and green parts), finely chopped

2 garlic cloves, minced

4 cups thawed frozen corn kernels (see Note, page 76)

³/₄ cup heavy cream

1¹/₂ cups milk

5 large eggs, beaten

1 teaspoon salt

¹/₂ teaspoon freshly milled white pepper

1. Position a rack in the center of the oven and preheat to 350°F. Lightly butter a 10 × 15-inch baking dish.

2. In a large skillet, melt the butter over medium heat. Add the bell pepper, scallions, and garlic. Cook, stirring often, until the bell pepper softens, about 4 minutes. Remove from the heat and set aside.

3. In a blender, process 3 cups of the corn with the heavy cream until smooth. Transfer to a large bowl. Add the remaining corn, the milk, eggs, salt, and white pepper. Stir in the vegetables. Transfer to the prepared dish.

4. Place the dish in a large roasting pan. Pour in enough nearly boiling water to come ½ inch up the outside of the dish. Bake until a knife inserted in the center of the pudding comes out clean, about 1 hour. Remove the dish from the roasting pan and let stand for 5 minutes before serving.

Southwestern Corn Pudding: Substitute 1 red bell pepper for the green pepper. Sauté 2 jalapeños, seeded and minced, with the vegetables.

Maque-Choux

Makes 8 servings

Make Ahead: The maque-choux can be prepared up to 1 day ahead.

This Cajun side dish has so much going for it, I hardly know where to begin. First, it adds a welcome splash of color to the Thanksgiving menu, which, frankly, can be somewhat bland-looking. Also, its spiciness complements, not overwhelms, the other dishes. Next, it can be made well ahead and reheated. Finally, it has bacon in it, which adds an old-fashioned flavor

that my guests love in these fat-challenged times. In fact, this simple dish has been the sleeper hit at many of my Thanksgiving spreads.

While choux *means cabbage in French, there is no literal translation of* maque-choux *in either French or Cajun patois. The word (and the basis for the recipe) probably comes from the Indians who lived in the Louisiana bayou. In other words, it is the Cajun version of succotash, the corn and bean dish that the northeastern Indians taught the Pilgrims.*

6 strips thick-sliced bacon

1 medium onion, chopped

1 medium red bell pepper, cored, seeded, and chopped

2 medium celery ribs, chopped

4 cups thawed frozen corn kernels (see Note)

2 garlic cloves, minced

1½ teaspoons Cajun Seasoning (page 4)

2 large ripe tomatoes (such as Holland or Israeli), seeded and chopped

Salt

1. Cook the bacon in a 12-inch skillet over medium heat, turning occasionally, until crisp and brown, about 5 minutes. Using a slotted spatula, transfer to paper towels to drain.

2. Pour out all but 3 tablespoons of the bacon fat from the pan. Add the onion, bell pepper, and celery to the pan and cook until the onion is golden brown, about 10 minutes. Add the corn, garlic, and Cajun seasoning and cook, stirring frequently, until the corn is heated through, about 5 minutes. (The maque-choux can be prepared up to this point 1 day ahead, cooled, covered, and refrigerated. Reheat gently in a large skillet over low heat, stirring often.)

3. Stir in the tomatoes and cook, stirring occasionally, until they are heated through, about 5 minutes. Chop the bacon, and stir it into maque-choux. Season with salt to taste. Serve immediately.

Note: Even if you can get fresh corn in November, I don't recommend it at that time of year. It would probably be a super-sweet hybrid, and too sugary. Frozen corn kernels are from a less-sweet variety, and much better at this time of year.

Not-Your-Grandmother's Succotash

Makes 8 servings

Make Ahead: The succotash, without the cherry tomatoes, can be prepared up to 1 day ahead.

Succotash was one of the mainstays of the Native American diet. Originally, it consisted of corn and beans cooked with bear fat. The original word was from the Narraganset Indian word misickquatash, *which meant both "stew pot" and "ear of corn." Many versions of succotash are uninspiring, to say the least. This updated version has its roots in tradition, but is flavor-packed to satisfy today's tastes.*

5 ounces salt pork, rind removed, and cut into
   $1/2$-inch cubes
1 large onion, chopped
$1^1/_2$ cups Homemade Turkey or Chicken Stock
   (page 22 or 24) or reduced-sodium canned
   chicken broth
3 cups thawed frozen corn kernels (see Note in
   previous recipe)
Two 10-ounce packages frozen lima beans,
   thawed
2 teaspoons chopped fresh thyme or
   1 teaspoon dried thyme
1 pint cherry tomatoes, halved

$1/4$ teaspoon freshly milled black pepper
Salt

1. Cook the salt pork in a large nonstick skillet over medium-high heat, stirring often, until golden brown, about 5 minutes. Add the onion and cook, stirring often, until golden, about 5 minutes. Add the stock and bring to a boil. Cook until the stock is reduced to about $1/4$ cup, 12 to 15 minutes.

2. Add the corn, lima beans, and thyme. Cook, stirring often, until heated through, about 3 minutes. (The succotash can be prepared to this point up to 1 day ahead, cooled, stored in self-sealing plastic bags, and refrigerated. Reheat gently in a large skillet over low heat, stirring occasionally.)

3. Add the cherry tomatoes and cook, stirring often, until they are heated through but not collapsing, about 2 minutes. Season with the pepper and add salt to taste (be careful, as the salt pork may have seasoned the succotash enough). Transfer to a heated serving dish and serve hot.

Classic Recipe: Green Bean Bake

Makes 6 to 8 servings

Make Ahead: The bake, without the onion topping, can be prepared up to 1 day ahead.

Here it is, one of America's favorite recipes. It was invented in 1955 by a Campbell's Soup Company home economist, Dorcas Reilly. Here are some amazing Green Bean Bake statistics.

• *Campbell's Soup Company estimates that more than twenty million Green Bean Bakes are served during the holiday season.*

- *A recent survey showed that over fifty percent of all Americans have tasted Green Bean Bake. Over thirty-eight percent said that the best time to serve it is at Thanksgiving or during the holidays, but thirty-five percent serve it all year.*

- *More than three hundred and twenty-five million cans of Campbell's Cream of Mushroom Soup are sold annually. Over eighty percent of the soup is used as an ingredient in recipes.*

One 10³/₄-ounce can Campbell's Cream of
  Mushroom Soup
¹/₂ cup milk
1 teaspoon soy sauce
Dash of freshly milled black pepper
One 20-ounce bag frozen cut green beans,
  thawed (see Note)
One 2.8-ounce can French-fried onions

1. Preheat the oven to 350°F.

2. In a 1¹/₂-quart casserole, combine the soup, milk, soy sauce, and pepper. Stir in the green beans and half of the onions. (The casserole can be prepared to this point up to 1 day ahead, covered, and refrigerated.)

3. Bake until bubbling, about 25 minutes. Top with the remaining onions and bake for 5 more minutes. Serve hot.

Note: Instead of the frozen green beans, use two 15¹/₂-ounce cans green beans, drained. Or, cook 1¹/₂ pounds fresh green beans in lightly salted water until tender, about 5 minutes, and drain.

Green Beans with Portobello Mushrooms and Bacon

Makes 8 servings

Make Ahead: The green beans can be blanched up to 1 day ahead; the mushrooms can be prepared up to 2 hours ahead.

Green beans and bacon go together like, well, turkey and gravy. Portobello mushrooms, full of meaty flavor, are a fine addition to this classic dish. However, sautéed portobellos often give off a lot of dark liquid, which some cooks feel ruins the look of a dish. Scraping the dark gills out of each portobello cap with a spoon solves the problem.

1¹/₂ pounds green beans, cut into 2-inch lengths
4 large portobello mushrooms (about 1 pound)
3 tablespoons vegetable oil
¹/₄ cup finely chopped shallots
4 ounces sliced smoked bacon (usually 1 slice
  equals 1 ounce)
¹/₂ teaspoon salt
¹/₄ teaspoon freshly milled black pepper

1. Bring a large pot of lightly salted water to a boil over high heat. Add the green beans and return to the boil. Cook until crisp-tender, about 3 minutes. Drain and rinse under cold running water. (The green beans can be prepared up to 1 day ahead. Pat the green beans dry with paper towels. Roll up the green beans in a double thickness of more paper towels, place in a large self-sealing plastic bag, and refrigerate.)

2. Cut off the stem from each mushroom and slice crosswise into ¹/₂-inch-thick rounds. Using a teaspoon, scrape out the dark brown gills from the underside of each mushroom cap and cut the caps into ¹/₄-inch-thick strips.

3. In a 12-inch nonstick skillet, heat 2 tablespoons of the oil over medium heat. Add the mushroom stems and caps and cook, stirring often, until lightly browned and tender, about 5 minutes. Add the shallots and cook, stirring often, until the shallots soften, about 2 minutes. Transfer to a plate and set aside. (The mushrooms can be prepared up to 2 hours ahead, covered, and kept at room temperature.)

4. Add the remaining 1 tablespoon oil to the skillet and tilt to coat the pan. Add the bacon and cook over medium heat, turning occasionally, until the bacon is crisp and brown, about 5 minutes. Using a slotted spatula, transfer to paper towels to drain. Leave the bacon drippings in the skillet. When the bacon is cool, coarsely chop and set aside. (The bacon can be prepared up to 2 hours ahead, covered, and kept at room temperature.)

5. Place the skillet over medium heat and heat until the bacon drippings sizzle. Add the green beans and mushrooms, cover, and cook, stirring occasionally, until heated through, about 5 minutes. Stir in the bacon and season with the salt and pepper. Transfer to a warmed serving dish and serve immediately.

Creamed Onions 101

Makes 8 to 12 servings

Make Ahead: The creamed onions can be prepared up to 1 hour ahead.

When I serve creamed onions, I make the Cheddar-Scalloped Baby Onions at the end of this recipe, which I love so much that I sometimes worry I might eat the whole dish by myself. Yet for many Americans it just isn't Thanksgiving without a blindingly white bowl (and bland, to my taste) of creamed onions on the table. Once I made a huge bowl at the request of my friend Rose. When I proudly presented them to her, she took exactly two onions. "I didn't say I liked them. I said it wouldn't be Thanksgiving without them!"

• *My version uses milk and broth for a deeper flavor—the sauce turns out light beige, but the flavor makes the compromise worthwhile. If you want Mom's white-sauce-on-white-onions version, use all milk.*

• *Practical cooks use frozen baby onions (which are excellent) with no apology. If you want to use fresh pearl onions, they must be peeled and cooked. There are three kinds of pearl onions available. White pearl onions are the most common, but many specialty produce markets also carry yellow and red pearl onions, and a bowl of creamed onions is especially attractive and tasty if you use all three colors. You can also use small white boiling onions (sixteen to twenty onions to a pound).*

• *To cook fresh baby onions, bring a large pot of water to a boil over high heat. Add the onions and cook pearl onions for 1 minute or boiling onions for 2 minutes (the water may not return to a boil). Drain well and rinse under cold running water. Using a small sharp knife, trim off the tops and bottoms of the onions, peel them, and pierce the side of each onion with the tip of the knife (this helps the onions keep their shape during cooking). Place the onions in a 12-inch skillet and add 2 cups chicken stock (preferably homemade, or use reduced-sodium canned chicken broth) and enough water to barely cover the onions. Bring to a boil over high heat, cover, and reduce the heat to medium. Cook until the onions are tender when pierced with the tip of a small, sharp knife, about 8 minutes for pearl onions or 12 minutes for boiling onions. Drain well, reserving the broth to make the creamed onion sauce, if desired. The fresh onions can be cooked up to 1 day ahead, cooled, stored in self-sealing plastic bags, and refrigerated.*

1 cup milk

1 cup Homemade Turkey or Chicken Stock
(page 22 or 24) or reduced-sodium canned
chicken broth

1 bay leaf

4 tablespoons ($^1/_2$ stick) unsalted butter

$^1/_4$ cup all-purpose flour

$^1/_4$ teaspoon salt

$^1/_4$ teaspoon freshly milled white pepper

Two 1-pound bags thawed frozen baby onions,
or 2 pounds pearl or white boiling onions,
peeled and cooked (see above)

1. In a small saucepan over medium-low heat, heat the milk, stock, and bay leaf until tiny bubbles appear around the edges, about 5 minutes. Remove from the heat and set aside for 5 minutes. Discard the bay leaf.

2. In a medium saucepan, melt the butter over low heat. Whisk in the flour and let bubble, without browning, for 1 minute. Whisk in the hot milk mixture. Bring to a simmer. Cook, stirring often, until the sauce thickens and no taste of raw flour remains, 2 to 3 minutes. Season with the salt and white pepper. Remove from the heat. Set the sauce aside. (The sauce can be prepared up to 2 hours ahead and kept at room temperature. Press a piece of plastic wrap directly onto the surface of the sauce, and pierce a few times with the tip of sharp knife to release the steam. This keeps a skin from forming on the sauce. Reheat gently over low heat, stirring often, until hot.)

3. Meanwhile, bring a large pot of lightly salted water to a boil over high heat. Add the onions and return to a boil. Cook, stirring occasionally, until the onions are tender, about 3 minutes. Drain very well. Return to the warm cooking pot. Add the hot sauce and mix well. Transfer to a warmed serving dish and serve immediately. (The creamed onions can be prepared up to 1 hour ahead and set aside at room temperature. Reheat over low heat, stirring often, until heated through.)

Cheddar-Scalloped Baby Onions: Preheat the oven to 350°F. Prepare Creamed Onions 101, preferably with 2 pounds mixed fresh white, yellow, and red pearl onions. Stir 1$^1/_2$ cups (6 ounces) grated extra-sharp Cheddar cheese into the hot creamed onions until melted. Transfer to a lightly buttered 9 × 13-inch baking dish. Mix $^2/_3$ cup fresh bread crumbs (preferably from day-old French or Italian bread) and $^1/_3$ cup freshly grated Parmesan cheese and sprinkle over the onions. Dot with 2 tablespoons unsalted butter, cut into small cubes. (The onions can be prepared to this point, up to 1 day ahead, cooled, covered, and refrigerated.) Bake, uncovered, until the sauce is bubbling and the top is golden brown, about 30 minutes.

Old-Fashioned Mashed Potatoes 101

Makes 8 to 12 servings

Make Ahead: The potatoes can be peeled and cut ahead, placed in the cooking pot, covered with cold water, and stored in a cool place for up to 4 hours.

Mashed potatoes are as American as Thanksgiving itself. Restaurants chefs seem to have newly discovered mashed potatoes, and there are lots of mouthwatering variations on the theme. But, at Thanksgiving, nothing beats a bowl of well-made classic mashed potatoes. As with many other deceptively simple dishes, there are reasons why sometimes you have good mashed potatoes, and other times you have great mashed potatoes. Here are my secrets to making those great ones, served piping hot, and ready for that big ladleful of gravy.

- *Potatoes with a high starch content (the kind used for baking) give the traditional flavor and texture. The same starch that gives a baked potato its fluffy interior contributes to perfect mashed potatoes. Yellow-fleshed varieties like Yukon Golds or Yellow Finns are excellent as well, but they turn out the same color as mashed turnips, which can be disconcerting to potato purists. If you live near a farmers' market, take the potato farmers' advice on local favorites—they may suggest an interesting heirloom variety that will become your favorite too.*
- *If possible, buy your potatoes a week or so ahead of time and age them in a cool, dark place (not the refrigerator)—mature potatoes are drier and mash up lighter.*
- *Always make mashed potatoes just before serving. Warmed-over mashed potatoes leave me cold, although the Make-Ahead Mashed Potato Casserole on page 83 is delicious.*

- *Don't overcook the potatoes—they should just yield to a sharp knife when pierced. If the drained potatoes seem soggy, return them to the pot and cook over low heat, stirring constantly, until they begin to stick to the bottom of the pot, about 2 minutes. This step forces the excess steam out of the potatoes and dries them out.*
- *Mash the drained potatoes in the still-warm cooking pot with hot milk—a cold bowl and cold milk make for lumpy, lukewarm potatoes. The exact amount of milk is a matter of taste, so use more or less to reach your desired consistency.*
- *Use an efficient mashing utensil. Some cooks swear by a potato ricer, which does make the smoothest potatoes. I use an electric hand mixer. If you want to use a low-tech, old-fashioned hand potato masher, go to a restaurant supply store and get a large one, or the chore will take forever, with the potatoes cooling off by the second. Never mash potatoes in a food processor, which will give you gummy mashed potatoes quicker than you can say "Cuisinart."*
- *Season the mashed potatoes well with salt and pepper. I have suggested amounts, but use your taste. White pepper (which is actually spicier than black) will give you pristine mashed potatoes, but certainly use black if you have to.*

5 pounds baking potatoes (such as russet, Idaho, Burbank, or Eastern)
Salt
4 tablespoons (¹/₂ stick) unsalted butter, at room temperature
³/₄ cup milk, heated
¹/₂ teaspoon freshly milled white pepper

1. Fill a large pot (5 quarts or larger) halfway with cold water. Peel the potatoes, cut into chunks about 1¹/₂-inch square, and drop them into the pot. Add more cold water to completely cover the potatoes by

1 to 2 inches. (The potatoes can be prepared to this point up to 4 hours ahead and stored at cool room temperature.)

2. Stir in enough salt until the water tastes mildly salted. Cover tightly and bring to a full boil over high heat, about 20 minutes.

3. Reduce the heat to medium-low and set the lid askew. Cook at a moderate boil until the potatoes are tender when pierced with the tip of a small sharp knife, 15 to 20 minutes; add more boiling water, if needed, to keep the potatoes covered. Do not overcook the potatoes.

4. Drain the potatoes well and return to the warm cooking pot. Add the butter. Using an electric hand mixer, mash the potatoes, gradually adding the milk. Season with 1 teaspoon salt and the pepper. Transfer to a warmed serving dish and serve immediately.

Make-Ahead Mashed Potato Casserole

Makes 8 to 12 servings

Make Ahead: The casserole can be prepared up to 1 day ahead.

I was a mashed potato snob who held tight to the belief that mashed potatoes are only worth eating when they were freshly made, until caterer/food stylist/restaurateur Katy Keck set me straight. Katy, who rarely cooks Thanksgiving dinner for fewer than thirty people, would never dream of trying to mash that many potatoes in one batch. She gave me this recipe for a delicious make-ahead mashed potato casserole. Cream cheese, sour cream, milk, and butter keep the potatoes light and fluffy.

5 pounds baking potatoes (such as russet, Idaho, Burbank, or Eastern)

Salt

One 8-ounce package cream cheese, cut into chunks, at room temperature

1 cup sour cream

$1/2$ cup milk, heated

$1/2$ teaspoon freshly milled white pepper

Chopped fresh chives or parsley, optional

1. Fill a large pot (at least 5 quarts) halfway with cold water. Peel the potatoes, cut into chunks about $1/2$ inches square, and drop them into the pot. Add more cold water to cover the potatoes by 1 to 2 inches. (The potatoes can be prepared to this point up to 4 hours ahead and stored at cool room temperature.)

2. Stir in enough salt until the water tastes mildly salted. Cover tightly and bring to a full boil over high heat, about 20 minutes. Reduce the heat to medium-low and set the lid askew. Cook at a moderate boil until the potatoes are tender when pierced with the tip of a small sharp knife, 15 to 20 minutes; add more boiling water, if needed, to keep the potatoes covered. Do not overcook the potatoes.

3. Drain the potatoes well and return to the warm pot. Add the cream cheese. Using a hand-held electric mixer, mash the potatoes until the cream cheese melts. Beat in the sour cream and milk. Season with 1 teaspoon salt and the pepper. Transfer to a buttered 9 × 13-inch baking dish. Cool completely. (The potatoes can be prepared up 4 hours ahead, covered loosely with plastic wrap, and stored at cool room temperature; or, cool, cover tightly with plastic wrap, and refrigerate for up to 1 day.)

4. Preheat the oven to 375°F.

5. Bake the casserole until the potatoes are heated through, 30 to 40 minutes. Serve hot, sprinkled with the chives, if using.

Candied Yam and Marshmallow Casserole 101

Makes 8 to 12 servings

Make Ahead: The yams can be prepared up to 8 hours ahead.

I wonder how many candied yam and marshmallow casseroles are trotted out every Thanksgiving? The combination is so entrenched in the American psyche that it seems centuries old—surely one of those dishes served at the first Thanksgiving. But although candied yams had been popular for years, it wasn't until the 1920s that cooks began to top them with marshmallows. Personally, I prefer sweet potatoes that aren't so sweet, but I know I'm in the minority.

- *Many cooks use canned yams in syrup to make their casseroles. If you prefer a less sweet version, use cooked fresh yams. Cook 3½ pounds (about 5 medium) yams in lightly salted water just until barely tender, 20 to 25 minutes. Do not overcook them—they will cook further in the oven. Drain well and rinse under cold water until cool enough to handle, then peel and cut into 1-inch chunks.*
- *It is best to broil the marshmallow topping on the yams just before serving. If the weather is humid and the casserole is allowed to stand, the browned marshmallows can melt into a syrup. If you put the marsh-*

mallows on the casserole and accidentally overbake it (which can happen in the flurry of kitchen activity), the marshmallows can also dissolve. I learned this firsthand when I once popped my sister-in-law's sweet potato casserole into the oven and then came back to find that the marshmallows had disappeared! Even though we jokingly served it as "yams with marshmallow sauce," Linda never let me near her yams again.

Two 40-ounce cans yam (sweet potato) chunks in light syrup, drained
¹/₃ cup packed light brown sugar
5 tablespoons unsalted butter, cut into pieces
¹/₄ cup water
2¹/₂ cups miniature marshmallows (about 5 ounces)

1. Preheat the oven to 350°F. Lightly butter a 9 × 13-inch baking dish.

2. Spread the yams in the prepared dish. Sprinkle with the brown sugar, then dot with the butter and drizzle with the water. (The yams can be prepared up to 8 hours ahead and stored in a cool place.)

3. Bake, stirring occasionally, until syrupy and bubbling, about 45 minutes. Remove from the oven. Position the broiler rack 6 inches from the source of heat and preheat the broiler.

4. Spread the marshmallows on top of the yams. Broil until the marshmallows are lightly toasted, 1 to 2 minutes. Serve immediately.

It Wouldn't Be Thanksgiving Without . . . Marshmallows

In the nineteenth century the roots of the marshmallow plant *(Althaea officinalis)* were used to make a homemade confection that took the plant's name. When confectioners developed a mass-produced version around the turn of the century, they switched to corn syrup and egg whites to create the bouncy consistency of the original. It didn't take long for marshmallows to establish themselves as a truly American food, spawning such offspring as marshmallow Fluff and a range of marshmallow-filled, chocolate-coated cookies. While their sweetness is appropriate in dessert icons like Rice Krispie Treats and S'mores, their presence in gelatin salads, fruit salads, and sweet potato casseroles is truly a testament to the tenacity of the American sweet tooth.

Scalloped Yams with Praline Topping

Makes 8 to 12 servings

Make Ahead: The yams can be parboiled up to 8 hours before baking; the praline topping can be prepared up to 8 hours ahead.

This is one of my favorite dishes to demonstrate how yams don't have to be cloyingly sweet to be good. Whenever I make it, it never fails that someone remarks (or in words to this effect), "I don't even like yams, but I could eat a whole dish of these!"

1/4 cup packed light brown sugar

3 tablespoons unsalted butter, at room
  temperature

3 tablespoons all-purpose flour

1/3 cup finely chopped pecans

6 medium yams (about 3 pounds), peeled and
  cut into 1/2-inch-thick rounds

1 1/2 cups heavy cream, heated

1. In a small bowl, using your fingers, work the brown sugar, butter, and flour together until well combined, then work in the pecans. Set aside. (The praline topping can be prepared up to 8 hours ahead and stored at room temperature.)

2. Bring a large pot of lightly salted water to a boil over high heat. Add the yams and cook just until crisp-tender, about 5 minutes. Do not overcook—they should be able to hold their shape when drained. Drain and rinse under cold running water.

3. Preheat the oven to 375°F. Lightly butter a 9 × 13-inch baking dish.

4. Arrange the yams, overlapping in vertical rows, in the prepared dish. (The yams can be arranged in the baking dish up to 8 hours before baking, covered tightly with plastic wrap, and refrigerated.)

5. Pour the cream over the yams. Bake for 20 minutes. Crumble the pecan mixture over the yams and continue baking until the yams are tender and the topping is browned, 20 to 30 more minutes. Serve hot.

It Wouldn't Be Thanksgiving Without . . . Yams

Life used to be so simple. When Thanksgiving rolled around, there was only one kind of sweet potato to be found. It had a light brown skin and was orange on the inside. Sometimes it was called a yam. No one but botanists knew the difference between the true sweet potato and the orange-fleshed yam, and no one cared.

Times change. One year, during my annual Thanksgiving cooking class marathon at five schools from Seattle down to Long Beach, California, I wrote "10 pounds sweet potatoes" on the shopping list that was sent ahead to each school. When I arrived, every grocer had provided sweet potatoes, all right—the true sweet potato, sometimes called *batata* or *boniato,* beloved by Latino and Japanese cooks. I guess I should have asked for yams.

Let's straighten out the situation, as best as possible. When Columbus arrived in the Caribbean, he found the natives eating a yellow-fleshed tuber, the *batata.* It was brought back to Europe, where it gained some popularity as a "potato." Even Shakespeare mentions the potato, but he was talking about the sweet potato. When a white-fleshed tuber (originally from Ecuador or Peru) was introduced to the Old World in the 1500s, its resemblance to the yellow sweet potato was so strong that people began to call it a potato too. As we know, the white potato became a staple of the European diet. It wasn't until 1775 that "sweet potato" was entered into the *Oxford English Dictionary,* distinguishing it permanently from the white one. The white potato established itself on tables throughout the world, while the farmers in the American South remained faithful to the sweet potato.

Yet another tuber was eaten by the Caribbean natives. The *igname* (ig-NYAM-eh) has dark brown, almost black skin, pale flesh with streaks of gray-purple, and a bland flavor not unlike that of the white potato. Eventually, the igname found its way to Africa, where it was cultivated. When the African slaves were brought to America, they found the sweet potato, which they dubbed igname, as the two tubers resembled each other. Eventually, *igname* contracted to *yam.* In today's Latino markets, you will find the igname, the "true" yam, labeled *name* or Colombian yam.

What most Americans call a yam is really a sugary sweet potato. True sweet potatoes are not very sweet at all. They cannot be substituted for the orange yam in our traditional Thanksgiving dishes (they take too long to bake and taste quite starchy, like regular potatoes). The Louisiana yam, developed by the farmers of that state to be especially sweet, is the most familiar variety. Well-stocked produce markets also sell beautiful Garnet or Jewel yams with purple skins and deep orange flesh, which make wonderful substitutes for the tried-and-true Louisiana. Yams should be stored in a cool, dark place, even the refrigerator, for no longer than 1 week. Even though they look like potatoes, they don't have the same long-keeping qualities.

I doubt that you'll ever send someone to the store to get yams, only to have them return with a bag full of *ignames.* On the other hand, it was only a few years ago that hardly any Americans knew what cilantro was. In my multiethnic neighborhood, the supermarket carries Louisiana yams, sweet potatoes, *and* true yams.

Cider-Mashed Yams

Makes 8 to 10 servings

Make Ahead: The yams can be prepared up to 8 hours ahead.

These yams take the mashed route, and deliciously. They also are one of the best low-fat side dishes around, and the one to serve if you're not a fan of overly sweet yams. In order to intensify the apple flavor, I boil the cider until reduced by half; you could also use one third cup thawed frozen apple juice concentrate. If you want, this is easy to marshmallow-ize.

²/₃ cup apple cider

5 large yams (about 4¹/₂ pounds), scrubbed but
   unpeeled

4 tablespoons (¹/₂ stick) unsalted butter

2 tablespoons light brown sugar

¹/₂ teaspoon salt

   1. In a small saucepan, boil the cider over high heat until reduced by half, about 7 minutes. Set aside.

   2. Bring a large pot of lightly salted water to a boil over high heat. Add the yams and cook until tender, 30 to 40 minutes, depending on the size of the yams. Drain well. Using a kitchen towel to protect your hands, peel the yams and return to the warm pot. Add the reduced cider, butter, brown sugar, and salt. Mash until well blended. (The mashed yams can be prepared up to 8 hours ahead, cooled, covered tightly with plastic wrap, and refrigerated. To reheat, place in a buttered 9 × 13-inch baking dish. Cover loosely with aluminum foil and bake in a preheated 350°F oven until heated through, about 30 minutes. Serve from the baking dish.) Serve hot.

Mashed Yams with Marshmallows: Spread half of the hot yams in a buttered 9 × 13-inch casse-role. Sprinkle with 1¹/₂ cups miniature marshmallows. Top with the remaining yams. Bake in a preheated 350°F for 20 minutes. Sprinkle the top with another 1¹/₂ cups marshmallows. Broil in a preheated broiler, about 4 inches away from the source of heat, until the marshmallows are lightly browned, about 1 minute. Serve immediately. (This casserole can be prepared up to 8 hours ahead, made with cooled mashed yams, following the reheating instructions in the main recipe and then broiling the marshmallow topping just before serving.)

Parmesan-Mashed Yellow Turnips

Makes 8 servings

Make Ahead: The turnips can be pared up to 8 hours ahead.

Like succotash, mashed yellow turnips (also called wax turnips, rutabagas, or Swedes) are a Thanksgiving must-have for many people on the East Coast. They are usually plain as can be, just mashed with milk and butter like potatoes, but they take nicely to some garlic, onion, and freshly grated Parmesan cheese.

2 medium yellow turnips (about 3¹/₄ pounds total)

1 large, plump head garlic cloves, separated and
   peeled

1 large onion, chopped

¹/₂ cup freshly grated Parmesan cheese (see
   Note)

4 tablespoons (¹/₂ stick) unsalted butter, at room
   temperature

1 teaspoon salt

¹/₂ teaspoon freshly milled black pepper

Approximately 1 cup milk, heated

1. Using a sturdy vegetable peeler, remove the thick skin from the turnips. Using a large knife, cut the turnips into pieces about 1 ½ inches square. Place the turnips and garlic in a large pot and add enough lightly salted water to cover. Cover tightly, and bring to a boil over high heat. Uncover and reduce the heat to medium-low. Boil gently for 20 minutes.

2. Add the onion and continue cooking until the turnips are tender when pierced with the tip of a small sharp knife, 15 to 20 more minutes. Drain well, then return to the warm cooking pot.

3. Add the Parmesan cheese, butter, salt, and pepper. Using a large masher or an electric hand mixer, mash the turnips, gradually adding enough milk to reach the desired consistency. Transfer to a warmed serving dish. (The mashed turnips can be kept warm in a 170°F oven, loosely covered with aluminum foil, for up to 20 minutes.) Serve hot.

Note: Use authentic Parmesan cheese for the best flavor. Unless the cheese is labeled "Parmigiano-Reggiano" (look on the rind, where these words are stamped in brown letters), it's not from Parma, Italy. Regular "Parmesan" cheese can be from Argentina or Wisconsin, and it just isn't the same.

Classic Recipe: Spiced Cranberry-Orange Jell-O Mold

Makes 10 servings

Make Ahead: The mold can be prepared up to 3 days ahead.

One of Jell-O's most requested recipes, this graces countless Thanksgiving tables every year.

Two 3-ounce packages Jell-O Brand Cherry Flavor Gelatin Dessert
One 16-ounce can whole-berry cranberry sauce
1 tablespoon fresh lemon juice
¼ teaspoon ground cinnamon
⅛ teaspoon ground cloves
1 seedless navel orange, peeled, sectioned, and cut into ½-inch cubes
½ cup chopped walnuts

1. In a medium bowl, stir 1½ cups boiling water into the gelatin, and continue to stir until the gelatin is completely dissolved, about 2 minutes. Stir in the cranberry sauce, 1 cup cold water, the lemon juice, cinnamon, and cloves. Refrigerate until thickened and almost set (a spoon drawn through the mixture will leave a definite impression), about 1½ hours.

2. Stir in the orange and walnuts. Spoon into a 5-cup mold. Cover and refrigerate until firm, at least 4 hours, or overnight. (The mold can be prepared up to 3 days ahead.)

3. To unmold, dip the mold into a large bowl of hot water and hold for 5 seconds. Dry the outside of the mold and invert onto a serving dish.

It Wouldn't Be Thanksgiving Without . . . Cranberries

No one is sure that cranberries were served at the first Thanksgiving, but the cranberry was a very important food to the Pawtuxet Indians, so historians assume that they would have offered it as a contribution to the feast. Instinct must have taught the Indians that the tart berries are an excellent source of Vitamin C, because they used them in many dishes. They ate them raw and boiled with maple syrup, but perhaps the most common use was in *pemmican,* which was a kind of low-tech energy bar made with berries, dried venison meat, and melted animal fat. Pemmican kept well, and went with the Indians on long journeys. (It can't have been much worse than some of the instant modern food I've had on camping trips.)

The Pilgrims probably referred to cranberries as "fenberries," a common fruit in old England which they resembled. The cranberry, however, gets its modern name from the Dutch and German settlers, who called it a "crane berry." When the cranberry vines bloom, the blossom looks like the head and bill of a crane. Eventually, the name became cranberry. Colonial Americans called them "bounce berries," referring to their bounciness. (Bouncing berries are an indication of freshness—bruised, old berries don't bounce.)

A recipe for cranberry sauce is included in the very first printed American cookbook, Amelia Simmons's *American Cookery,* which appeared in 1796. Canned cranberry sauce first hit the shelves in 1912, a product of the Cape Cod Cannery Company, which eventually became the Ocean Spray Preserving Company. The president of the company was a Boston lawyer, Marcus L. Urann. In 1930, Urann organized a merger between his company and two other cranberry canneries to form the Cranberry Canners, Incorporated, a cranberry farming cooperative. The cooperative, which eventually acquired Urann's former company name, after a few months of squabbling, now provides more than seventy percent of the world's cranberries. The world's supply of cranberries is grown on only about forty-two thousand acres, an area equal to the size of Manhattan. (If you've ever wondered how many cranberries are in a twelve-ounce bag, the number is three hundred and sixty, give or take a few berries.)

The high amount of Vitamin C in cranberries makes homemade cranberry sauce a long keeper—it can be refrigerated for at least one week before serving. To prepare cranberries for cooking, simply rinse them off and sort through them, discarding any bruised or soft ones. Cranberries are one of the best fruits for freezing. Just rinse them off, pat them dry, and store in self-sealing plastic bags. Don't thaw frozen berries before using.

Cranberries can react when they come in contain with aluminum and pick up the metal's taste. Be sure to cook them in pots with nonreactive metal surfaces, such as stainless steel or nonstick coating.

It Wouldn't Be Thanksgiving Without . . . Gelatin Molds

In the nineteenth century, cold, jellied aspics and desserts were the height of fashion. They also relied on the talents of a dedicated cook. Most thickeners, such as isinglass (the dried air bladder of sturgeon), agar-agar (a seaweed), and various mosses, weren't readily available to the home cook. Gelatin had to be painstakingly extracted from veal bones or calves' feet. This was absolute drudgery, and the long simmering, skimming, and clarification procedure took hours and hours.

By the 1880s, technology had advanced enough that gelatin was available in sheets (a version is still preferred by some professional pastry chefs), but it had to be soaked before use, and it still took a certain amount of guesswork to figure out how much to use to jell the food. In 1890, Charles B. Knox bought a gelatin company in Johnstown, New York. At first, it was business as usual, and Knox Gelatin Company sold gelatin sheets. Fatefully, Knox met a true innovator in American cooking, Sarah Tyson Rorer, principal of the Philadelphia Cooking School. Mrs. Rorer suggested that Knox granulate the gelatin so it would dissolve easily without soaking. This brainstorm was enhanced with the idea to sell the powdered gelatin in individual premeasured packets. This was the beginning of America's love affair with the bouncy, jiggly, transparent gelatin salad.

The affair heated up in 1897, when cough medicine manufacturer Pearl B. Waite introduced Jell-O (his wife Mary thought up the name). Waite improved the product from a recipe developed in 1845. Initially, his sweetened gelatin product failed as miserably as his predecessor's, but as Knox Gelatin became popular, Jell-O did too. By 1906, it was approaching one million dollars in annual sales (back when a million bucks meant something).

Fruits and vegetables were not very popular with cooks of the early twentieth century, and were often cooked to disguise their identity (a tradition that lives on in sweet potato casseroles and the like). And, as refined sugar became cheaper and more available, our nation quickly became hooked on sweets. It became perfectly acceptable to mix savory vegetables into sweet Jell-O. In 1905, when Knox conducted a national salad contest, the third place winner was Mrs. John Cooke's "Perfection Salad." It didn't have Jell-O, but it could have, being a sweet-and-sour gelatin salad with shredded cabbage, celery, green pepper, and pimientos. Knox printed the recipe in its popular recipe booklets, and one of the contest judges, Fannie Farmer, put it in the next edition of her cookbook. From this American classic, cooks created endless variations on a theme, and their popularity lives on, especially at Thanksgiving.

Classic Recipe: Jell-O Cream Cheese Mold

Makes 12 servings

Make Ahead: The mold can be prepared up to 3 days ahead.

This two-toned mold combines two Thanksgiving favorites, Jell-O and cream cheese. I love it.

1½ cups boiling water

Two 3-ounce packages Jell-O Brand Cranberry
 Flavor Gelatin Dessert (or any red flavor)

½ teaspoon ground cinnamon

1 medium apple, chopped

1 cup whole-berry cranberry sauce, optional

One 8-ounce package Philadelphia Brand
 Cream Cheese, at room temperature

   1. In a medium bowl, pour the boiling water over the gelatin and stir until the gelatin is completely dissolved, about 2 minutes. Stir in 1½ cups cold water and the cinnamon. Reserve 1 cup of the gelatin at room temperature. Refrigerate the remaining gelatin until thickened and partially set (a spoon drawn through the gelatin will leave a definite impression).

   2. Stir the apple and optional cranberry sauce into the thickened gelatin. Spoon into a 6-cup mold. Refrigerate until thickened and beginning to set (it will stick to your finger when touched, and a small spoonful will mound on a plate), about 30 minutes.

   3. In a medium bowl, gradually whisk the reserved gelatin into the cream cheese until smooth. Pour over the gelatin in the mold.

   4. Cover and refrigerate until firm, at least 4 hours, or overnight. (The mold can be prepared up to 3 days ahead.)

   5. To unmold, dip the mold into a large bowl of hot water and hold for 5 seconds. Dry the outside of the mold and invert onto a serving dish.

Reduced-Fat, Low-Calorie Cranberry Cream Cheese Mold: Substitute Sugar-Free Low-Calorie Jell-O for the regular variety, and Philadelphia Brand Neufchatel Cheese for the cream cheese.

Cranberry, Ginger, and Lemon Chutney

Makes about 3 cups   12 servings

Make Ahead: The chutney can be prepared up to 1 week ahead.

This is my most requested cranberry sauce recipe. As a matter of fact, many friends of mine now make quarts of this chutney at Christmastime for gift-giving. Crystallized ginger can be purchased inexpensively at Asian markets. It can also be found at many supermarkets and specialty food stores, where it gets pricey.

1 medium lemon

One 12-ounce bag fresh or frozen cranberries

2 cups sugar

½ cup diced (¼-inch) crystallized ginger (about
 2½ ounces)

⅓ cup finely chopped onion

1 garlic clove, minced

1 jalapeño pepper, seeded and minced

1 cinnamon stick

½ teaspoon dry mustard

½ teaspoon salt

   1. Grate the yellow zest from the lemon. Using a small sharp paring knife, cut away and discard the thick white pith. Cut the lemon crosswise in half and pick out the seeds with the tip of the knife. Dice the lemon into ¼-inch pieces.

   2. In a medium nonreactive saucepan, combine the

cranberries, diced lemon and zest, sugar, ginger, onion, garlic, jalapeño, cinnamon stick, mustard, and salt. Bring to a boil over medium heat, stirring often to help dissolve the sugar. Reduce the heat to low and simmer until the sauce is thick and the cranberries have burst, 10 to 15 minutes. Cool completely. (The chutney can be prepared up to 1 week ahead, covered tightly, and refrigerated.)

3. Remove the cinnamon stick just before serving. Serve at room temperature.

Cranberry-Tomato Chutney

Makes about 4 cups; 12 to 16 servings

Make Ahead: The chutney can be prepared up to 2 weeks ahead.

Here's another contender for the cranberry chutney crown. Cranberries and tomatoes may sound like an odd combination, but when you consider that tomatoes are a fruit and take well to sugar and spice, the pairing makes sense. Not only is this a terrific side dish for turkey, but I often offer it as an appetizer, spooned over cream cheese and served with crackers.

One 12-ounce bag fresh or frozen cranberries
One 28-ounce can tomatoes in juice, drained
1 cup packed brown sugar
¹/₂ cup raisins
1 medium onion, chopped
1 tablespoon shredded fresh ginger (use the large holes on a box grater)
1 jalapeño, seeded and minced
1 teaspoon yellow mustard seeds
1 cinnamon stick
1 garlic clove, minced

In a heavy-bottomed medium nonreactive saucepan, bring all of the ingredients to a simmer over medium heat, stirring often to dissolve the sugar. Reduce the heat to low and simmer until thickened, about 10 minutes. Cool completely and remove the cinnamon stick. (The chutney can be prepared up to 2 weeks ahead, covered, and refrigerated.) Serve at room temperature or chilled.

Grand Marnier Cranberry Sauce

Makes about 3 cups; 12 servings

Make Ahead: The cranberry sauce can be prepared up to 1 week ahead.

There is nothing like the incomparable flavor and aroma of Grand Marnier—it's the only orange liqueur made from bitter oranges and cognac. While you can make this with less-expensive Triple Sec or Cointreau (or even orange juice concentrate), it won't be quite the same. If you don't want to buy a large bottle, see if your liquor store carries mini-bottles (they are not available in all states).

2 large navel oranges
One 12-ounce bag fresh or frozen cranberries
1¹/₂ cups sugar
2 tablespoons Grand Marnier or other orange-flavored liqueur or thawed orange juice concentrate

1. Grate 2 teaspoons of zest from the oranges and set aside. Using a sharp knife, cut away and discard the thick white pith. Carefully cut between the membranes to release the orange sections. Set the orange sections aside.

2. In a medium heavy-bottomed nonreactive saucepan, combine the cranberries, sugar, 1 cup water, and the zest. Bring to a boil over medium heat, stirring often to help dissolve the sugar. Reduce the heat to low and simmer until the sauce is thick and the cranberries have burst, 10 to 15 minutes. During the last few minutes, stir in the orange sections. Remove from the heat and stir in the Grand Marnier. Cool completely. (The cranberry sauce can be prepared up to 1 week ahead, covered, and refrigerated.) Serve at room temperature or chilled.

Classic Recipe: Homemade Cranberry Sauce

There are really three "classic" cranberry sauce recipes. The first two, whole-berry and jellied, are cooked. Cranberry-orange relish is prepared from raw berries. Which of these three is your idea of classic just depends on which one you grew up on. Thanks to Ocean Spray Cranberries for providing the following archetypal versions of these timeless classics.

Fresh Cranberry Sauce

Makes 2 1/4 cups; 8 to 10 servings

Make Ahead: The sauce can be prepared up to 1 week ahead.

1 cup sugar

One 12-ounce bag fresh Ocean Spray Cranberries

In a medium nonreactive saucepan, bring 1 cup water and the sugar to a boil over high heat, stirring to dissolve the sugar. Stir in the cranberries and return to a boil. Reduce the heat to low and boil gently, stirring occasionally, until all the cranberries have popped and the sauce is thick, about 10 minutes. Transfer to a small bowl and cool completely. The sauce will thicken upon standing. Cover tightly with plastic wrap and refrigerate until ready to serve. (The sauce can be prepared up to 1 week ahead.) Serve chilled or at room temperature.

Homemade Jellied Cranberry Sauce

Makes 1 cup; 4 to 6 servings

Make Ahead: The sauce can be prepared up to 1 week ahead.

1 cup sugar

One 12-ounce bag fresh Ocean Spray Cranberries

1. In a medium nonreactive saucepan, bring 1 cup water and the sugar to a boil over high heat. Stir in the cranberries and return to a boil. Reduce the heat to low and boil gently, stirring occasionally, for 10 minutes.

2. Place a wire sieve over a medium bowl. Pour the sauce into the strainer. Mash and press the sauce through the sieve with the back of a large spoon, frequently scraping the outside of the sieve, until there is no pulp left in the sieve. Stir well and transfer to a small bowl. Cool completely. Cover tightly with plastic wrap and refrigerate until ready to serve. (The sauce can be prepared up to 1 week ahead.) Serve chilled or at room temperature.

The Cranberry Sauce Incident

O f course, many people consider canned cranberry sauce more classic than any homemade version. While I always serve some kind of homemade cranberry sauce (or chutney or salsa), I have learned that I'd better have a backup of canned sauce too.

A couple of Thanksgivings ago, when visiting my family in California, I was designated head chef (Mom was taking a break that year). As I was pulling food out of the refrigerator, my brothers noticed something missing.

"Where's the cranberry sauce?!" they demanded.

"This *is* cranberry sauce," I calmly replied, presenting the Cranberry, Ginger, and Lemon Chutney (page 91) that my New York friends eat by the barrel.

They looked at me as if I had gone crazy. "No, not that fancy stuff. The kind we always put on Grandma's glass plate!"

"Well, just give this a try . . ."

But they would have none of it. They hopped into the car and drove to the convenience store around the corner, and returned, minutes (or was it seconds?) later, with their prize—a can of cranberry sauce.

They carefully unmolded the quivering tube of canned sauce onto Grandma's cut-glass oblong serving dish (which, to my knowledge, has not been used to serve anything else in more than fifty years). Cutting into the sauce was ritualistic, each serving carefully designated by the rings on the tube—again proving that nostalgia is one of the most important ingredients served up at Thanksgiving.

Fresh Cranberry-Orange Relish

Makes about 3 cups; 12 servings

Make Ahead: The relish can be prepared up to 1 day ahead.

1 medium orange
One 12-ounce bag fresh Ocean Spray
  Cranberries
3/4 to 1 cup sugar

Cut the unpeeled orange into eighths, and pick out any seeds. Place half of the orange pieces and half of the cranberries in the work bowl of a food processor. Process until the mixture is evenly chopped. Transfer to a bowl. Repeat with the remaining orange and cranberries. Stir in sugar to taste. (The relish can be prepared up to 1 day ahead, covered tightly with plastic wrap, and refrigerated.) Serve chilled or at room temperature.

Rick's Cranberry-Double Orange Relish: Substitute 1 cup orange marmalade for the sugar, adding 1/2 cup to each batch in the food processor.

Rick's Cranberry-Kumquat Relish: Substitute 1 cup sliced fresh kumquats (about 5 ounces) for the orange.

Cranberry-Pineapple Salsa

Makes about 3 ½ cups; 12 servings

Make Ahead: The salsa is best prepared no longer than 2 hours before serving.

The fresh, crisp texture of this sweet-and-tangy salsa is very refreshing, and just the foil for Southwestern flavors like grill-smoked turkey. The ingredients are all mixed together in a food processor, but it is best to coarsely chop some of them before they go into the work bowl, or they won't chop to the proper consistency. Don't make this salsa too far ahead of time, or the scallions and garlic will overwhelm the fruit.

One 12-ounce bag fresh cranberries

¹/₂ medium pineapple, peeled, cored, and
  coarsely chopped (about 2 packed cups)

¹/₄ cup sugar

1 scallion (white and green parts), coarsely
  chopped

2 tablespoons chopped fresh mint or cilantro

1 to 2 jalapeños, seeded and minced

1 garlic clove, minced

¹/₄ teaspoon salt

Place all of the ingredients in a food processor fitted with the metal blade. Pulse until the cranberries are coarsely chopped. Transfer to a serving dish and cover tightly with plastic wrap. Refrigerate for at least 30 minutes but no longer than 2 hours. Serve chilled.

Cranberry and Fig Sauce

Makes about 3 cups; 10 to 12 servings

Make Ahead: The cranberry sauce must be prepared 1 day before serving; it can be refrigerated for up to 1 week.

This recipe is inspired by mostarda de Cremona (candied fruits in a mustard syrup), a wonderful Italian condiment for turkey and ham. For the best flavor, use an English hot mustard, such as Coleman's. Make it at least one day ahead to allow the mustard flavor to blossom.

One 12-ounce bag fresh cranberries

2 cups sugar

7 ounces Calimyrna figs, cut into ¹/₄-inch cubes
  (about 1¹/₂ cups)

2 teaspoons yellow mustard seeds

¹/₄ teaspoon crushed hot red pepper

1 tablespoon dry English mustard

1. In a medium nonreactive saucepan, combine all of the ingredients except the dry mustard. Bring to a boil over medium heat, stirring often to help dissolve the sugar. Reduce the heat to low and simmer until the sauce is thick and the cranberries have burst, 10 to 15 minutes. Remove from the heat.

2. Dissolve the dry mustard in 1 tablespoon cold water. Stir into the cranberry sauce. Cool completely. Cover tightly with plastic wrap and refrigerate overnight. (The cranberry sauce can be prepared up to 1 week ahead.) Serve chilled or at room temperature.

Four Gravies to Go

When I first moved to Manhattan, my kitchen was the size of most people's bedroom bureaus. The best thing about the apartment was the neighborhood—the Upper West Side. I lived near the block where Macy's blew up the balloons for the parade. Every Thanksgiving Eve, my friends and I would leave our restaurant jobs and meet at about 1 A.M. to watch the amazing sight of those enormous rubber sculptures being inflated. Of course, we'd get to bed around 3:30 A.M., only to get up a couple of hours later to reserve our spaces along the parade route. Then we would stagger back to my place and start Thanksgiving dinner. (Once, we were so behind schedule, we split the turkey lengthwise and roasted the halves. It worked.)

There was a door in the apartment that led out to the back hall, down the stairs, and then out to the street. Everyone was in the living room, and I was making gravy. While I was balancing the pan on the minuscule stove, the pan fell to the floor, spilling the gravy with a loud crash.

My friends tried to run into the kitchen to see what went wrong, but I diverted them. "Everything's fine. Have some more wine. I'll be right out." Then I sneaked down the back stairs and ran straight into the twenty-four-hour coffee shop on the corner. Luckily, the friendliest waiter on the staff was working behind the counter.

"Nick! Happy Thanksgiving! Do you have any turkey gravy?"

"Sure. How much do you need?"

"Enough for eight people."

So he filled up four coffee cups with canned turkey gravy (what else?) and put them in a bag. I ran upstairs, poured them into a pot, and stirred in a slug of bourbon. Without telling a soul of my trials, I poured the gravy into a sauceboat, and calmly served it.

Everyone told me it was the best gravy I had ever made. And I have put bourbon in my gravy ever since.

Pan Gravy 101

You'll find details for making the appropriate gravy or sauce with each of the turkey recipes, but here are basic instructions to use as an overview. There are a lot of different ways to make gravy—thickening with a flour-water paste or cornstarch, using a saucepan or a roasting pan, etc. But here's how to make the most delicious, greasefree, lumpless, dark mahogany brown gravy in the world.

• *Treat gravy as a classic French roux-based sauce, which has exact proportions of fat, flour, and liquid. Many cooks just stir enough flour into the pan drippings to make a paste and add water to make a gravy. The problem here is that one never knows how much fat will be released during roasting, and if the proportions are off, the paste gets lumpy or greasy. And in the flour-water paste method (where the paste is whisked into simmering drippings), the flour does not combine properly with the fat, so the gravy still turns out greasy. My recipe uses a measured amount of the fat skimmed from the drippings and turkey stock to give rich turkey flavor. I prefer a flour-based gravy to a cornstarch-thickened one, which turns out glossy rather than opaque and is really a sauce.*

• *The proportions for gravy are 1½ tablespoons each fat and all-purpose flour to each cup of liquid, part of which should be the pan drippings. Use these proportions for any size turkey and any amount of gravy. For example, to yield slightly less than 4 cups of gravy (some of the liquid will evaporate during simmering), use 6 tablespoons each fat and flour and 4 cups of liquid. If your family likes thicker gravy, increase the fat and flour by 2 tablespoons— you can always thin it down with more stock.*

• *The secret to dark, rich gravy? Dark, rich pan drippings. Let the drippings evaporate into a dark brown glaze during roasting, but don't let them burn. Whenever the pan looks dry, moisten the drippings with more turkey stock, wine, or water so they don't scorch. The darker and heavier your roasting pan, the darker and richer the drippings. Thin aluminum roasters make wimpy drippings.*

• *Always degrease the drippings and stock before making gravy, reserving the skimmed fat. Pour the pan drippings into large glass bowl or measure. (I find glass bowls and cups more efficient to use than gravy separators. The separators are often too small for the amount of drippings, but if you like them, use them, and at least buy a 1-quart separator if you roast large birds.) Let stand for 5 minutes so the clear yellow fat can rise to the top of the drippings. Use a large spoon to skim off the fat and transfer to a small bowl. If you don't have enough fat to make the amount of gravy needed, add melted butter.*

• *The degreased drippings add color and flavor to the gravy. Combine them with turkey stock or chicken broth to get the desired amount of liquid. You'll never resort to commercial gravy coloring again.*

• *Use a whisk to avoid lumpy gravy. A flat paddle-shaped whisk works better than a balloon whisk to reach into the corners of the pan. If you have a non-stick roasting pan, use a heatproof plastic whisk, available at kitchenware stores: Mine has become an indispensable tool.*

• *Allow ⅓ cup gravy per person, more if you want leftover for sandwiches.*

Makes about 3 1/2 cups

Pan drippings from roast turkey
About 3½ cups Homemade Turkey Stock (page 22) or canned reduced-sodium chicken stock
6 tablespoons all-purpose flour
Salt and freshly milled black pepper

1. When the turkey is done, transfer it to a serving platter and set aside. Pour the pan drippings into a

1-quart glass measure or medium bowl, leaving any browned bits in the bottom of the roasting pan. Let stand for 5 minutes. Using a large spoon, skim the clear yellow fat that has risen to the surface and reserve. (If the drippings don't seem dark enough, pour half back into the roasting pan and set over two burners. Bring to a boil over high heat. As the drippings reduce and darken, occasionally pour in the remaining drippings until the liquid in the pan is as dark as you want. The amount of drippings will decrease, but the finished gravy will be darker and taste better, without having to resort to bottled gravy coloring.) Add enough stock to the drippings to measure 4 cups total.

   2. Set the roasting pan on two burners over moderately low heat. Add 6 tablespoons of the reserved fat to the pan. Sprinkle the flour into the pan, whisking constantly. Let the mixture bubble, whisking constantly, until it turns beige, 1 to 2 minutes. It is important to let the mixture cook for a minute or two to allow the flour to loses its raw taste, but adjust the heat as needed to keep it from burning. Whisk in the stock/drippings mixture, scraping up the browned bits on the bottom of the pan. Simmer for 2 to 3 minutes, whisking occasionally. If the gravy seems too thin, increase the heat to medium and boil until it is as thick as you wish. If the gravy seems too thick, thin with additional stock. Season with salt and pepper. If desired, strain the gravy through a wire sieve to remove any extraneous browned bits of drippings.

Giblet Gravy: If you have made Homemade Turkey Stock, finely chop the cooked giblets and neck meat. Or, simmer the giblets and neck with $3\frac{1}{2}$ cups canned reduced-sodium chicken broth, $2\frac{1}{2}$ cups water, 1 small onion, sliced, and 1 small carrot, coarsely chopped, until tender, about 2 hours, then cool and chop the meat. Strain the mixture and use in place of the Homemade Turkey Stock.

Roast Garlic Gravy: For every 4 cups finished gravy, stir in 1 head garlic, roasted and puréed (see pages 74–75).

Wine Gravy: Substitute dry white or hearty red wine for up to one-quarter of the cooking liquid. For example, for about 4 cups of gravy, use 3 cups cooking liquid and 1 cup wine.

Spiked Gravy: For every 1 cup of cooking liquid, add 1 to 2 tablespoons dry sherry, ruby or tawny port, Madeira, brandy or cognac, or bourbon. Do not overdo the alcohol, or the gravy will taste too strong.

Herbed Gravy: For every 4 cups finished gravy, stir in up to 2 tablespoons minced fresh herbs, such as thyme, sage, rosemary, parsley, or tarragon, or a combination.

Head Start Gravy

When you have a crowd coming, you may want to get a head start on the gravy before the troops arrive. Here's my strategy: A couple of days ahead, make a turkey gravy base with butter instead of turkey fat. On Thanksgiving, color and enrich the base by stirring it into the degreased drippings from the roasted bird. Voilà! Not exactly "instant" gravy, but pretty close.

Follow the proportions for Pan Gravy 101 (page 97), substituting butter for the skimmed turkey fat. Melt the butter in a large heavy-bottomed saucepan over medium heat. Whisk in the flour and cook until very lightly browned, 2 to 3 minutes. Whisk in the stock or broth and bring to a simmer. Reduce the heat to medium-low and cook until lightly thickened, about 10 minutes. The gravy base will be pale and thin-bodied. Cool the gravy base completely, cover, and refrigerate for up to 2 days. Don't worry about a skin forming, as it will melt away when the gravy is reheated.

After the Thanksgiving turkey has roasted, pour the drippings into a glass bowl or measuring cup and let stand for 5 minutes. Skim off and discard the fat that has risen to the surface. Pour the degreased drippings back into the pan and place on two burners over medium heat. Whisk in the gravy base and bring to a boil, stirring up the browned bits in the pan. Cook, stirring often, until the gravy reduces and thickens, about 10 minutes. Season with salt and pepper. (If you have too much gravy base to fit into the pan, whisk in 1 quart of base, and pour this mixture back into the remaining gravy base. Transfer to a large pot and reheat over medium heat, stirring often.) Skim, if desired, and serve hot.

The base can also be served as a turkey sauce (I can't call it gravy without drippings) with turkeys that don't produce drippings, such as Smoke-Grilled Cider-Basted Turkey (page 47). It also acts an insurance policy against recipes that might not produce perfect drippings, like Oven-Blasted Turkey on page 44.

Yeast and Quick Breads

Rising to the Occasion

If there is one day of the year when home-baked breads should be served, it's Thanksgiving. To me, the ritual of passing a basket of hot rolls is as important as carving the turkey. Baking bread is one of the most satisfying things a cook can do, and it doesn't have to be complicated. All of the recipes in this chapter are designed for beginning bakers, although practiced bread makers will appreciate their old-fashioned flavor. Only two recipes use yeast, and only one of them requires kneading. In other words, you'll have scant excuse for not serving fragrant, warm, home-baked bread at your meal. Here is a guide to some ingredients in this chapter:

Flour: For most yeast doughs, use unbleached or bread flour. Organic unbleached flour, available at natural food stores, gives the bread an incredible flavor and chewy texture. Quick breads, leavened with baking powder or baking soda, are best made with bleached all-purpose flour.

Cornmeal: Stone-ground cornmeal has a coarser texture than mass-processed cornmeal, which translates into a fuller flavor. Stone-ground cornmeal is available (usually in paper sacks) in natural food stores and many supermarkets. Some cooks feel that white cornmeal is sweeter than yellow cornmeal and has a fuller corn flavor. All cornmeal is fairly perishable and should be stored in the refrigerator. However, the stone-ground variety is even more delicate, as it contains more oils that can turn rancid, than its overprocessed kin, and should be stored in a plastic bag in the freezer. Let the frozen cornmeal stand at room temperature for about 30 minutes to warm up before using.

Yeast: I use active dry yeast because it is easier to find than fresh compressed yeast. If you prefer, use twice as much compressed yeast as dry, crumbled and packed into the measuring spoon. Rapid-rise and "instant" yeast can be substituted for active dry yeast. Surprisingly, these quick-rising yeasts do not seriously affect the flavor of the dough. (Good bakers know that the longer the bread rises, the more flavor develops.) If you want the full advantage of the reduced rising periods these yeasts provide, follow the instructions on the package.

Unless you follow their instructions (for hot liquids and the like), the yeast will not work as quickly as it should. Store yeast in the refrigerator and use by the expiration date on the package. Freezing yeast does not extend its shelf life.

Yeast is a living thing, and hot water will kill it. Use warm water that feels slightly warmer than body temperature. If you are nervous about the correct temperature, test the water with an instant-read thermometer.

Buttermilk: Buttermilk makes bread with a deliciously tender crumb. The acids in the tangy buttermilk tenderize the gluten proteins in the flour. (I know that not everyone loves to drink buttermilk, but it is inexpensive, so if you have leftovers that you have to throw out, you won't go broke.) Dried buttermilk powder, which can be reconstituted with water, is available at some supermarkets and natural food stores. In a pinch, substitute $2/3$ cup plain yogurt whisked with $1/3$ cup low-fat or whole milk for each cup of buttermilk.

Dinner Rolls 101

Makes 1 ¹/₂ dozen

Make Ahead: See the various suggestions below.

Fresh-baked rolls, right out of the oven . . . I bet your mouth is watering just reading those words. Here is my favorite dinner roll recipe—chewy, with a thin crust and unsurpassable homemade flavor. Once you have the basic dough, you can form it into balls, cloverleaf rolls, or knots. (I am partial to the knots, because even though they are easy to make, they look as if you bought them from a bakery.) Leave the rolls plain, or take a couple of seconds to sprinkle them with poppy or sesame seeds. You can make the dough by hand, in the food processor, or in a heavy-duty electric mixer. There are a bunch of make-ahead options, but I prefer to time the rolls to come out of the oven just before serving.

• *The dough can be prepared the night before baking, using only 1¹/₂ teaspoons yeast. Divide the dough in half, close each half in a self-sealing plastic bag, and refrigerate overnight. The next morning, punch down the dough and refrigerate again until ready to shape the rolls. Punch down the dough, shape the rolls as desired, and cover loosely with plastic wrap. Allow the shaped rolls to stand at warm room temperature for about 2 hours to come to room temperature and rise until doubled. Bake as directed. (Some bakers freeze the dough, but it takes so long for the dough to defrost and warm up enough to rise, it is not worth the hassle.)*
• *The rolls can be baked up to 1 week ahead, cooled completely, stored in self-sealing plastic bags, and frozen. Allow the rolls to defrost for 1 hour at room temperature before reheating. To reheat, wrap the rolls in aluminum foil, six rolls to a package. Bake in a preheated 350°F oven until heated through, 10 to 15 minutes.*

• *The rolls can be baked early in the day, up to 8 hours before serving. Cool completely. To serve, wrap the rolls in aluminum foil packages and reheat as directed above.*

One ¹/₄-ounce package active dry yeast
1¹/₂ cups buttermilk
6 tablespoons unsalted butter, melted, plus
   additional for brushing the rolls
2 large eggs
3 tablespoons sugar
³/₄ teaspoon baking soda
5 cups bread or unbleached flour
1¹/₂ teaspoons salt
Approximately 2¹/₂ teaspoons poppy seeds or
   sesame seeds, for sprinkling (optional)

1. In a small bowl, sprinkle the yeast over ¹/₄ cup warm (100° to 110°F) water and let stand until creamy, 5 to 10 minutes. Stir to dissolve the yeast.

2. In a medium saucepan, heat the buttermilk, stirring constantly, just until warm (100° to 110°F). Or, place the buttermilk in a 1-quart glass measuring cup and microwave on High for 1 minute, or until warm. Transfer the buttermilk to a 1-quart measuring cup, if necessary, and stir in the dissolved yeast mixture, the melted butter, eggs, sugar, and baking soda.

3. *To make the dough by hand,* mix the flour and salt in a large bowl and make a well in the center. Pour in the liquid ingredients and mix to form a shaggy dough. Turn out onto a lightly floured work surface. Knead the dough, adding more flour as needed, until the dough is smooth and elastic, 8 to 10 minutes. Form the dough into a ball.

To make the dough in a heavy-duty standing mixer, place the liquid ingredients and the salt in the mixer bowl, and attach the paddle blade. With the machine on low speed, gradually add enough of the flour to make a stiff dough that collects around the blade. (You may not need all of the flour.) Change to the dough hook. Knead the dough in the machine, adding more flour as needed to make a elastic dough, about 8 minutes. Transfer to a lightly floured work surface and knead by hand until smooth, about 2 minutes. Form the dough into a ball.

To make the dough in a food processor, fit an 11-cup-capacity (or larger) machine with the metal blade. Make the dough in two batches. Place 2½ cups of the flour and salt in the machine and pulse to combine. With the machine running, pour about half of the liquid ingredients through the feed tube and process to form a soft ball of dough that rides on top of the blade. Process for 45 seconds to knead the dough. Transfer the dough to a lightly floured work surface and cover with plastic wrap. Repeat with the remaining ingredients. Knead the two portions of dough together by hand until smooth and combined. Form the dough into a ball.

4. Place the dough in a large buttered bowl. Turn the dough to coat with the butter, and turn the dough smooth side up. Cover tightly with plastic wrap and let stand in a warm place until doubled in volume (if you poke the dough with your finger, an impression will remain), about 1¼ hours.

5. Lightly butter two 9-inch round cake pans. Punch down the dough and knead briefly on an unfloured work surface. Cut the dough into eighteen equal pieces. (This is easiest to do by cutting the dough into thirds, then cutting each third in half, and each half into three pieces.) Place a piece of dough on the work surface. Using the sides of your hands, tuck the dough underneath itself, turning the dough as you tuck, stretching the top surface, and eventually forming a taut ball. Repeat with the remaining dough, transferring the rolls to the prepared pans as you form them, allowing nine balls per pan. Cover loosely with plastic wrap and let stand in a warm place until almost doubled in volume, about 40 minutes.

6. Preheat the oven to 400°F.

7. Brush the tops of the rolls lightly with melted but-

ter and sprinkle with the seeds, if using. Bake until golden brown, about 20 minutes. Remove from the pans and serve warm.

Knot Rolls: Lightly butter two baking sheets. Work with one piece of dough at a time, keeping the others covered with plastic wrap. Roll the dough between your palms into a thick rope. Place the rope on an unfloured work surface. Put your hands on top of the dough and roll it back and forth, stretching the dough into a 9-inch-long rope. Tie the dough into an overhand knot, with the knot positioned in the center of the rope. Place the knots 2 inches apart on the prepared baking sheets. Cover loosely with plastic wrap and let rise until almost doubled in size. Bake as directed above.

Cloverleaf Rolls: Lightly butter eighteen muffin cups. Cut each piece of dough into thirds and form each piece into a small, taut ball. Place three balls, smooth sides up, in each muffin tin. Cover loosely with plastic wrap and let rise until almost doubled. Bake as directed.

Angel Biscuits

Makes about 2 1/2 dozen

Make Ahead: The dough can be prepared up to 2 days ahead; the biscuits are best freshly baked but can be baked up to 8 hours ahead.

A variation on the biscuit theme, with a bit of yeast to add fluffiness. Not only does the recipe make sensational biscuits, but the dough can be mixed a couple of days ahead of baking. While Buttermilk Biscuits 101 uses a homemade baking powder, use a store-bought one in this recipe, as the homemade version will lose its leavening power if the dough stands for too long. All-purpose flour rather than bread flour will yield the tenderest biscuits.

1 teaspoon active dry yeast

5 cups all-purpose flour

¹/₄ cup sugar

1 tablespoon baking powder, preferably an
    aluminum-free brand, such as Rumford's

1 teaspoon baking soda

1¹/₂ teaspoons salt

1 cup solid vegetable shortening, chilled, cut
    into pieces

2 cups buttermilk

1. In a small bowl, sprinkle the yeast over 2 tablespoons of water and let stand until creamy, about 5 minutes. Stir until the yeast is dissolved and set aside.

2. In a large bowl, mix the flour, sugar, baking powder, baking soda, and salt. Using a pastry blender, cut in the shortening until the mixture resembles coarse crumbs. (If the shortening sticks to the pastry blender, just scrape it off.) Add the dissolved yeast and the buttermilk and stir to make a shaggy dough. Knead in the bowl to form a soft, sticky dough. Divide the dough between two self-sealing plastic bags, close, and refriger-

ate for at least 3 hours and up to 2 days. If it is refrigerated for longer than 3 hours, punch down the dough whenever it occurs to you, but no less than twice every 24 hours.

3. Position the racks in the center and top third of the oven and preheat the oven to 450°F.

4. Turn the dough out onto a lightly floured surface and knead briefly. Pat it out with lightly floured hands (or dust the top of the dough with flour and roll out) until ¹/₂ inch thick. Using a 2¹/₂-inch round biscuit or cookie cutter or a juice glass, cut out biscuits and place 1 inch apart on ungreased baking sheets. Gather up the dough scraps, knead briefly to combine, and repeat the procedure as needed to make about 30 biscuits.

5. Bake, switching the positions of the baking sheets from top to bottom halfway during baking, until the biscuits are barely golden, about 15 minutes. (Although the biscuits are best freshly baked, they can be baked up to 8 hours ahead and reheated. Wrap in aluminum foil, six biscuits to a package, and reheat in a preheated 350°F oven for about 15 minutes.) Serve immediately.

Buttermilk Biscuits 101

Makes 1 dozen

Make Ahead: The biscuits can be baked up to 8 hours ahead.

Here they are, the most tender, delicious, buttery, old-fashioned biscuits in the land. For the classic biscuit shape and texture, roll out the dough and cut into rounds or squares. Or, add some whole milk to mix a softer dough that can be dropped from a spoon to create biscuits with a crispy surface. Either way, you will be serving an American classic.

• *Ask any Southern cook for the secret to tender biscuits, and the answer is usually the flour. Southern flour (like White Lily brand) is milled from soft wheat and has a very low gluten content, whereas the rest of the country uses higher-gluten hard-wheat flour. To approximate soft-wheat flour, mix cake flour (made from very soft wheat) with all-purpose flour. Of course, if you live in the South, just use White Lily.*

• *Many biscuits use baking powder as a leavening, which starts with a simple combination of acid (cream of tartar) and alkali (baking soda). When moistened, the mixture forms carbon dioxide gases that make the biscuits rise. Most commercial baking powders include aluminum derivatives too, which can give your baked goods a metallic taste. (An exception is my favorite brand, Rumford's, which is available at natural food stores and many supermarkets.) This recipe uses a homemade baking powder made from the cream of tartar and baking soda already in your kitchen cabinet.*

• *Handle the biscuit dough as little as possible to keep the gluten in the flour from toughening. (See Perfect Pie Crust 101 on page 111 for a more detailed discussion of gluten.)*

• *Use a ruler to measure the dough's thickness. If the dough is rolled too thin, the biscuits will be skimpy.*

• *To cut out round biscuits, use a 2½-inch round biscuit or cookie cutter or a small juice glass. With round biscuits, you will always have scraps. Taking care not to overhandle the dough, gently knead the scraps together and roll out again. Although the subsequent batches will not be quite as tender as the first, most people won't be able to tell the difference.*

• *To make square biscuits (which avoid the scrap problem altogether), roll or pat the dough into a ¾-inch-thick square, and cut into twelve squares.*

• *To make drop biscuits, mix in an additional ¼ cup whole milk, not buttermilk, to make a loose, sticky dough. Drop the dough by heaping tablespoons onto ungreased baking sheets, spacing them 1 inch apart.*

1½ **cups cake flour (not self-rising)**
1½ **cups all-purpose flour**
1 **tablespoon cream of tartar**
1½ **teaspoons baking soda**
¾ **teaspoon salt**
12 **tablespoons (1½ sticks) unsalted butter, cut into ½-inch cubes**
1 **cup plus 2 tablespoons buttermilk**

1. Position a rack in the top third of the oven and preheat to 400°F.

2. In a large bowl, whisk together the cake flour, all-purpose flour, cream of tartar, baking soda, and salt. Using a pastry blender, cut in the butter until it resembles coarse crumbs. Mix in the buttermilk until combined. Knead lightly in the bowl to make a soft dough. Do not overwork the dough.

3. On a lightly floured work surface, pat out the dough with floured hands to a ¾-inch thickness. (Or, lightly dust the top of the dough with flour and roll it out.) Using a 2½-inch round biscuit or cookie cutter or a juice glass, cut out biscuits and place on an ungreased baking sheet. Gather up the scraps, knead gently to combine, and repeat the procedure to get a total of 12 biscuits.

4. Bake until the biscuits are risen and golden brown, about 15 minutes. (The biscuits can be baked up to 8 hours ahead, cooled, and stored at room temperature. To reheat, wrap the biscuits, six to a package, in aluminum foil. Reheat in a preheated 350°F oven for about 15 minutes.) Serve hot or warm.

Southern Corn Bread

Makes 12 servings (or 10 cups crumbled corn bread for stuffing; see Note)

Make Ahead: Corn bread is best when freshly baked, but it can be made up to 8 hours ahead.

More solid and crumbly than Yankee Corn Bread (next recipe), this is the one to use for dressing, or if your tastes run to firm corn bread.

2¹/₂ cups white or yellow cornmeal, preferably stone-ground
1¹/₂ cups all-purpose flour
1 tablespoon plus 1 teaspoon baking soda
1 teaspoon salt
2 cups milk
6 tablespoons (³/₄ stick) unsalted butter, melted
2 large eggs, beaten

   1. Position a rack in the center of the oven and preheat to 375°F. Lightly butter a 9 × 13-inch baking pan.
   2. In a large bowl, whisk the cornmeal, flour, baking soda, and salt to combine. Make a well in the center and pour in the milk, butter, and eggs. Stir just until combined. Pour into the pan and smooth the top.
   3. Bake until golden brown and a toothpick inserted in the center comes out clean, 25 to 30 minutes. (The corn bread can be baked up to 8 hours ahead. To reheat, cut the corn bread into serving pieces, wrap in aluminum foil, six pieces to a package, and bake in a preheated 350°F oven for about 15 minutes.) Serve warm.

Note: If you're making it for stuffing, the corn bread can be baked up to 1 month ahead, cooled, wrapped tightly in plastic wrap and an overwrap of aluminum foil, and frozen. Or, bake it up to 2 days ahead, and store at room temperature.
   To use for stuffing, crumble the corn bread and transfer to baking sheets. Let stand overnight at room temperature to dry out. Or, bake in a preheated 350°F oven, stirring occasionally, until slightly dried but not toasted, about 20 minutes.

Yankee Corn Bread

Makes 12 servings

Make Ahead: Corn bread is best when freshly baked, but it can be made up to 8 hours ahead.

While Southern corn bread eschews sugar, Northerners like their corn bread on the sweet side. Some bakers increase the sugar to ¹/₄ cup in this recipe, but I prefer a lighter hand. With the minimum of sugar, it can be turned into two excellent variations: one with chiles and cheese, and the other with bacon.

1¹/₃ cups yellow cornmeal, preferably stone-ground
1¹/₃ cups all-purpose flour
2 tablespoons sugar
1 teaspoon salt
1 teaspoon baking soda
2 cups buttermilk
8 tablespoons (1 stick) unsalted butter, melted
2 large eggs, beaten

   1. Position a rack in the center of the oven and preheat to 375°F.
   2. In a large bowl, whisk the cornmeal, flour, sugar, salt, and baking soda. Make a well in the center. Pour in the buttermilk, 4 tablespoons of the melted butter, and the eggs. Stir just until smooth. Do not overbeat.
   3. Pour the remaining 4 tablespoons butter into a 9 × 13-inch baking dish and place in the oven. Heat until the butter is very hot, but not browned, about 2

minutes. Pour the batter into the hot pan. Bake until the top is golden and a toothpick inserted in the center comes out clean, 25 to 30 minutes. Cool for 5 minutes. (The corn bread can be baked up to 8 hours ahead. To reheat, cut the corn bread into serving pieces, wrap in aluminum foil, six pieces to a package, and bake in a preheated 350°F oven for about 15 minutes.)

4. Cut the corn bread into serving pieces, and remove from the pan with a spatula. Serve warm or at room temperature.

Southwestern Chili and Cheese Corn Bread: Stir 1½ cups grated extra-sharp Cheddar cheese (6 ounces) and 2 jalapeño peppers, seeded and minced, into the batter.

Old-Fashioned Bacon Corn Bread: In a large skillet over medium heat, cook 6 strips of bacon until crisp. Reserving the bacon drippings, transfer the bacon to paper towels. Cool and chop the bacon. Combine ¼ cup of the bacon drippings with ¼ cup melted butter and substitute for the melted butter in the batter.

Rosemary and Cracked Pepper Corn Sticks

Makes 1 dozen

Make Ahead: The corn sticks can be baked up to 8 hours ahead.

Savory with rosemary and cracked peppercorns, this is corn bread with a delicious difference. You'll need cast-iron corn stick molds to make the corn sticks. Before using any cast-iron utensil for the first time, it needs to be "seasoned" according to the manufacturer's instructions to build up a patina of oil on the cooking surface.

And, after baking, never wash the molds with soap and water, or you'll wash off the seasoning and have to reseason them again. If you don't have corn stick molds, the batter can also be baked as muffins, according to the instructions following the recipe.

1¼ cups all-purpose flour
1 cup yellow or white cornmeal, preferably
   stone-ground
2 teaspoons chopped fresh rosemary
   or 1 teaspoon crumbled dried rosemary
1 teaspoon baking powder
1 teaspoon salt
³/₄ teaspoon coarsely cracked black
   peppercorns (use a mortar and pestle, or
   crush under a heavy skillet)
1½ cups milk
4 tablespoons (½ stick) unsalted butter, melted
1 large egg
Nonstick vegetable oil spray

Special Equipment
Two 6-stick corn stick molds

1. Position a rack in the top third of the oven and place the corn stick molds in the oven to heat while the oven is preheating. Preheat the oven to 425°F.

2. In a medium bowl, whisk the flour, cornmeal, rosemary, baking powder, salt, and pepper to combine. Make a well in the center. Pour in the milk, melted butter, and egg. Beat the egg to break it up, then stir the wet ingredients into the dry, just until combined. Do not overbeat.

3. Carefully remove the hot molds from the oven and spray with the oil. Spoon the batter into the molds (it will almost fill the molds completely). Return the molds to the oven. Bake until the tops are golden brown and the corn sticks pull away from the sides of the molds, about 20 minutes. Let cool in the pan for 2 minutes, then unmold. (The corn sticks can be baked up to 8 hours before serving. Cool completely, then wrap in aluminum foil, six corn sticks to a package. To reheat, bake in a preheated 350°F oven until heated through, 10 to 15 minutes.) Serve immediately.

Old-Fashioned Corn Sticks: Delete the rosemary and cracked peppercorns. Add 1 tablespoon sugar to the batter.

Rosemary and Cracked Pepper Muffins: Spoon the batter into 9 buttered muffin cups. So the muffins will bake evenly, add about 2 tablespoons water to each empty cup. Bake until a toothpick inserted in the center comes out clean, about 20 minutes.

Spiced Yam and Pecan Muffins

Makes 1 dozen

Make Ahead: The muffins can be baked up to 8 hours ahead.

Yams add their distinctive taste and color to these not-too-sweet muffins. When preparing mashed yams to use in batters and doughs, baked yams are better than boiled or steamed ones. Baked yams have more flavor and are drier than boiled ones, which can get water-logged and throw off the liquid measurements. Even so, the moisture in these muffins makes them bake longer than typical recipes. Use nonstick muffin cups, or paper muffin liners, so the muffins unmold easily.

3 medium yams (1¹/₄ pounds), scrubbed but
  unpeeled
¹/₂ cup packed light brown sugar

1 cup milk
4 tablespoons (¹/₂ stick) unsalted butter, melted
2 large eggs
2 cups all-purpose flour
2 teaspoons baking powder
1 teaspoon ground cinnamon
¹/₂ teaspoon freshly grated nutmeg
¹/₂ teaspoon salt
¹/₂ cup coarsely chopped pecans, plus 12 pecan
  halves

1. Preheat the oven to 400°F. Lightly butter 12 nonstick muffin cups (butter them even though they are nonstick), or line with paper muffin liners.

2. Pierce each yam a few time with a fork. Place on a baking sheet and bake until tender, about 1 hour. Cool until easy to handle. Remove the skins and discard. Rub the yams through a wire sieve into a small bowl. Cool completely.

3. Transfer 1 cup of the yam purée to a medium bowl; discard remaining purée. Rub the brown sugar through a dry wire sieve into the bowl (this removes any lumps and allows the brown sugar to dissolve easily in the batter) and mix well. Add the milk, melted butter, and eggs and mix well. Sift together the flour, baking powder, cinnamon, nutmeg, and salt and stir into the wet ingredients, just until combined. Fold in the chopped pecans. Do not overmix. Spoon equal amounts of the batter into the muffin cups. Top each muffin with a pecan half.

4. Bake until the muffins are lightly browned and a toothpick inserted in the center comes out clean, about 40 minutes. Cool slightly, then unmold. (The muffins can be baked up to 8 hours before serving. Cool completely, then wrap in aluminum foil, six muffins to a package. To reheat, bake in a preheated 350°F oven until heated through, 10 to 15 minutes.) Serve warm.

Desserts

How Many Ways Can You Say "Pumpkin"?

The turkey dinner may have been wonderful, but afterwards comes another indelible symbol of the Thanksgiving feast: pie. It doesn't have to be pumpkin pie—it could be chocolate, apple, or pecan. You can serve other desserts too, but don't try to get away with leaving out the pie.

Desserts are chemistry that tastes good. More than other kinds of cooking, which can be instinctive, dessert making calls for a careful balance of the right ingredients. Use a quarter teaspoon too much of baking soda (something very easy to do if you measure improperly), and the shortcake could be crumbly and flat instead of rising to tender, golden heights.

I don't say this to intimidate you, but to let you in on a few not-so-secret secrets. The happiest bakers follow two basic rules:

1. Measure all ingredients properly. When I cook at friends' homes, I am surprised to see that many people only have one glass measuring cup to do all their measuring chores. These are the same people who are afraid of baking because they have had a few failures. If they had measured properly, they would have had successes.

2. Use the right ingredients for the job. This means butter (not margarine), the correct type of flour, the right size eggs.

Here are some tips on techniques and ingredients to help you make blue-ribbon desserts every time.

Measuring: To measure accurately, use metal measuring cups for dry ingredients, glass measures for liquids, and measuring spoons for small amounts. You can never correctly measure a half-cup of milk in a metal cup, because to get the full measure, the milk would probably overflow. Conversely, you can never get a level cup of flour in a glass measure.

I use the dip-and-sweep method to measure flour. Even though there are other ways to measure, I prefer dip-and-sweep because I am convinced it is the one that most home cooks use. Just dip the measuring cup or measuring spoon into the bag of flour and fill the cup without packing the ingredient. Using the flat side of a knife, sweep the excess from the top of the cup to get a level measurement. When following a recipe in other cookbooks, read the introductory remarks to see what dry measuring method that cook prefers. Some bakers insist that you spoon the flour into the cup and level it off, but that makes a mess. Others suggest that you weigh the flour on a kitchen scale.

Measure liquid ingredients in glass measuring cups. Plastic cups can warp when filled with hot ingredients. Hold the cup at eye level to check the measurement.

Your Oven: The position of the oven rack makes a difference. Foods cooked in the top third of the oven brown more efficiently. If you cook a pie in the lower third of a gas oven, nearest the heat source, the crust will crisp better. (For some of the savory recipes in the book, when you will no doubt be crowding many things into the oven to reheat them, I have left out the rack positions for practicality's sake.) Position the rack as directed before preheating the oven. Preheat the oven for at least 15 minutes for it

to reach the correct temperature. To verify the oven temperature, use an oven thermometer—oven thermostats are notoriously inaccurate.

Mixers: I use a hand-held electric mixer in many of these recipes, because it is what most cooks own. If you have a heavy-duty standing mixer, you can certainly use it, but remember that it has a stronger motor, and the ingredients will mix in less time.

Flour: Supermarkets now carry many different types of flour. Each flour is meant to do a specific job, even if the mills like to use the word "all-purpose." Gluten is a substance found in wheat that gives a dough strength. The more gluten, the tougher the dough. Bakers call high-gluten flours "hard," and low-gluten flours "soft." If you are baking a yeast dough that will be kneaded, you want a strong, hard flour, like unbleached or bread flour. If you are baking a pie with a tender crust, you want a moderately strong flour, like bleached all-purpose. (The bleaching process reduces the gluten's strength. Unbleached flour isn't versatile at all, and should be reserved for yeast doughs. I am on a campaign to remove the "all-purpose" from bags of unbleached flour.) Cake flour is the softest of all, to give a delicate crumb. Many bakers use unbleached flour in their pie crust and wonder why it turns out tough. *Use the flour indicated in the recipe.* In this book, "all-purpose flour" means the *bleached* kind.

Sugar Products: *Granulated* sugar is a generic product, and you can use any brand. *Brown* sugar comes in two varieties, light and dark. The dark sugar has a deeper flavor, but essentially they are interchangeable. Brown sugar is always dry-measured in packed, level amounts. *Molasses* is a by-product of sugar refining. It is important to use the right kind, as the acidity is different in each of the three varieties and could react differently with the leavenings in the batter. I use unsulphured molasses, which has the most rounded flavor. The other two types are sulphured (sometimes labeled "robust") and blackstrap (which is very bitter; it can be found at natural food stores, as what it lacks in delicacy, it makes up for in vitamin content), but I only mention them so you don't use them by accident. As with brown sugar, *corn syrup* comes in light and dark varieties, and can be switched according to taste. To measure molasses and corn syrup, use a glass cup sprayed lightly with nonstick vegetable oil so the liquid won't stick to the cup.

Butter: Using unsalted butter allows the baker to control the amount of salt in the recipe. Also, salting hides off flavors, so unsalted butter has a shorter shelf life, and is therefore likely to be fresher. Do not substitute margarine for butter in any of these desserts. Margarine has a totally different consistency from butter, and the recipes, especially piecrusts, may not work.

Eggs: Use USDA Grade A "large" eggs. There is a big difference between small and jumbo eggs, and using the wrong size will lead to problems.

Decorating: When it comes to decorating desserts, keep it simple. A few swirls of whipped cream or a dusting of confectioners' sugar is all most desserts need. However, with very little trouble, you can pipe the cream through a pastry bag and give the dessert a professional, finished look.

Buy a moderately large capacity pastry bag, so you only have to fill it once. A makeshift pastry bag can be created from clipping the corner from a heavy-duty plastic storage bag.

I use only a handful of decorating tips for almost all garnishing jobs. Large open-star tips, such as Ateco numbers 4, 5, and 6, are the most versatile,

and their size allows you to cover a lot of surface quickly. With a small twist of the wrist, you can produce rosettes, stars, and curls. I don't feel I even need to give instructions, because when you give it a try, your imagination will take over. Pastry bags and large decorating tips are available at restaurant supply outlets and most kitchenware stores.

Cooking Desserts for a Crowd: If you want to bake two or more cakes, you should make them one at a time; don't double the recipe. If the batter includes baking soda or baking powder, the leavening needs will change with the volume of batter. Pie fillings, cheesecakes, and other desserts are much more forgiving, and recipes can be multiplied as needed.

Perfect Piecrust 101

Makes one 9- or 10-inch single or double piecrust depending on proportions used

Make Ahead: See the various suggestions below.

Granted, many Thanksgiving cooks rely on frozen or refrigerated piecrusts, but homemade piecrust tastes immeasurably better. Piecrust is one of those kitchen skills that make a cook's reputation.

Leave any doubts you may have about making piecrust behind. I have taught hundreds of people how to make this dough. It has all of the qualities that make a perfect crust—it's flaky yet crisp, tender, and golden. The recipe is lengthy not because it's difficult, but because the key to making good piecrust is understanding the details.

• *Cold temperatures help a piecrust maintain its flakiness and shape. The fats for a piecrust should be chilled (in warm kitchens, the flour can be chilled as well) and the water ice-cold (but with ice cubes removed). The idea is to work the fat into the flour to create tiny, flour-coated pellets. The dough is held together with ice water, which helps keep the fat distinct—warm water would soften the fat. When the dough is rolled out, the fat is flattened into flakes. When the dough is baked, the fat creates steam, which lifts the dough into flaky layers.*

• *Handle the dough as little as possible. As dough is mixed, the gluten is activated and starts to strengthen, so use a light hand. Mix the dough just until it is completely moistened and begins to clump and hold together without crumbling when pressed between your thumb and forefinger. Then chill the dough for at least 20 minutes to allow the activated gluten to relax (a cool place keeps the fat flakes chilled and distinct). If the dough is rolled out too soon, the gluten contracts and the crust shrinks. After the piecrust is fitted into the pan, it should be refrigerated for at least 30 minutes to allow the gluten to relax again.*

• *The type of fat used in the dough is another important factor. Americans love flaky piecrust, which is made with vegetable shortening (or lard). Butter makes a crisp crust with a texture closer to crisp, crumbly French tart crust or shortbread. This recipe benefits from both fats. For an excellent crust with an old-fashioned flavor that works beautifully with apple or mincemeat pie, substitute lard for the shortening and butter. Measure shortening in a dry measure in level amounts. Or, use stick shortening—a real boon to the piecrust maker.*

• *Some recipes use only ice water to bind the dough. I add an egg yolk (a fatty protein that adds richness and color) and vinegar (an acid that tenderizes the gluten). I also use a little sugar for tenderness and for browning. A bit of salt is imperative to enhance the flavors.*

• *A pastry blender (usually made of flexible wire, but some models have stiff metal blades) is the best*

tool for cutting the fat into the flour. An electric hand mixer also works well, set at low speed. Or, use a food processor, but freeze the fats first—the friction from the spinning metal blade can melt the fat. If you mix the dough in the work bowl, pulse just until the dough clumps together. If overprocessed into a ball, the dough will be tough. It's safer to transfer the dry fat/flour mixture to a mixing bowl and stir in the chilled liquids by hand.

• *The amount of liquid will always vary because of the humidity in the atmosphere when you mix the dough. Stir in just enough liquid to make the dough clump together. If you need more liquid, use additional ice water.*

• *A large heavy rolling pin is better than a small light one, because its weight makes it easier to roll out the dough. If you have a small (12-inch) rolling pin, be careful that the edges of the pin don't dig into the dough as you roll it out.*

• *Allow enough space to roll out the dough—at least 2 feet square. When I had a small kitchen with no counter space, rolling out pie dough was a feat for a contortionist. I finally went out and bought a large wooden pastry board to set up on my dining room table and roll out the dough with some elbow room. My life as a baker was changed, and I have been happily baking pies ever since.*

• *The technique for rolling out the dough (starting at the center of the dough and moving it a quarter turn after each roll) gradually creates a well-shaped pastry round that doesn't stick to the work surface. To be sure it isn't sticking, occasionally slide a long metal spatula or knife under the dough. If needed, sprinkle more flour under and on top of the dough.*

• *Pyrex pie pans give the best results. Their transparency allows the baker to see how the bottom crust is browning, and their thickness allows the heat to be more evenly distributed than metal pans.*

• *These recipes yield generous amounts of dough. When I was a beginning baker, nothing was more* exasperating than making recipes that yielded barely enough dough to line the pan. After you line the pan, simply trim the excess dough from the edges.

• Dough scraps can be cut into decorative shapes to decorate the top of a double-crust pie. Gather up the scraps, knead briefly, and reroll into a ½-inch-thick circle. Using cookie cutters or a cardboard template, cut out the desired shapes, such as leaves or stars. Arrange them on the glazed crust, then brush the shapes lightly with more glaze.

• To bake crisp bottom crusts, bake the pie on a preheated baking sheet. The pie will be sitting on a hot flat surface, instead of the oven rack, and crisp better.

• Baking an empty pie shell is called "baking blind." Sometimes an unfilled crust is only partially baked, which sets the shape and dries the surface, discouraging a soggy bottom crust from developing when it comes in contact with a wet filling. Other recipes call for the pie shell to be completely baked, until golden brown, usually to hold a finished filling, like the one in Dark Chocolate Cream Pie on page 121. In either case, the raw pie crust would collapse in the oven if not supported with aluminum foil and some kind of weights until it baked long enough to hold its shape. The amount of fat in the piecrust keeps the foil from sticking, so there's no need to grease it. Aluminum or ceramic pie weights are a very good investment, if you like to bake pies, as they absorb the oven heat and help crisp the crust. They aren't cheap, but they last for years. Dried beans and raw rice are inexpensive alternatives, and can be saved in a jar to use again and again.

• The dough can be prepared up to 2 days ahead, wrapped in wax paper, and refrigerated. Let stand at room temperature for 10 minutes before rolling out, or it may crack.

• The dough can be frozen, wrapped in wax paper and an overwrap of aluminum foil, for up to 1 month. Defrost in the refrigerator overnight.

• Unbaked pie shells can be kept in the pie pans,

covered tightly with a double covering of plastic wrap, for up to 2 weeks. Do not defrost before baking. Bake the frozen piecrust as directed, allowing an extra 5 minutes. However, unless you have a big freezer, it may be more space-efficient to freeze the unrolled dough.

Single Crust (for a 9- to 10-inch pie)
1½ cups all-purpose flour
1 tablespoon sugar
¼ teaspoon salt
⅓ cup plus 1 tablespoon vegetable shortening, chilled and cut into ½-inch cubes
3 tablespoons unsalted butter, chilled and cut into ½-inch cubes
¼ cup ice-cold water
1 large egg yolk
½ teaspoon cider or wine vinegar

Double Crust (for a 9- to 10-inch pie)
2¼ cups all-purpose flour
1½ tablespoons sugar
½ teaspoon salt
½ cup plus 1 tablespoon vegetable shortening, chilled and cut into ½-inch cubes
5 tablespoons unsalted butter, chilled and cut into ½-inch cubes
⅓ cup plus 1 tablespoon ice-cold water
1 large egg yolk
¾ teaspoon cider or wine vinegar

1. In a large bowl, mix the flour, sugar, and salt until combined. Using a pastry blender, rapidly cut in the shortening and butter until the mixture is the consistency of coarse bread crumbs, with some pea-sized pieces. Do not blend to a fine cornmeal-like consistency. If the fats stick to the wires of the blender, scrape them off.

2. In a glass measuring cup, mix the ice water, egg yolk, and vinegar. Tossing the flour mixture with a fork, gradually add the ice water mixture, sprinkling it over the ingredients in the bowl. Mix well, being sure to moisten the crumbs on the bottom of the bowl. Add just enough liquid so the dough clumps together. It does not have to come together into one big ball. To check the consistency, press some dough between your thumb and forefinger. The dough should be moist but not wet, and not crumbly. If necessary, gradually mix in more liquid or additional ice water, 1 teaspoon at a time, until you reach the correct consistency.

3. Gather up the dough into a thick disk and wrap in wax paper. (Wax paper is better than plastic wrap, because the plastic wrap can trap moisture in the pastry and create a sticky exterior.) *If making a double-crust pie,* divide the dough into two disks, one slightly larger than the other. Refrigerate the dough for at least 1 hour and up to 2 days. Let the dough stand at room temperature for 10 minutes before rolling out.

4. *To roll out a single crust,* sprinkle the work surface (preferably a pastry or cutting board) lightly but completely with flour, then spread out the flour with the palm of your hand into a very thin layer. Place the dough on the work surface, then sprinkle the top of the dough with a little flour. Don't bother to sprinkle the rolling pin with flour—it just falls off. Starting at the center of the disk, roll the dough away from you. Do not roll back and forth. (See illustration 1, page 115.) (If the dough cracks as you are rolling out, it may be too cold. Let it stand for a few minutes to warm up slightly, then try again.) Turn the dough a quarter turn. (Illustration 2.) Roll out again from the center of the dough. Continue rolling out the dough, always starting from the center of the dough and turning it a quarter turn after each roll, until the dough is about 13 inches in diameter and $\frac{1}{8}$ inch thick. (If you aren't sure what $\frac{1}{8}$ inch looks like, stand a ruler up next to the dough and check. This sounds elementary, but many bakers make the mistake of rolling out the

dough too thin or too thick, and until you learn by practice, a ruler is the best insurance.) Be sure that the dough is the same thickness throughout, especially at the edges, which tend to be thicker than the center. Work as quickly as possible so the dough doesn't get too warm. (Illustration 3.)

5. Carefully fold the dough into quarters. (Illustration 4.) If you think the dough is too warm to fold without tearing, transfer the entire board to a cool place—if it's a cold day, outside, on a windowsill, or in an unheated room is fine—for a few minutes to firm up. Transfer the dough to the pie pan, with the point in the center of the pan. Unfold the dough, letting the excess dough hang over the sides of the pan. Gently press the dough snugly into the corners of the pan. (If the dough cracks, just press the cracks together. Gaps can be patched with scraps of dough, moistened lightly around the edges so they adhere to the crust.) Using kitchen scissors or a sharp knife, trim the dough to extend only $\frac{1}{2}$ inch beyond the edge of the pan.

6. *To flute the crust,* fold over the dough so the folded edge is flush with the edge of the pan. Use one hand to pinch the dough around the knuckle or fingertip of your other hand, at 1-inch intervals around the crust. (Illustration 6.) Cover the dough with plastic wrap and refrigerate until ready to use, for at least 20 and up to 30 minutes. (To reduce crust shrinkage, refrigerate for 20 minutes, then freeze for 20 more minutes.)

7. *To roll out a double crust,* roll out the larger dough disk, place in the pan, and trim the edges so they hang about $\frac{1}{2}$ inch over the pan. Fill the pie with the cooled filling, if necessary. Immediately roll out the smaller disk of dough into a 10- to 11-inch round about $\frac{1}{8}$ inch thick. Fold the dough in half, position it over the filling, and unfold. (Illustration 7.) Press the edges of the two crusts together to seal. Using kitchen scissors or a sharp knife, trim the dough to extend only $\frac{1}{2}$ inch beyond the edge of the pan. Flute the dough as directed in Step 6.

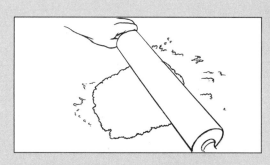

1. Starting at the center of the disk, roll the dough away from you in one direction. Do not roll back and forth.

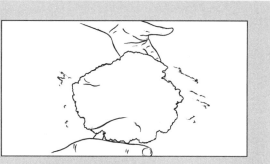

2. Turn the dough a quarter turn.

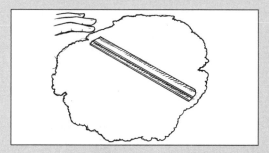

3. Continue rolling out the dough, always starting from the center of the dough and turning it a quarter turn after each roll, until the dough is about 13 inches in diameter and ⅛ inch thick. Be sure that the dough is the same thickness throughout. Work quickly so the dough doesn't become too warm.

4. Carefully fold the dough into quarters. If the dough is too warm to fold without breaking, and the dough is on a cutting board, move the board to a cool place for a few minutes to firm up. Transfer the dough to the pie pan, with the point in the center of the pan.

5. Unfold the dough, letting the excess dough hang over the sides of the pan.

6. Use one hand to pinch the dough around the knuckle or fingertip of your other hand at 1-inch intervals around the crust.

7. For a double crust, fold the dough in half, position over the filling, and unfold.

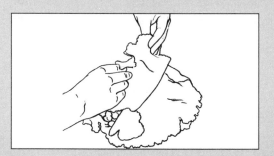

Classic Recipe:
Famous Pumpkin Pie

Makes 8 servings

Make Ahead: The pie can be baked up to 1 day ahead.

This recipe has been on the can of Libby's Solid Pack Pumpkin for more than thirty years—mildly spiced, smooth, and just about perfect. Not for nothing is it truly "famous." Libby's estimates that more than fifty-five million pumpkin pies are made from their canned pumpkin every Thanksgiving. For classic results, mix the ingredients by hand in the order given.

There are a number of crust options, all with slightly different oven temperatures and cooking times. Homemade piecrust makes the best pie, so I start with those directions, giving variations for frozen deep-dish and regular piecrusts. To be sure the crust holds all of the filling, it is important to flute the pie crust to stand high around the edge of the pan. If you still have a little too much filling, just discard it.

A crack will appear in the filling where the pie was tested with the knife. To disguise it, just spread a thin layer of whipped cream over the top. With experience, you will be able to test the pie without cutting into it—when the pie is shaken, only the very center of the pie should jiggle.

Perfect Piecrust 101 for a Single-Crust Pie
 (page 111)

2 large eggs, slightly beaten

One 15-ounce can Libby's Solid Pack Pumpkin
 (1³/₄ cups)

³/₄ cup sugar

¹/₂ teaspoon salt

1 teaspoon ground cinnamon

¹/₂ teaspoon ground ginger

¹/₄ teaspoon ground cloves

One 12-ounce can evaporated milk or 1¹/₂ cups
 half-and-half

Sweetened Whipped Cream (page 137)

1. Following the instructions on page 114, line a 9-inch pie pan with the pie dough. Flute the dough so the edge stands about ¹/₂ inch above the rim. (Libby's does not suggest this, but to reduce crust shrinkage, loosely cover the shell with plastic wrap, refrigerate for 30 minutes.)

2. Position a rack in the bottom third of the oven and place a baking sheet on the rack. Preheat the oven to 425°F.

3. In the order given, place all the remaining ingredients except the whipped cream in a large bowl and mix well. Pour the filling into the pie shell. Place on the hot baking sheet. Bake for 15 minutes. Reduce the oven temperature to 350°F and bake until a knife inserted near the center comes out clean, 40 to 50 minutes. Cool completely on a wire cake rack. Cover with plastic wrap and refrigerate until ready to serve. (The pie can be baked up to 1 day ahead.) Serve chilled, with the whipped cream.

Deep-Dish Pumpkin Pie (made with frozen crust): Substitute one 9-inch (4-cup capacity) deep-dish frozen pie shell for the homemade crust. Preheat the oven, and a baking sheet, as above, to 375°F. While the oven preheats, allow the crust to thaw for 20 minutes. Recrimp the pie shell so the edge stands ¹/₂ inch above the rim. Pour the filling into the crust and bake until the pie tests done with a knife as above, about 70 minutes.

Double-Batch Pumpkin Pie (made with frozen crusts): The pumpkin mixture will fill two regular (not deep-dish) piecrusts. Let the crusts thaw slightly while you mix the filling. Preheat the oven, and a baking sheet, as above, to 375°F. Pour the filling into the crusts and bake until the pies test done as above, about 45 minutes.

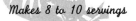

Berkshire Pumpkin Pie

Makes 8 to 10 servings

Make Ahead: The pie can be baked up to 1 day ahead.

For many years, I spent Thanksgiving with my friend Ron Dier in the picture-perfect Berkshire Mountains on the border between New York and Massachusetts. Ron always made this pumpkin pie according to his mom's recipe. Its light texture and generous spicing had everyone coming back for more. In fact, many times when there was pie left when we cleared the table, it would be gone the next morning because we had all tiptoed into the kitchen during the night and devoured it in the time-honored tradition of the Thanksgiving Midnight Snack. If you are looking for an extra-special pumpkin pie, look no further.

Perfect Piecrust 101 for a Single-Crust Pie
   (page 111)
One 15-ounce can solid pack pumpkin (1³/₄
   cups)
1 cup heavy cream
²/₃ cup granulated sugar
¹/₂ cup packed light brown sugar
2 tablespoons all-purpose flour
1¹/₂ teaspoons ground cinnamon
1 teaspoon ground ginger
1 teaspoon freshly grated nutmeg
¹/₄ teaspoon ground cloves
¹/₄ teaspoon salt
3 large eggs, at room temperature
Sweetened Whipped Cream (page 137)

1. Following the instructions on page 114, line a 10-inch pie pan with the pie dough. Cover loosely with plastic wrap. Refrigerate for 30 minutes.

2. Position the rack in the top third of the oven.

Place a baking sheet on the rack and preheat the oven to 400°F.

3. Line the pastry shell with aluminum foil, then fill with pie weights, dried beans, or raw rice. Bake on the hot baking sheet until the pastry seems set, about 12 minutes. Remove the foil and weights and set the pie shell aside. Leave the oven on.

4. In a medium bowl, whisk together all of the filling ingredients except the eggs (and whipped cream) until smooth. In another medium bowl, using a hand-held electric mixer set at high speed, beat the eggs until very light and tripled in volume, about 3 minutes. Fold the eggs into the pumpkin mixture. Pour into the pie shell.

5. Place on the hot baking sheet and bake for 15 minutes, then reduce the heat to 350°F. Continue baking until a knife inserted into the filling 2 inches from the center comes out clean, 40 to 50 minutes. The center will seem slightly unset when the pie is shaken, but will firm upon standing. Let cool completely on a wire cake rack, then cover with plastic wrap and refrigerate until chilled, at least 2 hours, or overnight. Serve chilled or at room temperature, with the whipped cream.

Down-Home Pecan and Bourbon Pie

Makes 8 servings

Make Ahead: The pie can be baked up to 2 days ahead.

Pecan pie is another one of those American desserts that seem to have been around forever. Pecans, a native nut, were grown on the estates of Washington and Jefferson. But, Jean Anderson, in her American Century Cookbook, *says that she cannot find a cookbook reference to it until the 1940s. Food historian Meryle Evans*

It Wouldn't Be Thanksgiving Without . . . Pumpkin Pie

Pumpkin pie was certainly not included in the first feast. The *Mayflower*'s stores of wheat had long been depleted, and the first planting had failed. No wheat, no piecrust. As with so many other foods, the Indians taught the Pilgrims about pumpkin. Along with beans and corn, it was one of the three major foods in the Native American diet throughout the continent. There is some argument over the pumpkin's origin. Some botanists say it is a New World vegetable, and others claim it was known in Europe before the Exploration Age. It is likely, however, that the European "pumpkins" in the pre-Columbus era were really gourds, and that we can truly claim the pumpkin as an American native that deserves a place of honor at the Thanksgiving meal.

The Indians probably roasted pumpkin over an open fire or boiled it with maple syrup. Pumpkin pudding became one of the favorite dishes of the Puritan era. The pumpkin flesh was scooped out, mixed with milk, spices, and syrup, then returned to the pumpkin shell, where it was roasted for hours in hot ashes. It is easy to see where the basic recipe for pumpkin pie filling came from. Known to the settlers as *pompion* (the name given by French explorers in the late 1500s), pumpkin saved them from starvation in the lean early years of their colony.

One of the first recipes for pumpkin pie appeared in 1655 in a British book called *Queens Closed Open*. This version represents the then-current taste for highly seasoned foods, and includes thyme, rosemary, cinnamon, nutmeg, pepper, cloves, and apple. In 1672, an English-American merchant named John Josselyn was already calling pompion stew "an Ancient New-England dish." He says to take diced ripe squash and ". . . so fill a pot with them of two or three gallons, stew them upon a gentle fire a whole day, then as they sink . . . fill again with fresh pompions not putting any liquor to them and when it is stirred enough it will look like baked Apples, this Dish putting Butter to it and Vinegar and some Spice as Ginger which makes it tart like an Apple, and so serve it up to be eaten with fish or flesh." Josselyn's "stew" would be recognized today as the pumpkin butter put up by New England cooks. Amelia Simmons included "pompkin" pie in the first American cookbook, published in 1796.

The history of the modern pumpkin pie can be dated back to 1929. In that year, Libby, McNeil and Libby bought a small pumpkin pie cannery, Dickinson Canning Company. The little cannery's pride and joy was its special eating pumpkin, now called the Dickinson variety. Eating pumpkins, very different from the Jack-o'-lantern varieties grown for their size and appearance, are elongated and buff-colored with thin walls. The Dickinson is noted for its bright orange color, creamy texture, and fresh taste. Libby's took years to develop its own strain, improving upon the Dickinson, called "Libby's Select." Today, Libby's, a division of Nestlé, Inc., plants more than four thousand acres of pumpkins annually.

believes the first instance of the modern pie showed up in 1925, and thinks it may have been the invention of Karo syrup home economists. (Older recipes are made with brown sugar and without corn syrup.) Karo was introduced in 1902, during the early-twentieth-century American food revolution, when canned and bottled products were replacing homemade goods with alarming speed. Consumers were anxious to try these new foods that promised to increase their leisure time. Product-sponsored cookbooks were all the rage, and when a new recipe showed up on the back of, for example, a corn syrup can, it could quickly gain fans.

This version is less sweet than most. A little bourbon works wonders, cutting through the richness and adding a gentle aroma. If you'll have kids around, you can leave out the bourbon and still have a darned fine pie. There are two schools of thought about the pecans. One camp uses coarsely chopped pecans so the pie is easier to slice. The opposition arranges the whole pecan halves in concentric circles in the pie crust before pouring in the filling, so the pie has a beautiful symmetrical design after baking. For the nuttiest filling, sprinkle chopped pecans over the crust, then top with the pecan halves. Just have a good sharp thin-bladed knife handy for slicing.

Perfect Piecrust 101 for a Single-Crust Pie
  (page 111)

3 large eggs

¹/₂ cup packed light brown sugar

1 cup light corn syrup

4 tablespoons (¹/₂ stick) unsalted butter, melted

2 tablespoons bourbon

1 teaspoon vanilla extract

9 ounces pecan halves (2 heaping cups)

Sweetened Whipped Cream (page 137)

1. Following the directions on page 114, line a 9-inch pie pan with the pie dough. Cover loosely with plastic wrap. Refrigerate for 30 minutes.

2. Position a rack in the bottom third of the oven and place a baking sheet on the rack. Preheat the oven to 425°F.

3. In a medium bowl, whisk the eggs. Rub the brown sugar through a sieve into the bowl (this removes any lumps in the sugar). Add the corn syrup, melted butter, bourbon, and vanilla and whisk until well combined.

4. To gauge exactly how many pecan halves are needed to decorate the pie, arrange pecan halves in concentric circles in a 9-inch round on the work surface. Gather up the pecan halves and set aside. Coarsely chop the remaining pecan halves and sprinkle over the crust. Arrange the unchopped pecan halves in circles on top. Carefully pour the filling into the crust.

5. Place the pie on the hot baking sheet and bake for 15 minutes. Reduce the oven temperature to 350°F. Continue baking until the topping is puffed around the edges and a knife inserted 1 inch from the center comes out clean, 30 to 35 more minutes. Cool completely on a wire cake rack. (The pie can be baked up to 2 days ahead, cooled, covered tightly with plastic wrap, and refrigerated.) Serve at room temperature, with the whipped cream.

Florida Sweet Potato Pie

Makes 8 servings

Make Ahead: The pie can be baked up to 1 day ahead.

Down South, sweet potato pie holds the place of honor as the favorite Thanksgiving dessert. But if candied yams were served at dinner, a sweet potato pie might be overkill, even south of the Mason-Dixon line. One year, I solved the problem by serving small slivers of this pie (without the whipped cream) as a side dish, figuring that it's no sweeter than the usual recipes you often find next to the turkey on your plate, and my guests loved it. Oranges, in the form of marmalade, give this version a special fillip. (After all, Florida is a Southern state.)

Piecrust 101 for a Single-Crust Pie (page 111)

2 medium orange-fleshed sweet potatoes or
  yams (1 pound), scrubbed but unpeeled

2 tablespoons unsalted butter

$1/2$ cup orange marmalade

$1/3$ cup packed dark brown sugar

$1/4$ teaspoon ground cinnamon

$1/4$ teaspoon salt

2 large eggs plus 1 large egg yolk, beaten
  together

1 cup half-and-half

About 20 pecan halves

Sweetened Whipped Cream (page 137)

1. Following the directions on page 114, line a 10-inch pie plate with the piecrust and flute the edges. Cover loosely with plastic wrap and refrigerate for 30 minutes.

2. Position a rack in the bottom third of the oven and place a baking sheet on the rack. Preheat the oven to 400°F.

3. Remove the plastic wrap and line the pastry shell with aluminum foil, then fill with pie weights, dried beans, or raw rice. Bake on the hot baking sheet until the pastry seems set, about 12 minutes. Remove the foil and weights and set the pie shell aside. Leave the oven on.

4. Meanwhile, bring a large pan of salted water to a boil over high heat. Add the sweet potatoes and cook until tender, about 30 minutes. Drain and rinse under cold water until easy to handle, then peel and place in a medium bowl.

5. Add the butter to the sweet potatoes and mash with a hand-held electric mixer set at low speed until smooth. Beat in the orange marmalade, brown sugar, cinnamon, and salt, then beat in the eggs and half-and-half. Pour into the pie shell and smooth the top. Arrange the pecan halves around the edge of the pie.

6. Place on the hot baking sheet and bake for 10 minutes, then reduce the oven temperature to 350°F. Continue baking until a knife inserted into the center of the filling comes out clean, about 45 more minutes. Transfer to a wire cake rack and cool completely. (The pie can be baked up to 1 day ahead, covered with plastic wrap, and refrigerated.) Serve at room temperature, with the whipped cream.

Dark Chocolate Cream Pie

Makes 8 servings

Make Ahead: The pie, without the cream topping, can be prepared up to 1 day ahead.

Everyone knows that pumpkin, apple, and mince-meat pies are Thanksgiving favorites. I was surprised to hear how many of my friends included chocolate cream pie in their lineup. In my family, Mom's chocolate cream is the most beloved of all her pies. For the deepest chocolate flavor, use an imported bittersweet chocolate like Lindt or Valhrona, or a high-quality dark American brand like Chocolove.

Perfect Piecrust 101 for a Single-Crust Pie
 (page 111)

3 cups half-and-half

²/₃ cup plus 2 tablespoons sugar

¹/₈ teaspoon salt

3 tablespoons cornstarch

4 large egg yolks

4 ounces high-quality bittersweet or semisweet
 chocolate, finely chopped

2 tablespoons unsalted butter

1 teaspoon vanilla extract

1 cup heavy cream

1. Following the instructions on page 114, line a 9-inch pie pan with the pie dough and flute the edges. Cover loosely with plastic wrap. Refrigerate for 30 minutes.

2. Position a rack in the lower third of the oven and place a baking sheet on the rack. Preheat the oven to 400°F.

3. Remove the plastic wrap and line the pastry shell with aluminum foil, then fill with pie weights, dried beans, or raw rice. Bake on the hot baking sheet until the pastry seems set, about 10 minutes. Lift up and remove the foil and weights. Continue baking until the pie shell is golden brown, about 10 more minutes. Transfer to a wire cake rack and cool completely.

4. In a medium saucepan over medium heat, heat 2¹/₂ cups of the half-and-half, ²/₃ cup of the sugar, and the salt, stirring often to dissolve the sugar, until tiny bubbles appear around the edges. Remove from the heat.

5. In a medium bowl, sprinkle the cornstarch over the remaining ¹/₂ cup half-and-half and whisk until dissolved. Whisk in the egg yolks. Gradually whisk in the hot half-and-half mixture, and return to the rinsed-out saucepan. Cook over medium heat, stirring constantly with a flat wooden spatula (to keep the custard from scorching on the bottom of the saucepan), until the custard comes to boil. Reduce the heat to medium-low and simmer, stirring constantly, for 1 minute. Remove from the heat, add the chocolate, butter, and ¹/₂ teaspoon of the vanilla, and stir until the chocolate melts completely.

6. Pour into the cooled baked pie shell and smooth the top. Butter a piece of wax paper and place it, buttered side down, directly on the surface of the filling. Pierce a few slits in the wax paper with the tip of a sharp knife (this keeps a skin from forming on the filling). Cool completely. Refrigerate until chilled, at least 4 hours, or overnight.

7. Just before serving, in a chilled medium bowl, using a hand-held electric mixer set at high speed, beat the cream with the remaining 2 tablespoons sugar and ¹/₂ teaspoon vanilla just until stiff. Remove the waxed paper and spread the whipped cream over the filling. Serve chilled.

Chocolate Banana Cream Pie: Thinly slice 2 ripe bananas and place in the baked pie shell before adding the chocolate filling.

Apple Pie 101

Makes 8 to 10 servings

Make Ahead: See the suggestions below.

For American bakers, the perfect apple pie is the holy grail of desserts. A perfect apple pie has a sweet-tart, chunky, mildly spiced apple filling that doesn't collapse when baked. A number of my friends suggested precooking the apples for the filling—and the trick worked like a charm, as the apples shrink in the skillet, not in the crust. Also, the released apple juices reduce and thicken in the skillet, so the apple flavor intensifies. Allow about an hour for the apple filling to cool completely before putting it into the crust.

- *A good pie apple isn't too sweet and doesn't break up when cooked. Some apples, like Jonathan and McIntosh, are best for eating out of hand, or cooking into applesauce. Unfortunately, a raw apple won't reveal what it is like when it's cooked, even if it tastes delicious. I usually take the advice of the people at apple stands at my farmers' market—they often have some wonderful dark-horse, heirloom varieties that I would otherwise pass over. As far as supermarket apples go, Golden Delicious is my favorite. A lot of bakers like Granny Smiths, but they tend to shrink a lot. My friend Carole Walter, author of* Great Pies*, is partial to Mutsu and Cortlandt apples, separately or together. You can mix two or three varieties—Rome and Granny Smith is another good combination.*

- *For the best apple pie with a crisp, rich, old-fashioned crust, substitute lard for the shortening and butter in the dough.*

- *The filled unbaked pie can be prepared ahead, without its cream and sugar glaze, covered tightly in plastic wrap and an overwrap of aluminum foil, and frozen for up to 1 month. Glaze, then bake the frozen pie at 375°F until golden brown, about 1 hour and 15 minutes.*

- *The pie can be baked up to 2 days ahead, cooled, covered with plastic wrap, and refrigerated. Serve at room temperature.*

5 pounds Golden Delicious apples
2 tablespoons fresh lemon juice
6 tablespoons ($^3/_4$ stick) unsalted butter
$^2/_3$ cup plus 1 teaspoon sugar
3 tablespoons all-purpose flour
1 teaspoon ground cinnamon
Perfect Piecrust 101 for a Double-Crust Pie
  (page 113), preferably made with lard
2 teaspoons heavy cream or milk

1. Peel and quarter the apples, cutting out the core from each quarter. Cut each quarter into thirds and place in a large bowl. As they fill the bowl, occasionally sprinkle and toss the apples with the lemon juice. (Don't wait until all the apples are cut, or the first ones may already be turning brown.)

2. In a large nonstick skillet, melt 3 tablespoons of the butter over medium-high heat. Add half of the apples and $^1/_3$ cup of the sugar. Cook, stirring often, until the apples are barely tender when pierced with the tip of a sharp knife, about 7 minutes. Transfer to a large roasting pan or rimmed baking sheet. Repeat with the remaining butter and apples and another $^1/_3$ cup sugar. (If your nonstick skillet is smaller than 12 inches, cook the apples in three batches.) Cool completely, stirring occasionally.

3. Position a rack in the center of the oven and place a baking sheet on the rack. Preheat the oven to 375°F.

4. Sprinkle the flour and cinnamon over the cooled filling and toss well. Following the directions for a double-crust pie on page 113, line a 10-inch pie pan with the bottom crust. Fill with the apple mixture. Cover the filling with the top crust and flute the edges. Cut a small hole in the center of the top piecrust. (The unbaked pie can be prepared up to 1 month ahead, covered tightly in plastic wrap and an overwrap of aluminum foil, and frozen.) Brush the top of the pie lightly with the heavy cream. If desired, cut out decorative shapes from the dough scraps, place them on the top crust, and brush lightly with heavy cream. Sprinkle with the remaining 1 teaspoon sugar.

5. Place the pie on the hot baking sheet and bake until the top is golden brown, 40 to 50 minutes (about 1 hour and 15 minutes for a frozen pie). Cool on a wire cake rack for 30 minutes. Serve warm or at room temperature.

New-Fashioned Mincemeat Pie

Makes 8 to 10 servings

Make Ahead: The mincemeat can be prepared up to 1 week ahead; the pie can be baked up to 1 day ahead.

A simmering pot of mincemeat announces the holiday season with its heady, spicy aroma. As dried fruits were served at the first Thanksgiving, this fruit-packed pie is an appropriate dessert for today's feast. It's an updated mincemeat that breaks with tradition, but in ways that most people would approve of. To replace the store-bought candied peel that no one really likes anyway, use homemade. (It's very easy to do, but allow time for it to dry overnight.) The suet and beef from the old recipes are gone, and the fruit flavor has been increased with apple juice concentrate, which also acts as a sweetener. Some mincemeat is aged for months, but this one is ready to go the day after it's made. The result is a multicolored and deeply flavored mélange that tastes different with every bite.

1 large navel orange (see Note)

1 large lemon (see Note)

1 1/2 cups granulated sugar, plus extra (optional) for rolling

1/3 cup light corn syrup

2 Golden Delicious apples, peeled and grated (use the large holes on a box grater)

One 12-ounce can frozen apple juice concentrate, thawed

1 packed cup (3 ounces) chopped dried apples

3/4 cup (3 ounces) raisins

3/4 cup (3 ounces) golden raisins

3/4 cup (3 ounces) dried currants

3/4 cup (3 ounces) dried cranberries

1/2 cup packed dark brown sugar

1/2 cup dark rum

1/2 cup cognac or brandy

4 tablespoons (1/2 stick) unsalted butter

1/2 teaspoon ground cinnamon

1/2 teaspoon ground allspice

1/2 teaspoon freshly grated nutmeg

1/2 teaspoon ground cloves

Perfect Piecrust 101 for a Double-Crust Pie (page 113)

1. Using a sharp knife, cut the thick peel off the orange and lemon in wide strips, cutting down to the fruit. Cut into long strips about 1/2 inch wide. Place in a medium saucepan and cover with cold water. Bring to a boil over high heat, then reduce the heat to medium and cook at a gentle boil for 5 minutes. Drain and rinse under cold running water. Return the peel to the pan, cover with water, and repeat the procedure.

2. In a medium saucepan, bring the granulated sugar, corn syrup, and 1 1/4 cups water to a boil, stirring to dissolve the sugar. Add the orange and lemon peels and reduce the heat to medium-low. Simmer until the peels are translucent and tender, about 30 minutes. Drain the peels. Arrange the peels, not touching each other, on a wire cake rack set over a baking sheet. Let stand at room temperature overnight. (The candied peel can be prepared up to 5 days ahead. Roll the peels in granulated sugar, and store airtight at room temperature.)

3. Chop the candied citrus peels into ½-inch pieces. In a large Dutch oven, bring the candied peels, the apples, apple juice concentrate, dried apples, raisins, golden raisins, currants, cranberries, brown sugar, rum, cognac, butter, cinnamon, allspice, nutmeg, and cloves to a boil over medium heat, stirring often. Reduce the heat to medium-low and cook, stirring often, until the fruits are softened and the liquid has almost completely evaporated, about 25 minutes. Transfer to a medium bowl and cool completely. Cover tightly with plastic wrap and refrigerate overnight, or for up to 1 week.

4. Position a rack in the bottom third of the oven and place a baking sheet on the rack. Preheat to 375°F. Following the directions for a double-crust pie on page 113, line a 10-inch pie pan with the bottom crust. Fill with the mincemeat. Cover the filling with the top crust and flute the edges. Cut a small hole in the center of the pie.

5. Place the pie on the hot baking sheet and bake until the top is golden brown and you can see the mincemeat bubbling through the center hole, about 40 minutes. Cool on a wire cake rack for 30 minutes. Serve warm or at room temperature.

Note: If desired, substitute ⅔ cup store-bought candied orange peel (or the grated zest of 1 large orange) and ⅓ cup store-bought candied lemon peel (or the grated zest of 1 large lemon) for the homemade candied peels.

Cranberry-Ginger Tart with Chocolate Drizzle

Makes 8 servings

Make Ahead: The tart can be prepared up to 1 day ahead.

This is a sophisticated combination of ingredients that grownups will love—tart cranberries, zesty ginger, and bittersweet chocolate. (You may want to have another, less adult pie to serve to the kids.) And, it's easy to make, thanks to a sweet pastry dough that doesn't need to be rolled out before baking. Just press it into the buttered tart pan, and you're in business. In the recipe for Perfect Piecrust 101 (page 111), I warn against mixing pie dough in the food processor. But this dough uses more sugar, which tenderizes the crust and keeps the flour's gluten from toughening in the processor. Still, take care not to overprocess the dough.

Sweet Tart Dough
1 cup all-purpose flour
3 tablespoons sugar
¼ teaspoon salt
6 tablespoons (¾ stick) unsalted butter, chilled and cut into ½-inch cubes
1 large egg yolk

Cranberry Filling
One 12-ounce bag fresh cranberries
1 cup sugar
¼ cup finely chopped crystallized ginger
1 tablespoon cornstarch
1 ounce high-quality bittersweet chocolate, finely chopped
Sweetened Whipped Cream (page 137)

1. Position a rack in the center of the oven and place a baking sheet on the rack. Preheat to 400°F.

Lightly butter a 9-inch round tart pan with a removable bottom.

2. To make the tart dough, in a food processor, pulse the flour, sugar, and salt to combine. Add the butter and pulse 10 to 15 times, until the mixture resembles coarse crumbs. In a small bowl, mix the egg yolk with 2 tablespoons water. With the machine running, add the yolk mixture and process just until the dough is moistened. It will look crumbly, but should hold together when pressed between your thumb and forefinger. If necessary, sprinkle with 1 teaspoon water, pulse briefly, and check again. Do not overprocess the dough.

3. Press the dough evenly into the bottom and up the sides of the prepared tart pan. Using a fork, prick the dough a few times. Line the dough with aluminum foil and weight with pie weights, dried beans, or raw rice. Freeze for 10 minutes.

4. Place the pan on the hot baking sheet. Bake until the pastry seems set, about 10 minutes. Lift up and remove the foil and weights. Continue baking until the tart shell is golden brown, 10 to 15 more minutes. Transfer to a wire cake rack and cool completely.

5. In a large saucepan, bring the cranberries, 1 cup water, the sugar, and ginger to a boil over high heat, stirring to dissolve the sugar. Reduce the heat to medium. Cook, stirring often to avoid scorching, until the mixture is thick and reduced to about 2 ¼ cups.

6. In a small bowl, sprinkle the cornstarch over 2 tablespoons water and stir to dissolve. Stir into the cranberry mixture and boil briefly until very thick. Spread evenly in the cooled tart shell and cool completely.

7. Place the chopped chocolate in a small bowl, and set it over a small saucepan of very hot, but not simmering, water over very low heat. Melt the chocolate, stirring occasionally. Transfer to a small plastic sandwich bag. Force the chocolate into a bottom corner of the bag. Using scissors, snip off the corner to make a small opening. Squeeze the chocolate in a cross-hatch pattern over the top of the tart. Refrigerate for at least

1 hour until the chocolate is set and the tart is chilled. Serve chilled, with the whipped cream.

Caramel Cashew Tart

Makes 8 to 12 servings

Make Ahead: The tart can be prepared up to 1 day ahead.

Talk about a crowd-pleaser! There is something about the combination of caramel and cashews that everyone loves—it must remind us of a candy bar. I sent this tart off to a friend's office to get opinions, and it got such unanimous raves, I had to send a second tart to placate the disappointed people who missed the first one. A few tips: When making the caramel, be careful when adding the cream (it can bubble over if you're not alert), and allow time for the caramel to cool before adding the egg, or the filling will curdle. As good as this buttery tart is, it is candy-bar sweet, and should be served in thin slices.

Sweet Tart Dough (page 124)

³/₄ cup heavy cream

1 cup sugar

8 ounces unsalted roasted cashews (2 heaping cups)

3 tablespoons unsalted butter, melted

1 large egg, beaten

1 teaspoon vanilla extract

Sweetened Whipped Cream (page 137)

1. Position a rack in the center of the oven and place a baking sheet on the rack. Preheat to 400°F. Lightly butter a 9-inch round tart pan.

2. Press the dough evenly into the bottom and up the sides of the prepared tart pan. Using a fork, prick the dough a few times. Line the dough with aluminum foil and weight with pie weights, dried beans, or raw rice.

3. Place the pan on the hot baking sheet. Bake until the pastry seems set, about 10 minutes. Lift up and remove the foil and weights. Continue baking until the tart shell is lightly browned, about 8 more minutes. Cool the tart shell on a wire cake rack while you make the filling. Remove the baking sheet from the oven, and keep the oven at 400°F.

4. In a small saucepan, heat the cream over medium heat until small bubbles appear around the edges. (Or, heat the cream in a microwave oven, being careful that it doesn't boil over.) Set the hot cream aside.

5. In a tall medium saucepan over high heat, bring the sugar and ¼ cup water to a boil, stirring constantly to dissolve the sugar. As soon as the sugar comes to a boil, stop stirring. (Don't stir a boiling sugar syrup, or it will crystallize into a thick glop.) Boil the syrup until it turns deep amber, 3 to 5 minutes. While the syrup is boiling, occasionally swirl the pan by the handle to mix it, and wash down any sugar crystals that form on the sides of the pan by dipping a large pastry brush in cold water and rubbing the wet brush against the crystals. When the syrup is dark amber, reduce the heat to low. Being very careful, slowly stir in the hot cream. The mixture will bubbly dramatically but eventually subside. Simmer, stirring often, until slightly thickened, about 3 minutes. Pour into a medium bowl and place on another cake rack or a trivet. (The caramel will cool more quickly if air can circulate under the bowl.) Cool, stirring often, until tepid, about 1 hour.

6. Using the side of a large knife, coarsely crush about 1 cup of the cashews and spread in the tart shell. Top with the remaining whole cashews. Whisk the melted butter, egg, and vanilla into the tepid caramel. Pour the caramel mixture over the cashews.

7. Place the tart on a cool baking sheet. Bake for 15

minutes. Reduce the heat to 350°F and continue baking until the filling is bubbling in the center, about 15 more minutes. Cool the tart completely on a wire cake rack. (The tart can be baked 1 day ahead. Cover the cooled tart with plastic wrap and store at room temperature.) Serve with the whipped cream.

Drambuie Gingerbread

Makes 10 to 12 servings

Make Ahead: The cake can be prepared up to 3 days ahead.

Drambuie, a heady Scotch-based liqueur, is an excellent way to add interest to a spicy gingerbread. When I am asked to bring something to a holiday feast, my friends often request this cake. Don't cream the butter and sugar as long as you would for a typical batter, or it will become overly aerated and make the top of the cake crack. If that happens, don't worry—the imperfections won't show when the cake is unmolded, and it tastes just as good. Use a nonstick pan for the best results.

Gingerbread

½ **pound (2 sticks) unsalted butter, at room temperature**

1 **cup packed light brown sugar**

2 **large eggs, at room temperature**

1 **cup unsulphured molasses**

½ **cup Drambuie**

2¼ **cups all-purpose flour**

2 **teaspoons baking soda**

2 **teaspoons ground ginger**

2 **teaspoons ground cinnamon**

½ **teaspoon ground cloves**

½ **teaspoon salt**

Drambuie Glaze

4 tablespoons (¹/₂ stick) unsalted butter

¹/₃ cup Drambuie

1. To make the cake, position a rack in the center of the oven and preheat to 350°F. Lightly butter the inside of a 12-cup *nonstick* fluted tube pan, such as a Bundt pan. Dust the pan with flour and tap out the excess.

2. In a large bowl, beat the butter and brown sugar just until well combined, about 1 minute. (If necessary, first rub the brown sugar through a sieve to remove any lumps.) Do not overbeat. Beat in the eggs. Beat in the molasses and Drambuie.

3. Sift the flour, baking soda, ginger, cinnamon, cloves, and salt onto a piece of wax paper. Stir (do not beat) into the wet ingredients just until combined. Stir in ³/₄ cup hot water. Scrape into the pan and smooth the top.

4. Bake until a toothpick inserted in the center of the cake comes out clean, about 1 hour. Cool for 10 minutes on a wire cake rack.

5. To make the glaze, in a small saucepan, melt the butter over low heat. Remove from the heat and stir in the Drambuie. Brush the top of the cake with about 2 tablespoons of the mixture and let stand for 5 minutes. Invert onto the cake rack and unmold. Brush the cake with the remaining glaze. Cool completely. (The cake can be prepared up to 3 days ahead, covered with plastic wrap, and stored at room temperature.)

Pumpkin-Currant Cake

Makes 10 to 12 servings

Make Ahead: The cake can be prepared up to 2 days ahead.

For a pumpkin dessert when pie isn't in the picture, here's an easy spice cake packed with holiday flavors. Substitute dried cranberries for the currants, if you wish. I always pray that there are leftovers of this cake for my day-after-Thanksgiving breakfast.

2¹/₂ cups all-purpose flour

1¹/₂ teaspoons baking soda

¹/₂ teaspoon baking powder

³/₄ teaspoon ground cinnamon

³/₄ teaspoon ground cloves

³/₄ teaspoon salt

12 tablespoons (1¹/₂ sticks) unsalted butter, at room temperature

1 cup granulated sugar

1 cup packed light brown sugar

3 large eggs

One 15-ounce can solid pack pumpkin (1³/₄ cups)

³/₄ cup dried currants

³/₄ cup toasted and coarsely chopped pecans

1. Position a rack in the center of the oven and preheat to 350°F. Lightly butter a 12-cup fluted tube cake pan, such as a Bundt pan (preferably nonstick). Dust the pan with flour and tap out the excess.

2. Sift the flour, baking soda, baking powder, cinnamon, cloves, and salt onto a piece of wax paper. Set aside.

3. In a medium bowl, using a hand-held electric mixer at high speed, beat the butter until creamy, about 1 minute. Add the sugar and brown sugar and beat until light in color and texture, about 2 minutes.

What Do You Mean, Pumpkin Doesn't Grow in Cans?

Finicky cooks like to make their pumpkin desserts from freshly prepared pumpkin purée. It sounds like a good idea, but there are a few problems to be aware of.

The texture and flavor of canned pumpkin is the same from can to can. With fresh pumpkin, the amount of liquid varies, and the purée must always be drained to achieve the thickness of the canned variety. Using a watery purée in a recipe that was tested with firm canned pumpkin will wreak disaster.

It is very important to choose the right kind of fresh pumpkin. Jack-o'-lantern-type pumpkins are too large, watery, and bland to use in baking. Sugar or cheese pumpkins, available at many farmers' markets and produce markets, are the best for cooking. They are smaller (averaging 2 to 3 pounds) and denser than the familiar huge pumpkins. Ask the produce manager at your market—it's a good bet that the smaller pumpkins on display are eating pumpkins. Or use Hubbard squash—it's an excellent substitute. You will need about 2 ½ pounds of pumpkin to yield about 1 ¾ cups of purée, the equivalent of

a 15-ounce can. (If you have any doubts, err on the side of buying too much fresh pumpkin.)

Roasting is the preferred method for cooking fresh pumpkin that will be puréed, as it incorporates less water than steaming or boiling. Preheat the oven to 350°F. Using a large knife, remove the stem and cut the pumpkin into quarters. Scoop out and discard the stringy fibers and seeds. Cut the quarters into 2- to 3-inch pieces. Place in a large lightly oiled roasting pan, skin side down. Add ⅓ cup water, and cover tightly with aluminum foil. Bake until very tender, about 1 ¼ hours. Uncover and cool. Remove the pumpkin skin and purée the pumpkin in a food processor, or rub through a wire sieve. Place the pumpkin purée in a cheesecloth-lined wire sieve set over a bowl. Fold up the edges of the cheesecloth to cover the purée. Place a saucer on the purée and weight it down with a 1-pound can to force out the excess liquid. Let stand until the purée is the consistency of canned pumpkin, about 1 hour. The pumpkin purée can be frozen in an airtight container for up to 1 month.

Scrape down the bowl and, one at a time, beat in the eggs. Beat in the pumpkin. Reduce the mixer speed to low. In three additions, beat in the flour mixture. Stir in the currants and pecans. Scrape into the prepared pan and smooth the top.

4. Bake until a long wooden skewer inserted in the cake comes out clean, about 1 hour. Cool for 10 minutes on a wire cake rack. Invert the cake onto the rack, unmold, and cool completely. (The cake can be prepared up to 2 days ahead, covered tightly with plastic wrap, and stored at room temperature.)

Pumpkin-Walnut Roulade with Ginger Filling

Makes 8 to 10 servings

Make Ahead: The roulade can be made up to 2 days ahead.

A number of my cooking students report that this spicy pumpkin roll has replaced pumpkin pie at their house. Don't be nervous about rolling up the cake— it is very flexible, and if for some reason it does crack, the whipped cream garnish will cover any blemishes. Be sure the walnuts are very finely chopped (the best way is to pulse them in a food processor, being careful that they don't turn into walnut butter).

Roulade

³/₄ cup all-purpose flour

1 teaspoon baking soda

2 teaspoons ground cinnamon

1 teaspoon ground ginger

¹/₂ teaspoon freshly grated nutmeg

¹/₈ teaspoon ground cloves

¹/₂ teaspoon salt

1 cup granulated sugar

3 large eggs, at room temperature

²/₃ cup canned solid pack pumpkin

1 teaspoon fresh lemon juice

³/₄ cup finely chopped walnuts

Confectioners' sugar, for sifting

Filling

Two 3-ounce packages cream cheese, at room temperature

4 tablespoons (¹/₂ stick) unsalted butter, at room temperature

¹/₂ teaspoon vanilla extract

1 cup confectioners' sugar

2 tablespoons minced crystallized ginger

Spiked Cream

¹/₂ cup heavy cream

1 tablespoon confectioners' sugar

2 teaspoons dark rum or brandy, optional

¹/₄ teaspoon vanilla extract

3 tablespoons finely chopped walnuts

2 tablespoons minced crystallized ginger

1. To make the cake, position a rack in the top third of the oven and preheat to 375°F. Lightly butter a 10 × 15-inch jelly-roll pan. To line the bottom and sides of the pan, cut a 12 × 16-inch piece of parchment or wax paper. In each of the four corners, cut a diagonal slash about 2 inches long. Fit the paper into the pan, folding the cut ends over each other at the slashes to form neat corners. Lightly butter and flour the paper, tapping out the excess flour.

2. Sift the flour, baking soda, cinnamon, ginger, nutmeg, cloves, and salt, onto a piece of wax paper and set aside. In a large bowl, using a hand-held electric mixer at high speed, beat the sugar and eggs until light in color and texture, about 3 minutes. The mixture should form a thick ribbon that falls back on itself when the beaters are lifted about 2 inches from the bowl. Stir in the pumpkin and lemon juice.

3. With the mixer on low, gradually beat the flour mixture into the batter, scraping the sides of the bowl as needed. Spread the batter evenly in the prepared pan, being sure to reach into the corners. Sprinkle the batter with the walnuts.

4. Bake until the center of the cake springs back when lightly pressed with a finger, about 15 minutes. Sift confectioners' sugar over the top of the cake. Place a clean kitchen towel over the cake, then top with a baking sheet. Holding the baking sheet over the cake, turn the cake upside down and invert it onto the towel on the baking sheet. Carefully peel off the paper, then place it back on the cake. Using the towel as an aid, roll up the cake. Cool completely.

5. To make the filling, in a medium bowl, using a hand-held electric mixer at medium speed, beat the cream cheese, butter, and vanilla until combined. Gradually beat in the confectioners' sugar until smooth.

6. Unroll the cake and discard the paper. Spread the filling evenly over the cake and sprinkle with the crystallized ginger. Reroll the cake (you won't need to use the kitchen towel) and wrap in plastic wrap. Refrigerate until the filling is firm, at least 1 hour. (The cake can be refrigerated for up to 2 days.)

7. To make the spiked cream, in a chilled medium bowl, using a hand-held electric mixer set at high speed, beat the cream, confectioners' sugar, optional rum, and vanilla until stiff. Transfer to a pastry bag fitted with a large open star tip, such as Ateco number 5.

8. Transfer the roll to a long serving platter. Garnish the cake with swirls of the whipped cream, and sprinkle with the walnuts and crystallized ginger. To serve, cut the cake diagonally into thick slices.

Grandma's Steamed Persimmon Pudding

Makes 8 servings

Make Ahead: The pudding is best served within 45 minutes after steaming.

This recipe always makes new fans for the underappreciated persimmon. My grandmother made this every Thanksgiving. Of all my holiday dessert recipes, this is the one my friends always ask me to be sure and include on the menu, and I am happy to oblige, as I get a nice dose of nostalgia every time I make it. The pudding looks humble, but it has a spicy flavor and moist texture that will win you over. Pudding molds are available at kitchenware stores, and by mail-order from Sur la Table (1-800-243-0852).

2 very ripe, medium Hachiya persimmons

2 teaspoons baking soda

1 cup sugar

¹/₂ cup milk

2 tablespoons unsalted butter, melted

1 large egg

1 cup all-purpose flour

¹/₂ teaspoon ground cinnamon

¹/₂ teaspoon salt

Sweetened Whipped Cream (page 137)

1. Generously butter the inside of a 1¹/₂- to 2-quart fluted tube pudding mold. Dust the inside of the mold lightly with flour, and tap out the excess.

2. Cut the stems from the persimmons. Cut up the persimmons and remove any large seeds in the pulp. In a food processor or blender, purée the unpeeled persimmons. You should have 1 cup purée. Place in a medium bowl and sift in the baking soda. (For some reason, mixing the persimmon with the soda improves the texture of the pudding and keeps it from getting

Puckering Up: Persimmons

Persimmons are just beginning to come into season around Thanksgiving. Some varieties are not edible until they have been "kissed" with frost. There are two basic persimmon varieties, and they have totally different qualities. One is best for baking, the other for salads.

Hachiya persimmons are shaped like large deep-orange acorns. These are the persimmons I grew up with, and many of our neighbors in Northern California grew them in their gardens. Unripe, they are extremely tannic and will make you pucker up quicker than a lemon can. They must be ripened until *very* soft and translucent, at which point they take on a honeyed flavor. Hachiya persimmons are rarely ripe at the market when you need them. Buy them about 1 week before using, and let them ripen at room temperature in a paper bag. Once soft, they can be refrigerated for a few days. Because my persimmon timing is often off, I usually cook with thawed persimmon pulp that I have frozen at my convenience. Persimmon pulp can be frozen for up to 1 month, stored in an airtight container. Use Hachiya persimmons in desserts like Grandma's Steamed Persimmon Pudding (page 130).

Fuyu (the seedless variety is called Sharon) persimmons look like squat pale orange tomatoes. They do not have to be ripened and can be enjoyed when crisp-tender, thinly sliced into wedges. I serve them in salads (see Spinach and Persimmon Salad with Ginger Vinaigrette on page 25) and on cheese boards.

gummy—a common problem with persimmon desserts.) Immediately whisk in the sugar, milk, melted butter, and egg.

3. Sift together the flour, cinnamon, and salt. Add to the persimmon mixture and whisk until smooth. Scrape the mixture into the prepared pudding mold and smooth the top. Cover the mold with its lid or a double thickness of aluminum foil.

4. Place a collapsible vegetable steamer in a pot large enough to hold the mold, and put the mold on the steamer. Pour enough boiling water into the pot to almost, but not quite, touch the bottom of the steamer. Bring to a boil over high heat, cover the pot, and reduce the heat to medium-low. Steam the pudding, adding more boiling water as needed, until the pudding is dark brown and a toothpick inserted in the center comes out clean, about 2 hours.

5. Let the pudding stand for 10 minutes. (The pudding can stay in its mold for up to 45 minutes.) Run a sharp knife around the inside of the mold, and invert the pudding onto a platter. Slice and serve warm, with the whipped cream.

Note: The recipe can be doubled and steamed in a 10- to 12-cup fluted tube pan. Cover the pan tightly with aluminum foil. To lift the pan in and out of the kettle, tie the pan with kitchen string, like a package. The double-batch recipe can also be cooked in the oven. Place the pan in a roasting pan, add enough hot water to come 1 inch up the sides of the pan, and bake in a 350° F oven until a toothpick inserted in the pudding comes out clean, about 1½ hours.

Pumpkin-Ricotta Cheesecake with Amaretti Crust

Makes 12 to 16 servings

Make Ahead: The cheesecake must be chilled overnight; it can then be refrigerated for 2 more days.

This pumpkin-swirled dessert was inspired by the flavors of Italy, where ricotta cheese creates an especially light-textured cheesecake. The texture is also maintained by baking in a water bath. You'll get a lot of servings (and compliments) from this great-looking finale.

1½ cups finely crushed *amaretti* (see Note) or gingersnap cookies (about 7 ounces)

4 tablespoons (½ stick) unsalted butter, melted

½ cup packed light brown sugar

One 32-ounce container whole-milk ricotta cheese

One 8-ounce package cream cheese, at room temperature

1 cup granulated sugar

¼ cup cornstarch

5 large eggs

⅓ cup heavy cream

1 teaspoon vanilla extract

Grated zest of 1 lemon

One 15-ounce can solid pack pumpkin (1¾ cups)

1 large egg yolk

1 teaspoon ground cinnamon

1 teaspoon ground ginger

½ teaspoon ground cloves

1. Position a rack in the center of the oven and preheat to 325°F. Lightly butter a 9½-inch springform pan. Wrap the outside bottom of the pan tightly with aluminum foil.

2. In a small bowl, toss th e amaretti crumbs with the melted butter. Press evenly into the bottom and about 1 inch up the sides of the prepared pan. Bake for 10 minutes. Set aside on a wire cake rack. Leave the oven on.

3. Rub the brown sugar through a wire sieve to remove the lumps and set aside. Rub the ricotta cheese through the sieve to lighten the texture, and set aside.

4. In a large bowl, using a hand-held electric mixer set at high speed, beat the cream cheese and granulated sugar until smooth. Beat in the cornstarch. Reduce the speed to low. One at a time, beat in the whole eggs. Beat in the cream, vanilla, and lemon zest. Add the ricotta and beat just until smooth.

5. Pour 1½ cups of the cheese mixture into a medium bowl. Add the pumpkin, brown sugar, egg yolk, cinnamon, ginger, and cloves. Beat on low speed until smooth.

6. Pour the plain cheesecake batter into the prepared pan. Top with large spoonfuls of the pumpkin mixture. Using a table knife, swirl the two mixtures together to get a marbleized look.

7. Place the pan in a large roasting pan and put in the oven. Add enough nearly boiling water to come ½ inch up the sides of the pan. Bake until a sharp knife inserted 1 inch from the edge of the cake comes out clean, about 1¾ hours. The center may seem slightly unset, but it will firm upon chilling. Remove the cheesecake from the roasting pan and place on a wire cake rack. Run a sharp knife around the inside of the pan to release the cake from the sides but leave the sides attached. Cool completely.

8. Remove the foil from the pan. Cover the cheesecake with plastic wrap and refrigerate for at least 4 hours, or overnight. (The cheesecake can be prepared up to 2 days ahead.)

9. Remove the sides of the pan. Serve chilled, dipping a thin sharp knife into a tall glass of hot water before cutting each slice.

Note: *Amaretti* are crisp almond cookies, often wrapped in pairs with colorful tissue paper and sold in pricey tins. There are also brands that come in boxes, and they are a less expensive option for making crumb crusts. *Amaretti* can be found in Italian delicatessens, specialty food stores, and many supermarkets.

Cranberry Cheesecake

Makes 12 to 16 servings

Make Ahead: The cheesecake must be chilled at least 4 hours; it can then be refrigerated for 2 more days.

Cranberries give this cheesecake an attractive pink tint and a tartness that cuts through the rich, thick cream cheese filling. Like any cheesecake, part of its appeal is that it must be made well ahead of serving, so there is no last-minute fussing at serving time.

1½ cups crushed graham crackers (about 7 ounces)

1½ cups plus 2 tablespoons sugar

5 tablespoons unsalted butter, melted

One 12-ounce bag fresh cranberries

Three 8-ounce packages cream cheese, at room temperature

3 large eggs, at room temperature

1¼ cups sour cream

1 tablespoon cornstarch

1. Position a rack in the center of the oven and preheat to 350°F. Lightly butter a 9½-inch springform pan. Wrap the outside bottom of the pan tightly with aluminum foil.

2. In a small bowl, mix the cracker crumbs, $1/4$ cup of the sugar, and the melted butter until well combined. Press evenly into the bottom and about 1 inch up the sides of the prepared pan. Bake for 10 minutes. Set aside on a wire cake rack. Leave the oven on.

3. In a large nonreactive saucepan, combine the cranberries, 2 cups water, and $1/2$ cup of the sugar. Bring to a boil over medium-high heat, stirring to dissolve the sugar. Reduce the heat to medium-low and cook, stirring often to avoid scorching, until very thick and reduced to about 2 cups. Transfer to a bowl and cool completely, stirring often.

4. In a large bowl, using a hand-held mixer at medium speed, beat the cream cheese until smooth, about 1 minute. Add the remaining $3/4$ cup plus 2 tablespoons sugar and beat for 1 minute, scraping down the sides of the bowl as needed. One at a time, beat in the eggs. Beat in $1½$ cups of the cranberry mixture, the sour cream, and cornstarch. Pour into the prepared crust, and dot the surface with heaping tablespoons of the remaining cranberry mixture.

5. Bake for 15 minutes. Reduce the heat to 325°F and continue baking until the edges are puffed and lightly browned, 50 to 60 minutes longer. Remove from the oven and run a thin knife around the inside of the pan to release the cheesecake from the sides, but leave the sides attached. Cool completely on a wire cake rack.

6. Cover the pan tightly with plastic wrap and refrigerate for at least 4 hours, or overnight. (The cheesecake can be prepared up to 2 days ahead.)

7. Remove the sides of the pan and the foil from the bottom. Serve chilled, dipping a thin sharp knife into a tall glass of hot water before cutting each slice.

Pumpkin Crème Brûlée

Makes 8 servings

Make Ahead: The pumpkin custards must be chilled for at least 4 hours before serving; they can be prepared up to 2 days ahead.

Crème brûlée has taken restaurant dessert menus by storm. This version is a creamier, lusher rendition of pumpkin pie filling, topped with a caramelized brown sugar glaze. The glazing is a little tricky in the broiler—keep a close eye on the sugar so it doesn't scorch. The most efficient way to caramelize crème brûlée is with a hand-held propane torch. Inexpensive models are available at hardware stores, and many kitchenware stores carry lightweight models specifically designed for cooks. Wave the flame in a circular pattern about two inches above each brown sugar-dusted custard and let the flame melt the sugar, which will only take a few seconds.

2 cups heavy cream

$2/3$ cup packed light brown sugar, plus $1/3$ cup for caramelizing the custard tops

5 large egg yolks

One 15-ounce can solid pack pumpkin ($1¾$ cups)

1 teaspoon ground cinnamon

$1/2$ teaspoon ground ginger

$1/8$ teaspoon ground cloves

Special Equipment

Eight 6-ounce custard cups

Hand-held propane torch, optional

1. Position a rack in the center of the oven and preheat to 350°F.

2. In a medium saucepan, heat the cream over medium heat, stirring often, until tiny bubbles appear

Cheesecake Savvy

Cheesecakes are perfect holiday desserts because they are ready and waiting in the refrigerator at serving time. Everyone loves them, even if they are as rich as a dessert can get. Cheesecakes are especially popular on the East Coast, where a version of the recipe surfaced with the influx of Jewish immigrants around the turn of the century. Many recipes call for Philadelphia Brand Cream Cheese. Cream cheese itself was invented in Upstate New York in the 1870s. In 1880, A. L. Reynolds began selling foil-wrapped blocks of cream cheese under the name "Philadelphia." At the time, Philadelphia was the culinary capital of the nation, and consumers associated top-quality foods with the city. Eventually, Philadelphia cream cheese was acquired by Kraft Cheese Company, where it remains today.

The most common problem with cheesecakes is that the tops crack during cooling. Cheesecakes usually crack because the batter is baked onto the sides of the springform pan, and as the cake cools and contracts, tension creates the fissures. Running a knife around the inside of the pan releases the cake, and the tension. A bit of cornstarch also helps to stabilize the batter and make it less delicate and prone to cracking. Gently baking the cake in a water bath also prevents some cracking. Even if you think your springform pan has a tight fit, wrap the outside of the pan with aluminum foil so it doesn't get a wet crust from using a water bath. The foil also prevents the butter from leaking out of the crust.

around the edges. Remove from the heat and stir in $^2/_3$ cup brown sugar until it has dissolved.

3. In a medium bowl, whisk the egg yolks, pumpkin, cinnamon, ginger, and cloves. Gradually whisk in the hot cream mixture. Pour equal amounts (about $^1/_2$ cup) of the pumpkin custard into eight 6-ounce custard cups. Transfer the cups to a large roasting pan, and place the pan in the oven. Pour enough boiling water around the cups to come $^1/_2$ inch up the sides. Bake until a knife inserted in the center of the custard comes out almost clean (the custards will continue to cook when removed from the oven), about $1^1/_4$ hours. Remove the custards from the water and cool completely on a wire cake rack.

4. Cover each custard with plastic wrap and refrigerate until chilled, at least 4 hours, or preferably, overnight. (The custards can be prepared up to 2 days ahead.)

5. Position a broiler rack 6 inches from the source of heat and preheat the broiler. Rub the remaining $^1/_3$ cup brown sugar through a wire sieve over each custard to cover each one with a dusting of sugar. Put the custards on a baking sheet and broil, watching carefully to avoid scorching, until the brown sugar caramelizes, 1 to 2 minutes. Or, use a hand-held propane torch as directed above. Serve immediately.

Cranberry Granita

Makes 6 to 8 servings

Make Ahead: Granita is best the day it is made, but it can be prepared up to 1 day ahead.

To most of us, the more sinful the Thanksgiving dessert selection, the better. This low-fat treat is for those guests who insist on monitoring every mouthful, even at holidays. But even dessert hedonists will love it for its refreshing flavor and festive bright pink color. Note that the recipe makes only six healthy or eight moderate servings, so this is not a dessert for a crowd. If you want to double the recipe, freeze the granita in two pans, as the volume of a double recipe takes too long to freeze in one pan. (Or use the biggest shallow metal pan that fits into your freezer.) Serve the granita in well-chilled stemmed glasses—I freeze martini glasses for thirty minutes to get them good and cold.

One 12-ounce bag fresh cranberries
1 cup plus 2 tablespoons sugar
1 tablespoon fresh lemon juice
Mint sprigs

1. In a large nonreactive saucepan, bring 4 cups water, the cranberries, and sugar to a boil over high heat, stirring often to dissolve the sugar. Reduce the heat to medium and simmer for 10 minutes, or until all of the cranberries have burst. Pour into a wire sieve placed over a bowl and drain well. Press gently on the cranberries to extract as much juice as possible, but don't force the solids through the sieve. Stir the lemon juice into the cranberry liquid. Refrigerate, uncovered, until completely cooled, about 2 hours.

2. Meanwhile, place a metal 9 × 13-inch baking pan in the freezer to chill.

3. Pour the cranberry liquid into the chilled pan. Freeze until the mixture freezes around the edges, about 1 hour, depending on your freezer's temperature. Using a large metal spoon, mix the frozen edges into the center (leave the spoon in the pan.)

4. Freeze again, repeating the stirring procedure about every 30 minutes, until the mixture is frozen into a slushy consistency, 2 to 3 hours total freezing time. Serve immediately in well-chilled glasses, garnished with mint sprigs, or keep frozen until ready to serve, or overnight. (If the granita freezes solid, allow it to soften slightly in the refrigerator for about 10 minutes, and try stirring again. Or, break into large chunks and process in a food processor until slushy and serve immediately.)

Sweetened Whipped Cream

Makes about 1 3/4 cups

Make Ahead: Whipped cream can be prepared up to 1 day ahead.

Experienced cooks may think it's silly to give a recipe for whipped cream, but a lot of novice cooks are scared of this simple, important ingredient. When Thanksgiving comes around, fake whipped dessert topping goes on a lot of shopping lists. I hope this recipe convinces those cooks to scratch the artificial stuff and just buy a carton of good old heavy cream. Have we become so lazy that we can't take a couple of minutes to whip a bowl of delicious, thick, real cream? Here's how to do it right, and in record time. Of course, this recipe can be multiplied as needed.

- *For the very best whipped cream, use pasteurized (not ultrapasteurized) heavy cream, available at most dairies and natural food stores, and some supermarkets. This cream has been less processed than* ultrapasteurized, *and you can really taste the difference.*

- *Don't serve* unsweetened *whipped cream—it does nothing for your dessert. It tastes almost like butter.*

- *The heavy cream must be well chilled, to help it whip more quickly and hold its shape longer. To keep it cold during whipping, chill the mixing bowl and beaters in the freezer for at least 10 minutes.*

- *It doesn't matter if you use granulated sugar or confectioners' sugar. Granulated sugar must be added to the cream at the beginning so it dissolves by the time the cream is stiff. Confectioners' sugar dissolves rapidly, and can be mixed in at any time.*

- *Use a hand-held electric mixer to whip the cream quickly. A large balloon whisk with lots of thin wires is a good second choice, but don't expect a small whisk with thick wires to work as well—the many thin wires help beat lots of air into the cream. Large standing mixers only work for large amounts (over 2 cups) of cream.*

- *If desired, add up to 2 tablespoons brandy, cognac, dark rum, or bourbon for every cup of cream.*

- *If whipped cream stands for a few hours, liquid sometimes separates from the cream. Just beat the cream again until the liquid reincorporates itself.*

1 cup heavy cream, preferably not ultrapasteurized
2 tablespoons granulated or confectioners' sugar
$1/2$ teaspoon vanilla extract

Pour the cream into a chilled medium bowl and add the sugar and vanilla. Using a hand-held electric mixer set at medium speed, beat just until stiff peaks form. Do not overbeat, or the cream will separate. (The cream can be whipped up to 1 day ahead, covered, and refrigerated. Just before serving, rewhip the cream briefly to incorporate any liquid that may have separated out of the cream.)

Leftovers

There's Got to Be a Morning After . . .

Friday's leftover turkey sandwich is anticipated just as strongly as, if not more than, Thursday's big-deal dinner. Sandwiches are great, but that's just the tip of the leftover iceberg. When asked about their favorite leftover turkey uses, Americans gave sandwiches top honors, with soup, casseroles, salads, and stir-fries following behind.

There are so many ways to enjoy turkey leftovers, those alone could fill up a book. I have included recipes for some more involved dishes, and a detailed method for making the best turkey soup around. Leftover recipes should never be difficult—after all, you just cooked your head off the day before. The cook's creativity and what's at hand are the main elements that turn leftovers into meals. Mexican dishes are especially delicious with leftover turkey. When I'm faced with a mountain of turkey meat, there is usually a burrito, taco, or enchilada casserole in my future. And, sandwiches should be just as inspired. Here are a few ideas using about 4 cups (1 pound) of leftover turkey.

Turkey Soft Tacos: Roll strips of turkey into warm corn tortillas with salsa, guacamole, and shredded iceberg lettuce.

Turkey and Black Bean Burritos: In a medium saucepan, sauté a small chopped onion and a minced garlic clove in olive oil. Add one 15- to 19-ounce can black beans, drained and rinsed, and turkey strips and heat through. Roll up in warm flour tortillas with salsa, shredded cheese, and sour cream.

Turkey and Pepper Fajitas: In a large skillet, sauté sliced red onion, green and red bell pepper strips, and minced garlic until very soft. Add turkey strips and cook until heated through. Stir in chili powder to taste. Roll up in warm flour tortillas with salsa and sour cream.

Turkey Salad Niçoise: Arrange turkey strips on a bed of red leaf lettuce with tomato wedges, cooked crisp-tender green beans, cooked sliced new potatoes, and hard-boiled egg wedges. Serve with your favorite vinaigrette.

Curried Turkey Salad: Mix diced turkey with mayonnaise, a little yogurt, chopped apples, raisins, and curry powder. Serve on a bed of green leaf lettuce, or use as a sandwich or pita bread filling.

Hot Turkey, Cheddar, and Apple Sandwich: Place sliced turkey on a slice of lightly toasted bread and top with thinly sliced Cheddar cheese. Broil until the cheese melts. Add some thin slices of Granny Smith apples and top with another slice of toasted bread.

New Club Sandwich: Mix cranberry sauce with Dijon mustard to make a sweet-sour sandwich spread. Make a triple-decker sandwich on your favorite bread with turkey slices, crisp bacon, lettuce, and the cranberry-mustard sauce.

Leftovers Aren't Forever

On Thanksgiving, store your leftovers safely. Get any leftover turkey and stuffing into the refrigerator within two hours of serving. Never leave leftovers out overnight.

Slice all of the turkey meat from the carcass and place in shallow plastic containers or self-sealing plastic bags, or wrap tightly in plastic wrap. Scrape all of the stuffing from the carcass, and refrigerate it separately from the turkey meat. (If you plan to use the carcass for soup, chop or break it into manageable pieces and store in plastic bags.) Refrigerate at 40°F or below, and serve within two or three days, or freeze and use within three months.

Friday Turkey-Vegetable Soup 101

Makes 8 to 12 servings

Make Ahead: The soup base can frozen for up to 3 months, as can the soup.

The most common way of making leftover turkey soup is to toss the carcass and vegetables into a pot and simmer with water until the broth is flavorful. That's a good beginning, but the flavor is also cooked out of the turkey meat and vegetables (and you have to look out for little pieces of bone in your soup). It's a better idea to treat this broth as the first step in the soup-making process, using it to create a perfect pot of soup that will keep everyone in the house well fed at lunchtime for quite a few days to come. Freeze the soup in one-pint containers for those winter days when homemade turkey soup is just what the doctor orders.

- *Even if you don't want to turn the turkey carcass into a soup, make the soup base anyway and freeze to substitute for chicken broth in other recipes.*

- *Trim all edible meat from the turkey carcass. Cooked turkey should be added to the finished soup just before serving to heat through. If overcooked, it will be flavorless and tough.*

- *If there are bits of stuffing in the carcass crevices, leave them alone—the bread will dissolve into the broth and thicken it slightly. However, if the stuffing includes flavors that would not complement the broth (such as rice, fruit or nuts), rinse the stuffing off the carcass under cold running water.*

- *The carcass should be chopped into large pieces (3 inches square or so), to enable the bones to release more flavor into the broth. Also, it takes too much water to cover a whole carcass, resulting in a weak, watery broth. A heavy cleaver works best, but if you don't have one, use your hands to break up the carcass into*

manageable pieces. Of course, add any extraneous (drumstick or thigh) bones and skin to the pot too.

- *Sautéing the vegetables gives them more flavor. But don't overdo the vegetables for the soup base—let the turkey flavor come through.*

- *Use cold water to make your broth. It will take longer to come to a simmer, but it will draw more flavor from the ingredients. If you have any leftover turkey stock from your Thanksgiving turkey, use it in place of some of the water.*

- *Allow the broth to come to a simmer and skim off the foam before adding the seasonings. If you add the seasonings at the beginning, they'll float to the top and be skimmed off with the foam.*

- *While a stock is unsalted because it is going to be used in sauces that may be reduced, a soup broth base should be salted. Don't be afraid to add enough salt—it makes the difference between a well-flavored soup and a bland one.*

- *If your turkey soup base tastes weak even after seasoning, it is perfectly fine to bolster it with canned chicken broth or bouillon cubes. I won't tell anyone.*

- *Use a cheesecloth- or kitchen towel–lined colander to strain the solids from the broth. It's hard to clean the solids from a wire sieve, and most are too small to strain out the large bones anyway.*

- *Leftover gravy will thicken and enhance the color and flavor of any soup. Stir cold gravy into the soup (not the soup base) to taste during the last 10 minutes of simmering.*

Friday Turkey Soup Base

2 tablespoons vegetable oil

1 medium onion, chopped

1 medium carrot, chopped

1 medium celery rib with leaves, chopped

1 turkey carcass, chopped into large pieces

4 parsley sprigs

$1/2$ teaspoon dried thyme

1 bay leaf

1 teaspoon salt

¹/₄ teaspoon black peppercorns

Turkey Vegetable Soup

2 tablespoons unsalted butter

1 large onion, chopped

2 medium carrots, chopped

2 medium celery ribs with leaves, chopped

1 medium turnip, peeled and chopped

2 garlic cloves, minced

Friday Turkey Soup Base

2 tablespoons chopped fresh parsley

4 cups bite-sized pieces cooked turkey (about
  1 pound)

Salt and freshly milled black pepper

1. To make the soup base, in a large soup pot, heat the oil over medium heat. Add the onion, carrot, and celery, cover, and cook, stirring occasionally, until softened, about 5 minutes. Add the turkey carcass. Pour in enough cold water (about 3 quarts) to cover the carcass by at least 1 inch. Bring to a boil over high heat, skimming off any foam that rises to the surface.

2. Add the parsley, thyme, bay leaf, salt, and pepper. Reduce the heat to low. Simmer, uncovered, adding more water as needed to keep the carcass covered, until the broth is well flavored, at least 2 and up to 4 hours.

3. Place a colander over a large bowl or pot. Pour the soup base through the colander, and discard the solids. Let the base stand for 5 minutes, then skim any clear fat from the surface. (The soup base can be frozen for up to 3 months. Cool completely, then store in airtight containers.) Add enough water to make 2 quarts soup base; or, return to the pot and boil over high heat until reduced to 2 quarts.

4. To make the soup, in a large soup pot, melt the butter over medium heat. Add the onion, carrots, celery, turnip, and garlic, cover, and cook, stirring oc-

casionally, until the onions are golden, about 6 minutes. Add the soup base and parsley and bring to a boil. Reduce the heat to low and simmer until the vegetables are tender, about 1 hour. During the last 5 minutes, stir in the turkey. Season the soup with salt and pepper. Serve hot. (The soup can be frozen for up to 3 months. Cool completely and store in airtight containers.)

Amish Turkey-Vegetable Soup: Substitute 2 boiling potatoes, peeled and cut into 1-inch cubes, for the turnip, and add during the last 20 minutes of simmering. During the last 10 minutes, add 8 ounces dried wide egg noodles, and cook until tender. Season the soup with ¹/₄ teaspoon crumbled saffron threads, or more to taste.

Italian Egg Drop Soup: Mix 2 large eggs and 3 tablespoons freshly grated Parmesan. Season with salt, pepper, and freshly grated nutmeg. After adding the turkey to the soup, stirring constantly, add the egg mixture. Simmer until the egg mixture forms tiny flakes.

Tuscan Turkey Ribollita

Makes 6 to 8 servings

Make Ahead: *Here's an Italian rendition of the Friday Turkey Soup theme. In Tuscany, soup is often layered with slices of day-old bread and cheese to make a hearty baked dish called* ribollita *(literally, "reboiled"). Turkey is a natural addition to this hearty meal-in-a-dish, which is always served with a cruet of extra virgin olive oil for seasoning the soup. (In Italy, fine olive oil is used as a condiment as well as a cooking medium.) Make the soup in a flameproof casserole that can also go into the oven.*

1/4 cup extra virgin olive oil, plus more for
serving

1 large onion, chopped

1 medium carrot, cut into 1/2-inch cubes

2 medium celery ribs with leaves, cut into
1/4-inch-thick slices

1 large zucchini, cut into 1/2-inch cubes

2 garlic cloves, minced

4 cups packed finely shredded kale (about
10 ounces)

One 28-ounce can tomatoes in juice, drained
and chopped

1 teaspoon dried basil

1 teaspoon dried oregano

1/2 teaspoon salt

1/4 teaspoon crushed hot red pepper

5 cups Friday Turkey Soup Base (page 140)

1 cup hearty red wine, such as Chianti or
Zinfandel

4 cups bite-sized pieces cooked turkey (about
1 pound)

One 19-ounce can cannellini (white kidney)
beans, drained and rinsed

8 large slices crusty Italian or French bread

1/2 cup freshly grated Parmesan cheese

1. In a Dutch oven or flameproof casserole, heat 2 tablespoons of the oil over medium heat. Add the onion, carrot, celery, zucchini, and garlic. Cook, stirring occasionally, until softened, about 5 minutes. Add the kale, cover, and cook until the kale wilts, about 5 minutes. Stir in the tomatoes, basil, oregano, salt, and crushed red pepper.

2. Add the turkey soup base and wine and bring to a boil. Reduce the heat to medium-low and partially cover. Simmer for 30 minutes. During the last 5 minutes, stir in the turkey and beans.

3. Meanwhile, position a rack in the center of the oven and preheat to 400°F. Arrange the bread on a baking sheet and lightly brush with the remaining 2 tablespoons oil. Bake until the bread is lightly toasted around the edges, about 10 minutes. Set the toasted bread aside. Reduce the oven temperature to 350°F.

4. Add 4 bread slices to the soup, pressing them down with a large spoon or a ladle until completely submerged. Place the remaining bread on the top of the soup and sprinkle with the cheese. Bake until the cheese is golden brown, about 20 minutes. Serve in deep soup bowls, including a piece of the crusty bread topping in each serving. Pass a cruet of olive oil for drizzling.

Turkey Tetrazzini Gratin

Makes 6 to 8 servings

Make Ahead: The gratin should be prepared just before serving.

Turkey Tetrazzini is an old-fashioned leftover-turkey spaghetti casserole named for an opera star of the early 1900s. This is an easy-to-make spinoff of the traditional version. The golden brown top, with ends of the pasta baked to a crusty turn, is irresistible.

3 tablespoons unsalted butter

10 ounces cremini or button mushrooms, sliced

One 10-ounce package frozen artichoke hearts,
thawed

1/2 cup chopped shallots or white part of
scallions

4 cups bite-sized pieces cooked turkey (about
1 pound)

1/2 cup dry sherry, such as Manzanillo

1 pound penne

One 15-ounce container part-skim ricotta
cheese

1 cup freshly grated Parmesan cheese
  (4 ounces)

1 cup heavy cream or milk

³/₄ teaspoon salt

¹/₄ teaspoon freshly milled black pepper

1. Position a rack in the top third of the oven and preheat to 400°F. Lightly butter a 10 × 15-inch baking dish.

2. In a large skillet, melt 2 tablespoons of the butter over medium-high heat. Add the mushrooms and cook, stirring occasionally, until they give up their juice, it evaporates, and they begin to brown, about 6 minutes. Stir in the artichokes and shallots and cook, stirring often, until the shallots soften, about 2 minutes. Add the turkey and sherry and cook until the sherry has almost completely evaporated, about 5 minutes.

3. Meanwhile, bring a large pot of lightly salted water to a boil over high heat. Stir in the penne and cook, stirring occasionally, until the pasta is barely tender, about 8 minutes. Do not overcook the pasta, as it will cook further in the oven. Drain well.

4. Return the drained pasta to the warm cooking pot. Add the turkey mixture, the ricotta, ³/₄ cup of the Parmesan cheese, the heavy cream, salt, and pepper and mix well.

5. Transfer to the prepared baking dish. Sprinkle with the remaining ¹/₄ cup Parmesan cheese and dot with the remaining 1 tablespoon butter. Bake until the top is golden brown, 10 to 15 minutes. Serve hot.

Turkey Enchilada Casserole

Makes 6 servings

Make Ahead: The casserole should be prepared just before serving.

A warm, comforting casserole is a delicious way to take the chill off a cool evening. This innocent-looking dish can be quite spicy, depending on the heat level of the salsa you use. If you don't have green tomatillo salsa, use green taco sauce or your favorite red tomato salsa.

12 corn tortillas

One 15-ounce container sour cream

³/₄ cup milk

1 cup green tomatillo salsa, green taco sauce, or
  thick-and-chunky-style tomato salsa

2¹/₂ cups bite-sized pieces cooked turkey
  (about 12 ounces)

1 cup thawed frozen corn kernels

3 scallions (white and green parts), chopped

2 cups shredded sharp Cheddar cheese
  (8 ounces)

1. Position a rack in the center of the oven and preheat to 375°F. Lightly butter a 9 × 13-inch baking dish.

2. *If you have a gas stove,* turn a burner to medium heat. Place a tortilla directly on the burner grid and cook, turning once, until the tortilla is warm and softened, about 20 seconds total. Repeat with the remaining tortillas. *If you have an electric stove,* heat an empty skillet over medium heat. Place a tortilla in the skillet and cook, turning once, until softened, about 45 seconds total. Repeat with the remaining tortillas. Stack the warmed tortillas on a plate as you go and set aside.

3. In a medium bowl, whisk the sour cream and milk until smooth. Spread a thin layer of the salsa in the bottom of the prepared dish. Place 4 tortillas in the bottom of the dish, tearing them to fit. Scatter half of the turkey over the tortillas, then top with ½ cup of the corn and half the scallions. Drizzle with ¾ cup of the cheese, ½ cup of the salsa, and about one third of the sour cream mixture. Top with 4 more tortillas, then the remaining turkey, corn, scallions, and salsa. Drizzle with half of the remaining sour cream mixture and sprinkle with another ¾ cup of the cheese. Top with the remaining 4 tortillas, spread with the remaining sour cream mixture, and sprinkle with the remaining ½ cup cheese.

4. Bake until the casserole is heated through and the cheese is melted, about 30 minutes. Let stand for 5 minutes before serving.

Mongolian Turkey and Broccoli Stir-Fry

Makes 4 to 6 servings

Make Ahead: Make the stir-fry just before serving.

Szechwan peppercorns and crushed red pepper give this zesty stir-fry a heady aroma. Scotch may seem like an odd ingredient, but it actually resembles Mongolian liquor. Szechwan peppercorns can be found at Asian grocers and many supermarkets, but look closely. They should be wrinkled and rust-colored—I have seen white peppercorns mislabeled as Szechwan.

3 cups broccoli florets

1 tablespoon vegetable oil

2 scallions (white and green parts), chopped

1 medium red bell pepper, cored, seeded, and cut into ½-inch-wide strips

2 tablespoons shredded fresh ginger (use the large holes of a box grater)

2 garlic cloves, minced

3 cups cooked turkey, cut into ½ × 2-inch strips (1 pound)

1½ cups Homemade Turkey or Chicken stock (page 22 or 24) or reduced-sodium canned chicken broth

⅓ cup soy sauce

¼ cup Scotch or dry sherry

2 tablespoons dark Asian sesame oil

¾ teaspoon crushed Szechwan peppercorns (use a mortar and pestle, or crush under a heavy saucepan)

½ teaspoon crushed hot red pepper

1 tablespoon plus 1 teaspoon cornstarch

Hot cooked rice, for serving

1. In a large (12-inch) nonstick skillet, bring the broccoli and 1 cup water to a boil over high heat. Cover tightly and cook until the broccoli is crisp-tender, 2 to 3 minutes. Drain the broccoli and set aside. Dry the skillet and return to the stove.

2. Add the oil to the skillet and heat until very hot. Add the scallions, red bell pepper, ginger, and garlic. Stir until the mixture is fragrant, about 30 seconds. Add the turkey strips and ½ cup of the stock. Cover and cook until the turkey is heated through, about 2 minutes.

3. Meanwhile, in a medium bowl, mix the remaining 1 cup stock with the soy sauce, Scotch, sesame oil, Szechwan peppercorns, and crushed red pepper. Add the cornstarch and whisk to dissolve.

4. Stir the cornstarch mixture into the skillet and cook until the sauce is boiling and thickened. Stir in the reserved broccoli. Serve immediately, spooned over bowls of rice.

Turkey and Black Bean Tamale Pie

Makes 6 to 8 servings

Make Ahead: The tamale pie can be prepared up to 8 hours ahead, cooled, covered, and refrigerated.

My mom is the tamale pie queen, and to many of us children of the fifties, these represent the best of comfort food. Here's an updated version of this classic, which you can vary according to mood and what you have on hand. Try substituting hominy for the black beans, or adding a chopped green bell pepper to the saucepan with the onion.

2 tablespoons olive oil

1 medium onion, chopped

1 jalapeño pepper, seeded and minced

2 garlic cloves, minced

3 tablespoons all-purpose flour

2 tablespoons chili powder, or more to taste

2 cups Homemade Turkey or Chicken stock
   (page 22 or 24), or canned reduced-sodium
   chicken broth

One 8-ounce can tomato sauce

1 teaspoon salt

3 cups bite-sized pieces cooked turkey (about
   12 ounces)

One 15- to 19-ounce can black beans, drained
   and rinsed

1 cup thawed frozen corn kernels

1 1/2 cups yellow cornmeal, preferably stone-
   ground

1 cup shredded extra-sharp Cheddar cheese (4
   ounces), optional

1. Position a rack in the center of the oven and preheat to 350°F. Lightly oil a 9 × 13-inch baking dish.

2. In a medium saucepan, heat the oil over medium heat. Add the onion and jalapeño and cook, stirring often, until the onion is golden, about 4 minutes. Add the garlic and stir until fragrant, about 1 minute. Sprinkle with the flour and chili powder and stir until the vegetables are coated.

3. Gradually stir in the stock, then the tomato sauce and 1/4 teaspoon of the salt. Bring to a simmer, then reduce the heat to medium-low. Simmer, stirring often to avoid scorching, until the sauce thickens, about 5 minutes. Stir in the turkey, black beans, and corn. Pour into the prepared dish.

4. In another medium saucepan, bring 1 1/2 cups water and the remaining 3/4 teaspoon salt to a boil over high heat. In a small bowl, whisk the cornmeal with 1 1/2 cups cold water. Whisk into the boiling water and cook, whisking constantly, until the mixture is boiling and thick, about 1 minute. Spread over the turkey mixture as smoothly as possible. Sprinkle with the cheese, if using.

5. Bake until the turkey mixture is bubbling, about 30 minutes. Let stand for 5 minutes before serving.

Thanksgiving Menu Planner

Here are complete menus to fit a variety of Thanksgiving possibilities, from an elegant sit-down dinner to a large buffet that feeds a crowd. Also included are timetables to help you plan and prepare the meal from start to finish. It's a good idea to photocopy the timetable, tape it in a visible place, like the refrigerator door, and mark off the items as you finish them.

Be sure to read every recipe thoroughly. If you don't have a lot of counter space to hold the cookbook, photocopy the recipes, and tape at eye level on a kitchen cabinet door. This will also keep your cookbook clean from spills and splatters.

Of course, the timing of the meal hinges on when the turkey is done. It is always difficult to estimate the exact roasting time, so allow yourself a certain amount of leeway. Remember that the turkey needs to stand for at least twenty minutes before carving anyway, and you can use that window of opportunity to serve the first course and make or reheat the side dishes in the now-empty oven. I actually allow forty-five minutes from when the turkey comes out of the oven until carving, because the cook needs as much time as he can get for the other dishes, and the turkey will stay perfectly hot. In all of the menus, I use the time it takes to serve the first course as a grace period. By the time the guests have finished the first course, the side dishes will be heated through, and you can move on to finishing the rest of the meal.

Most of the recipes in the book are for eight servings. With the exception of desserts, the recipes can be easily multiplied or divided to fit your guest count. (For desserts, make two different recipes and enjoy the leftovers, rather than trying to make half a pie.) If you are reheating chilled dishes in the oven, add ten to fifteen minutes to the suggested cooking times. Detailed make-ahead instructions are given with each recipe.

Traditional Thanksgiving Feast

This lengthy menu has all of the dishes that most people feel they just must have on the Thanksgiving table. The feast is easiest to prepare with two ovens, but can be prepared in one large oven, if the baking dishes are carefully arranged to fit. There is a flurry of activity as soon as the turkey comes out of the oven, but most of it is reheating side dishes. Once the gravy is made, turn it on to the barest simmer to keep warm. Then make the oyster stew, which only takes a few minutes, and serve the stew. For beverages, serve a lightly chilled Beaujolais and have sparkling apple cider on hand for nondrinkers.

Savory Cheddar and Jalapeño Cookies (page 8)
Buttered Cajun Pecans (page 4)
New England Oyster Stew (page 15)
Perfect Roast Turkey with Best-Ever Gravy (page 43)
Bread Stuffing 101 (page 66)
Old-Fashioned Mashed Potatoes 101 (page 82)
Candied Yam and Marshmallow Casserole (page 84)
Green Bean Bake (page 78)
Angel Biscuits (page 104)
Spiced Cranberry-Orange Jell-O Mold (page 88)
Classic Recipe: Famous Pumpkin Pie (page 116)
Apple Pie 101 (page 122)
Hot Coffee and Tea

Timetable

Up to 1 month ahead:

Make turkey stock; freeze

Make piecrusts for pumpkin and apple pies; freeze one for pumpkin pie

Make apple pie; freeze

3 days ahead:

Make cranberry mold; refrigerate

2 days ahead:

Make the pecans; store airtight at room temperature

Make the biscuit dough; refrigerate

The night before:

Defrost piecrust in refrigerator

Shuck oysters (or pick up at fish store)

If using fresh bread for stuffing, cut into cubes and let stand overnight to dry

Make pumpkin pie; refrigerate

Bake the cookies; store airtight at room temperature

8 hours before serving turkey:

Bake apple pie; cool and store at room temperature

7 1/2 hours before serving turkey:

Bake biscuits; cool and wrap in two foil packets

Make green bean bake; refrigerate

Make yam casserole (without marshmallows); refrigerate

Make stuffing

5 1/2 hours before serving turkey:

Stuff turkey (place remaining stuffing in casserole, cover and refrigerate)

Roast turkey

4 hours before serving turkey:

Peel potatoes; store in cold water at room temperature

Whip cream for pies; refrigerate

When guests arrive:

Serve pecans and cookies

When turkey is done (about 45 minutes before serving):

Remove turkey from oven; increase oven temperature to 350°F

Pour turkey drippings into glass bowl and let stand until ready to make gravy

Reheat half of rolls to serve with stew

Bake remaining stuffing

Bake green bean bake

Bake yam casserole

Place potatoes on stove, bring to a boil, and cook

Make gravy; keep warm

Make oyster stew; serve

Just before serving turkey:

Reheat remaining rolls to serve with dinner

Unmold cranberry mold

Top yams with marshmallows; broil until browned

Drain and mash potatoes

After serving turkey:

Make coffee and tea

Serve pumpkin pie and apple pie with whipped cream

A Sophisticated Thanksgiving Dinner

Here's an elegant dinner for grownups. It touches all the bases, but doesn't serve overwhelming amounts of food. Keep in mind that wild turkeys are delicious, but they don't have as much meat on them as regular turkeys. Serve a California or Oregon pinot noir throughout the meal.

Glittering Spiced Walnuts (page 3)

Roasted Beet, Endive, and Blue Cheese Salad with Walnuts (page 26)

Wild Turkey with Wild Rice and Dried Cherry Stuffing (page 55)

Broccoli with Roast Garlic Butter (page 74)

Scalloped Yams with Praline Topping (page 85)

Cranberry, Ginger, and Lemon Chutney (page 91)

Pumpkin Crème Brûlée (page 134)

Hot Coffee and Tea

Timetable

Up to 1 month ahead:
Make turkey stock for wild turkey; freeze

Up to 1 week ahead:
Make cranberry chutney; refrigerate

Up to 5 days ahead:
Make spiced walnuts, store airtight at room
temperature

Up to 3 days ahead:
Make roast garlic butter; refrigerate

Up to 2 days ahead:
Toast walnuts for salad; refrigerate

The night before:
Roast beets for salad; peel and refrigerate
Make the wild rice stuffing; refrigerate
Make pumpkin custards for crème brûlée
(without topping); refrigerate
Cut broccoli into florets; refrigerate

Up to 8 hours before serving turkey:
Prepare yams for scalloped yams; place in
baking dish, cover and refrigerate
Make praline topping for yams

3 1/2 hours before serving turkey:
Reheat stuffing and stuff turkey (place remaining
stuffing in casserole, cover and refrigerate)
Roast turkey

When guest arrive:
Serve walnuts

**When turkey is done (about 45 minutes
before serving):**
Remove turkey from oven; transfer to
serving platter
Pour turkey drippings into glass bowl; let stand
until ready to make gravy
Finish scalloped yams; bake
Bring water to boil for broccoli
Reheat stuffing in casserole
Finish salad; serve

Just before serving turkey:
Make sauce for roast turkey
Cook broccoli, drain and finish with garlic butter

After serving turkey:
Make coffee and tea
Add brown sugar topping to pumpkin crème
brûlée and caramelize

A Chile-Lovers' Thanksgiving

Spicy flavors season this menu with regional favorites from the Cajun country and the Southwest. I usually serve smoke-grilled turkey with salsa, but you may prefer to offer gravy. If so, make the Head Start Gravy, because the drippings from the turkey may not be usable. Chilled hard cider or a semi-dry Gewurtztraminer would be perfect with these dishes.

Hot Crab Salsa Dip (page 7)

Sweet Potato and Peanut Soup (page 22)

Smoke-Grilled Cider-Basted Turkey (page 47)

Head-Start Gravy, optional (page 99)

"Tamale" Stuffing with Pork, Chiles, and Raisins (page 69)

Maque-Choux (page 77)

Maple-Glazed Baby Carrots with Pecans (page 76)

Cranberry-Pineapple Salsa (page 95)

Rosemary and Cracked Pepper Corn Sticks (page 107)

Florida Sweet Potato Pie (page 120)

Hot Coffee and Tea

Timetable

Up to 1 month ahead:
Make turkey stock for gravy and soup; freeze
Make piecrust; freeze

Up to 2 days ahead:
Make sweet potato soup; refrigerate
Toast pecans for carrots; refrigerate

The night before:
Defrost piecrust in refrigerator
Make polenta cubes for stuffing; refrigerate
Cube bread for stuffing; let stand at room
   temperature
Make maque-choux; refrigerate
Make sweet potato pie; refrigerate
Make gravy, if using

Up to 8 hours before serving turkey:
Make stuffing; refrigerate
Make crab dip; refrigerate
Bake corn sticks; cool and wrap in foil

5 1/2 hours before serving turkey:
Make basting mixture for turkey; cool
Stuff turkey with seasoning mixture; let stand

4 1/2 hours before serving turkey:
Light briquettes in charcoal grill or preheat
   gas grill

4 hours before serving turkey:
Grill turkey
Whip cream for pie; refrigerate

30 minutes before guests arrive:
Bake crab dip; keep warm
2 hours before serving turkey:
Make glazed carrots (without pecans)
Make cranberry-pineapple salsa

**When turkey is done (about 45 minutes
before serving):**
Transfer turkey to serving platter; set stand
If making gravy, discard drippings in
   aluminum pan,
leaving browned bits in pan
Place cornsticks in oven; reheat for 10 to
   15 minutes to serve with soup
Bake stuffing
Reheat soup; serve

Just before serving turkey:
Reheat carrots; add pecans
Reheat maque-choux
Reheat gravy; stir into turkey pan, scraping
   up browned
bits in pan

After serving turkey:
Make coffee and tea
Serve pie with whipped cream

Thanksgiving Buffet for a Crowd

When cooking for a crowd, think *big*. Big skillets, big baking dishes, big refrigerators, big pots, and big dishwashers. Regular-sized pots and pans are not very much help with this many mouths to feed—have at least one twelve- to fourteen-inch skillet (two is better) for sautéeing the succotash and stuffing ingredients, and a ten-quart stockpot for preparing the turkey stock and boiling the mashed potatoes. If you run out of refrigerator space, store the finished dishes in a cold, unheated area (like a spare room with an opened window or the garage).

This menu is geared for twenty-four guests. It is served as a buffet without a plated first course. You will need two ovens to reheat the side dishes. A twenty-four-pound turkey will make enough servings for dinner, but if you want leftovers, roast two two-and-a-half to three-pound turkey breast halves too. The turkey is roasted unstuffed—if you want to stuff the bird, add about an hour to the roasting time. Make at least three quarts of Pan Gravy 101. Figure on two-and-a-half batches of Corn Bread Stuffing and three batches of Mashed Potato Casserole. If you have to bake and serve the stuffing and mashed potatoes from large disposable aluminum foil pans, allow at least one hour at 375°F for reheating to compensate for the added bulk. Also make three batches of Not-Your-Grandmother's Succotash and three batches of Cranberry Sauce. Make Cider-Mashed Yams on top of the stove. Because it doesn't need refrigeration and keeps for a couple of days, Pumpkin-Currant Cake is a good dessert choice—bake two of them. If you want pies and rolls, order them from your favorite bakery. Serve inexpensive bulk wines and apple cider as beverages. If you are serving hot coffee, use a large-quantity coffee maker, and allow about one hour for the coffee to brew.

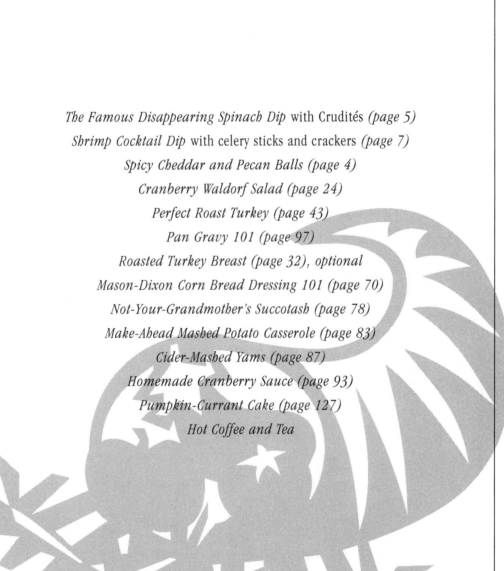

The Famous Disappearing Spinach Dip with Crudités *(page 5)*

Shrimp Cocktail Dip with celery sticks and crackers *(page 7)*

Spicy Cheddar and Pecan Balls (page 4)

Cranberry Waldorf Salad (page 24)

Perfect Roast Turkey (page 43)

Pan Gravy 101 (page 97)

Roasted Turkey Breast (page 32), optional

Mason-Dixon Corn Bread Dressing 101 (page 70)

Not-Your-Grandmother's Succotash (page 78)

Make-Ahead Mashed Potato Casserole (page 83)

Cider-Mashed Yams (page 87)

Homemade Cranberry Sauce (page 93)

Pumpkin-Currant Cake (page 127)

Hot Coffee and Tea

T i m e t a b l e

Up to 1 month ahead:
Make turkey stock for gravy; freeze

Up to 1 week ahead:
Make the cranberry sauce; refrigerate

Up to 3 days ahead:
Make cheddar cheese balls; refrigerate

Up to 2 days ahead:
Bake pumpkin cakes; store at room temperature
Make cocktail sauce for shrimp dip; refrigerate
Make the spinach dip; refrigerate
Make the cranberry salad; refrigerate

The night before:
Bake corn bread for stuffing; let stand at room
  temperature to stale
Cook shrimp for dip; refrigerate
Prepare the crudités; refrigerate
Chop ingredients for stuffing; refrigerate
Make the succotash (without the tomatoes);
  refrigerate

8 hours before serving turkey:
Make the stuffing; refrigerate
Make the mashed potatoes; refrigerate

About 7 hours before serving turkey:
Roast the turkey
Prepare yams; let stand at cool room temperature

When guests arrive:
Serve spinach dip, shrimp dip, and cheddar balls

**When the turkey is done (about 1 hour
before serving):**
Transfer turkey to serving dish

1 hour before serving:
Pour drippings into glass bowl; let stand until
  ready to make gravy
Bake stuffing
Bake mashed potatoes
Bake sweet potatoes
Make gravy; keep warm

1 hour before serving dessert:
Brew coffee

15 minutes before serving turkey:
Reheat succotash in skillet
Unmold cranberry salad

After serving turkey:
Boil water for tea
Serve pumpkin cake
Serve coffee

Index

The ultimate course for spectacular, stress-free holidays

Once again, Rick Rodgers takes you by the hand to help you entertain—and still be entertaining. Tackling the hectic Christmas-to-New Year's season, *Christmas 101* features 100 of Rick's never-fail recipes, from holiday classics such as egg nog, glazed ham, and gingerbread cookies, to contemporary ideas such as Shrimp Bisque with Confetti Vegetables, Chicken Cassoulet, and Pear Shortcakes with Brandied Cream. Whether you're preparing an intimate dinner or an open-house for the entire neighborhood, *Christmas 101* has holiday entertaining all wrapped up.